Corporate Communications

Corporate Communications

Convention, Complexity, and Critique

Lars Thøger Christensen
Mette Morsing
George Cheney

SAGE Publications
Los Angeles · London · New Delhi · Singapore

First published 2008

SAGE Publications Ltd
1 Oliver's Yard
55 City Road
London EC1Y 1SP

SAGE Publications Inc.
2455 Teller Road
Thousand Oaks, California 91320

SAGE Publications India Pvt Ltd
B 1/I 1 Mohan Cooperative Industrial Area
Mathura Road
New Delhi 110 044

SAGE Publications Asia-Pacific Pte Ltd
33 Pekin Street #02-01
Far East Square
Singapore 048763

Library of Congress Control Number: 2007930360

British Library Cataloguing in Publication data

A catalogue record for this book is available from the British Library

ISBN 978-1-4129-3102-1
ISBN 978-1-4129-3103-8 (pbk)

Typeset by C&M Digital Pvt Ltd, Chennai, India
Printed in India by Replika Press Pvt. Ltd
Printed on paper from sustainable resources

Contents

Preface

Today we find all sorts of organizations and collectivities speaking. Nevertheless, we know surprisingly little about messages by, from and for organizations. Put another way, we have difficulty both in coping with and understanding "corporate" messages, even though we are subject to and party to communications from corporate bodies all the time.

George Cheney (1992: 166)

Introducing the Field

The organizational and social significance of corporate communications has grown immensely over the last few decades. While corporate communications as a field and practice is not new, corporate messages are today ubiquitous across sectors, media and situations. Increasingly, these messages seek to draw our attention to the organizations that shape our lives through their provision of products, services, opinions, symbols and jobs. In contrast to other types of professional communication – for example advertising, employee communications and technical communications – that typically address specific audiences with discrete messages, the aim of *corporate* communications is to speak to many audiences *at once* with a consistent set of messages (Cornelissen, 2004a).

The ambition of corporate communications is to project a consistent image of the organization across multiple audiences.

The reasons why organizations embark on corporate communications programmes are many, but often centre on issues of identity and legitimacy. Contemporary managers seem to believe that in a globalized world of increased complexity, organizational existence hinges on the ability to establish and maintain the organization as a *unified and integrated whole* across different audiences. This belief increasingly shapes the communication strategies of contemporary organizations. As one manifestation of this trend, a growing number of organizations are branding *themselves* rather than their products. The fact that many organizations now place their communication activities under the umbrella of *corporate* communications, however, reflects more than a shift in branding strategies. The pursuit of the "corporate" in the communications of contemporary organizations illustrates an orientation with total images of organizations – images that are able to cover both symbolic and behavioural dimensions of an organization's life. This preoccupation is not entirely new; it has been evident in attempts by organizations to articulate shared values and visions, and in the programmes by many organizations to use design, aesthetics and symbolism to reach members and customers that span time and space. Today, the drive toward total or whole organizational image is most apparent in efforts to manage everything organizations say or do within *one* coherent and consistent expression. Behind these efforts, we find the conviction that *non*-integrated communications send disjointed messages that weaken impact and confuse, frustrate or irritate internal and external audiences. By contrast, the orchestration of messages is regarded as essential for businesses and other organizations to survive and prosper. With the notion of integrated communications, this conviction is translated into communication campaigns to encompass both internal and external dimensions of the organizational life.

The field of corporate communications assumes that it is possible and desirable for an organization to communicate as one unified whole.

The Purpose of the Book

We challenge this idea. To do so we draw on the "body" as a metaphor to understand better the assumptions and implications of corporate communications' omnipresence in contemporary society. Our point of departure is the fact that corporations and sometimes organizations are treated as persons in western legal systems and that the metaphor of the corpus, from which the word corporation originates, is still widely used. "Corporate" derives from the Latin *corpus* which means *body*; the derivative "incorporate" means to include or to integrate. And, the notion of "corporation" refers to a group of people combined into or acting as one body. In this book, we take the etymological roots of the corporation seriously by making it a recurrent theme in our discussion of corporate communications. More specifically, we use the notion of the body as an organizing framework to structure our analysis and critique of the field. Based on the body metaphor we argue that communication in and around contemporary organizations has become "corporeal". This is true especially for large incorporated organizations, although a growing number of organizations across sectors conceive of themselves as bodily totalities that need to be expressed and managed in terms communication. Being critical of this trend, our discussion suggests a move toward a more elaborate, complex and refined understanding of the corporate body. By making the organizational "anatomy" of corporate communications the primary object of analysis, the ambition of this book is to inspire new avenues of research, practice and teaching in the field – avenues that are far more sensitive to the organizational and social context in which projects of communication exist and unfold.

Corporate communications embraces the organization as a whole because it seeks to integrate all its communicative dimensions into one body.

The Perspective of the Book

We were motivated to write this book out of curiosity with the repeated call for consistency, coherence and unity to be guiding principles for contemporary organizations. Such prescriptions are never neutral. Our analysis and critique of corporate communications takes as its point of departure a philosophical tradition that regards communication as *consequential*: rather than simply describing the world, it *does* things. Communication, for example, makes people pay attention to certain things, while ignoring others; it frames situations and invites certain types of action. Organizations, thus, emerge in their communication (Taylor and van Every, 2000). Through the articulation of accounts, ideals, values and visions, managerial talk contributes to a continuous (re)creation of organizational reality. Of course, to say that an organization emerges within or is, in large part, defined by communication in no way means that things such as geography, architecture, technology, and physical presence and experience are unimportant. Rather, a communication-centred perspective on organization puts the accent on the interactional, symbolic and systemic aspects of the organization as something that requires communication for existence, maintenance and growth. Given this perspective, a critical assessment of corporate communications involves an examination and deconstruction of the dominant assumptions, logics and metaphors that characterize the field.

Organizations shape their own reality through the communication ideals they subscribe to.

To date, most work in the field of corporate communications has been limited to prescriptive accounts of an *ideal* state of organizing and communicating between the organization and its many audiences. Such accounts typically demonstrate very little interest in understanding the phenomenon called "organization". And most often, there is little insight into how organization and communication affect each other. Only a few analysts have provided a more comprehensive critical and theoretical framework for understanding the organizational and societal implications of corporate communications. By contrast, we want to probe, question and refine corporate communications theory by penetrating its foundational assumptions and exposing some of the difficulties in its application. While it may seem appealing to align all messages inside and outside an organization, a deeper examination of this position reveals logical, practical and even ethical problems. With our organizational approach, we want to demonstrate that plurality and diversity of opinions and expressions are necessary for organizations operating in complex environments and having multiple constituencies. Moreover, pluralism and diversity offer important counterpoints to monolithic images of organizations and their representations.

Our knowledge and applications of corporate communications are strengthened when we unveil underlying assumptions and consider their implications for organizations and society.

The Book's Readership

The book should be regarded as a cautionary note for students and scholars interested in corporate communications as well as for professionals working in the field. The book invites a critical perspective without rejecting the corporate communications project altogether. Our goal, thus, is not to answer the question of how to manage an efficient corporate communications programme. Most undergraduate students of business have already been exposed to numerous "how to" books on marketing, communication, management and related topics. As an alternative to such prescriptive approaches, this book raises a series of basic questions about corporate communications programmes:

- Where does the idea of corporate communications come from?
- What are its underlying assumptions?
- How did this project emerge in the last century?
- What sorts of activities are involved?
- What does it mean for an organization (or group, or society) to communicate as a whole? And, is that even possible, desirable and ethically sound?
- Who is responsible for the orchestration of the many dimensions of the company's communications and thus for communicating on behalf of the whole?

- What are the practical challenges faced by an organization that wishes to maintain "a united front" in a world characterized by a cacophony of messages and rapid change?

We raise these questions in order to further an understanding of corporate communications as an organizational ideal and practice.

To challenge means to confront, critique and question, especially by bringing to light previously hidden or taken-for-granted assumptions or by offering alternatives to what is often called "common sense".

The Organization of the Book

While we aim for a fairly comprehensive picture of corporate communications today, we cannot be encyclopaedic in our coverage of subtopics, research studies, scholars or cases. We see this book as an important thought experiment for the student or practitioner of corporate communications, as he or she reconsiders the discipline and it underlying logics. In order to stimulate new lines of thinking within the field, we have introduced a number of features that differentiate our book from conventional approaches to the field. Throughout the text, relevant sociological or philosophical concepts and theories that do not appear in standard textbooks on corporate communications are featured in textboxes or vignettes that stand out from the rest of the text and which tie in to cases in each chapter. Additionally, central points are provided as executive briefings, emphasized through the use of grey text and **bold** text in the boxes: a feature that simultaneously makes it easier to get a fast overview of the book. Instead of conventional introductions, each chapter is opened with three "points of challenge" that highlight the chapter's central ideas and urge the reader from the very beginning to think beyond conventional perspectives on corporate communications. Designed to stimulate further questioning and, thus, inspire a self-reflective approach to the field, these challenge points call for scholars and practioners to "test" their theories and ideals against their experiences and practices (Schön, 1983). Also, each chapter is introduced with a depiction of an artwork that illustrates the bodily theme of that particular chapter. In addition to numerous examples, each chapter has a lengthy case that exemplifies the chapter's major points. Our hope is to help build new understandings that inform our decisions and actions on the arena of professional communications.

In addition to this preface, the book consists of eight chapters, a Prologue and an Epilogue. While Chapters 1 through 4 provide a critical introduction to corporate communications as an ideal, a field and a principle of organizing, Chapters 5 to 8 move behind the ideal and its theoretical assumptions and practical consequences. The

Prologue offers an introduction to the notion of corporate communications followed by a discussion of metaphors of organization and communication. Drawing attention to the metaphor of the "body" in the social sciences, the prologue argues that corporate communications should be thought of as the "body of communication". Taking its point of departure in the ongoing quest for social legitimacy, a quest that has shaped the corporate landscape for more than a century, Chapter 1 argues that while corporate communications is a fairly old practice its new manifestations are dramatically changing the relations between organizations and their internal and external environments. The most important changes are communicative expansion, disciplinary convergence and strategic concentration. Chapter 2 takes a closer look at the notion of integrated communications. Showing that "integration" potentially has multiple meanings, the chapter illustrates how integrated communications has become an all-encompassing practice that claims to cover still more dimensions (formal as well as informal) of an organization's practice. Chapter 3 discusses and illustrates the ambition of contemporary organizations to present themselves as unified corporate brands. Taking its point of departure in the assumption that consumers increasingly "buy" the companies *behind* the products, the chapter challenges conventional notions of coherence between the brand promise and the organizational culture "behind". Chapter 4 provides a critical examination of corporate reputation management arguing that although images are ambiguous and unstable, the measurement of reputations plays a central role in dealings with organizational stakeholders. Chapter 5 challenges the diagnosis behind corporate communications, maintaining that its discourse on message "clutter", audience fragmentation, parity marketplace, critical stake holders, and so forth is seriously flawed. Chapter 6 explains that while all organization, to some extent, is about discipline and control, the corporate communications project has introduced a new type of bodily discipline that appeals to contemporary managers through its rhetoric of synergy, integration and consistency. Chapter 7 demonstrates that the corporate desire for integration is necessarily counteracted by processes of differentiation, buffers and loose couplings. In a world of growing complexity, organizations need to accept and appreciate these "barriers" to integration in order to retain sufficient diversity to perceive and respond to variations and changes in their surroundings. Chapter 8 extends this line of argument by questioning conventional understandings of explicitness, clarity and consistency in corporate messages. Introducing the notion of polyphony, the chapter illustrates how the desire to orchestrate all communications is challenged by the need for contemporary organizations to listen and learn from the many voices of its internal and external audiences. Returning to the notion of the body, the Epilogue argues that the whole and its parts are interdependent and should always be seen and approached in terms of each other.

xii Corporate Communications

Acknowledgements

We would like to thank the following people, who have in various ways helped, supported, encouraged and inspired us: Dominique Bouchet, Jette Brockstedt, Kenneth Burke, Nikolaj Buchardt, Joep Cornelissen, Delia Alfonso, Jonas Eder-Hansen, Thomas Kiar, Mette Lund Kristensen, Sally Planalp, Phillip K. Thompkins, Christina Thyssen, Ole Thyssen, Simon Torp, Murat Zubcevic as well as anonymous reviewers at SAGE. We extend a special thanks to Tanja Verbik and Samfundslitteratur in Copenhagen for their generosity, flexibility and support, both when we originally crafted these ideas for a Danish audience (Christensen and Morsing, 2005) and when we decided to develop them further for an international audience.

Prologue

Images of Corporate Communications

Definitions and Metaphors

… in contemporary societies the project of the self, as the principal legacy of individualism, has now been converted into the project of the body.

Bryan S. Turner (1996: 20)

Probing Disciplinary Definitions

What makes communication "corporate"? In other words, what difference does it make to conceive of communication as a specifically *corporate* endeavour? To many people working within marketing, public relations and related disciplines, "corporate communications" is merely a label for a field of practice, an umbrella term that encompasses the range of internal and external communication activities that organizations bring together and seek to manage under one banner. Thus, many textbooks take the notion of corporate communications *for granted* and define it only indirectly by listing the many types of activities it encompasses: for example, public relations, community relations, investor relations, employee communications, crisis communications, issues management and so forth (Argenti, 1998; Dilenschneider, 2000; Dolphin, 1999; Goodman, 1994). Even in cases where the theoretical exploration of these activities is more refined, we find corporate communications defined in terms of *other* communication disciplines like marketing communication, organizational communication and management communication (Riel, 1995).

Corporate communications is often defined indirectly as the sum of communication activities brought under one banner.

Increasingly, however, corporate communications is regarded as a discipline in its own right, that is, as a discipline with a distinct rationale and identity. In contemporary writings, corporate communications is understood as a *mindset,* a certain way of thinking about and approaching communication as a strategic management function. Marketing scholar Joep Cornelissen defines the field this way:

> *Corporate communications is a management function that offers a framework and vocabulary for the effective coordination of all means of communications with the overall purpose of establishing and maintaining favourable reputations with stakeholder groups upon which the organization is dependent.* (2004a: 23)

While corporate communications, according to this definition, is a management function that embraces all the organization's communication activities, its distinct nature has less to do with the growing number of communication functions and subdisciplines it subsumes than with the framework or mindset it provides. Corporate communications is defined primarily by its *vision,* that is, by its goals and implied assumptions for the communication project involved. In a number of important respects, these ambitions and assumptions set corporate communications aside from other management-oriented communication disciplines. In contrast to the fields of marketing communication and organizational communication, traditionally concerned with consumers and employees respectively, the aim of corporate communications as a distinct field of theory and practice is to manage *all* communications that involve the organization as a whole. The objective of corporate communications, thus, is different not simply because it claims to include a broader range of communication activities or to address more audiences across formal organizational boundaries but because its *raison d'être* is to organize the organization's communication activities as one coherent entity (Jackson, 1987).

Corporate communications above all is a mindset, an ambition to encompass all communications within one perspective.

Across their differences, most understandings and definitions of corporate communications are based on images of *wholeness* and *totality*, emphasizing the importance of managing everything the organizations says or does in a unitary and consistent manner (Åberg, 1990; Balmer and Greyser, 2003; Bernstein, 1984; Harrison, 1995). Rather than pursuing different identities vis-à-vis different audiences or letting different departments handle their communications autonomously, the vision of corporate communications is to project a coherent and unambiguous image of what the organization is and stands for. Obviously, this objective implies more than simply coordinating multiple communication activities within the organizational setting. To qualify as "corporate", all communications (symbols, messages, strategies and behaviours) must be conceived, coordinated, and handled as one organizational entity (Goodman, 2000; Yeshin, 1998). With its emphasis on total images of the organization, the concept of corporate communications draws on the notions of holism and synergy.

Corporate communications relies on a metaphor of holism: the desire to encompass everything within one perspective or framework.

BOX P.1   Holism and Synergy

Holism (from *holos*, a Greek word meaning whole) refers to "the idea that the properties of a system cannot be determined or explained by the sum of its components alone." Thinkers adopting a holistic perspective claim to avoid reductionism by studying organic or unified wholes that are greater than the simple sum of their parts. Although the notion of holism is frequently applied in a superficial and non-scientific sense, it has shaped the ideals of many scientific fields, including sociology, philosophy, biology and medicine.

The notions of holism and synergy refer to systemic properties or characteristics of the whole.

(Continued)

(Continued)

Synergy (from the Greek *synergos* meaning working together) refers to "the phenomenon of two or more discrete influences or agents acting in common to create an effect which is greater than the sum of the effects each is able to create independently"[1]. Applied to corporate communications, the notion of synergy suggests that the total image of the organization is an emergent quality: a quality that comes into existence produced through the continuous interaction between individual symbols and messages. The task of the corporate communicator is to make sure that the synergy is positive; that discrete symbols, messages or activities support each other to produce an enhanced combined effect.

According to sociologist Richard Sennett (1996: 25), wholeness, oneness and coherence are key words in the vocabulary of power. As we will demonstrate, corporate communications today has adopted a particular vocabulary of power to make a case for itself.

Metaphors of Organization and Communication

Our ideals and notions of communication have always been based on more or less implicit metaphors emphasizing different aspects of the communication process. A metaphor is a way of describing a phenomenon in terms of something else. A metaphor creates or asserts a link between two different domains and in this way helps us to acquire new insights and make sense of the world. As such, metaphors are fundamental to our understanding and shaping of social reality (Cornelissen, 2004b; Lakoff and Johnson, 1989). Metaphors are unavoidable: they are inherent to language and other symbol systems. Language itself can be seen as a metaphor, in that the word is not the thing described except when we are focusing on the word in its own right. That is, we are inevitably resorting to one thing in order to talk about something else; as is evident from a perusal of any dictionary.

Metaphors help us make sense of the world by allowing us describe one phenomenon in terms of another.

The nature of complex organizations requires an array of metaphors because organizations are not easily grasped with a single label or image. As organizational theorist Gareth Morgan has demonstrated, organizations have been described through the use of multiple metaphors, including machines, organisms, brains, cultures, political systems, psychic prisons, flux and transformation, and instruments of domination (Morgan, 1986). Other metaphors of organization include team, tribe, community, rubbish bin, and so forth. Each of these metaphors has its own strengths and weaknesses, illuminating certain parts of organizational life while downplaying or obscuring others. Although metaphors create insight they simultaneously carry blind spots. Thus, for example, when a woman calls her husband a donkey her intention is (probably) not to suggest that he has four legs and a tail, but to point out that her husband is stubborn – a quality often ascribed to the donkey. Adopting a metaphor, however, tends to push out of view other qualities of the person described. Likewise, when a marketing department refers to its recent market analysis as a "dialogue" with consumers, it draws attention to some qualities of the analysis – its two-way nature, for example – but overlooks simultaneously other parts of the interaction, for example the fact that the interaction was imbalanced by virtue of being controlled by the organization.

Metaphors highlight certain features of an object while downplaying or ignoring others.

Just as the organizational literature has produced a plethora of images of organization, so it has offered multiple metaphors for the communication that takes place in the organizational context. Organizational scholars have suggested that the most prevailing metaphors of organizational communication are the following: conduit, lens, linkage, performance, symbol, voice and discourse (Putnam et al., 1996). As one example, the metaphor of voice captures the idea of organizations and their members *speaking*. As mentioned earlier, each metaphor accentuates certain dimensions – processes, roles or ideals – of the communication process. Whereas the conduit metaphor, for example, emphasizes the transmission of messages in a linear and one-way fashion, the performance metaphor highlights social interaction and coordinated behaviour.

BOX P.2   Metaphors of the Whole vs. Metaphors of the Parts

In every social system there is a tension between the individual and the system, the parts and the whole (Morin, 1973). This tension is recognized, for example, in metaphors for US society. For many years the USA was described as a "melting pot", as an amalgamation of "the parts" into an end product where individual differences are subordinated to the new, unified

(Continued)

(Continued)

entity. Following this metaphor, one should expect US society to empha-size the inclusion of newcomers through processes of homogenization or other ways of downplaying differences of ethnicity, religion, gender or sexuality. In more recent years, alternative metaphors that allow us to focus on the identity and diversity of the parts have been introduced, for exam-ple "the salad bowl", "the vegetable soup", or "the mixed drink". These metaphors describe a product of combination while allowing us, in different ways, to focus on the unique ingredients that shape and add distinction ("flavour") to the end product. Using these metaphors, we can highlight dif-ferent characteristics of an integration process. Whereas the ingredients in the salad retain their unique identities even when the salad is finished, the ingredients in the soup tend to dissolve the longer the soup has been cook-ing. Finally, the metaphor of the mixed drink allows us to focus on power issues, recognizing that some ingredients occasionally play a more domi-nant role than others (Griffin, 1998).

Because metaphors produce one-sided representations of reality, it is important to use and combine different metaphors in order to understand the complexity of organizational life:

> *Ideas about organization are always based on implicit images or metaphors that per-suade us to see, understand, and manage situations in a particular way. Metaphors cre-ate insight. But they also distort. They have strengths. But they also have limitations. In creating ways of seeing, they create ways of not seeing. There can be no single theory or metaphor that gives an all-purpose point of view, and there can be no simple "correct theory" for structuring everything we do. The challenge facing modern managers is to become accomplished in the art of using metaphor to find new ways of seeing, under-standing, and shaping their actions.* (Morgan, 1993: xxi)

Following this call by organizational theorist Gareth Morgan, this book will bring a metaphor of corporate communications into play that at once recognizes the discipline's concern with wholeness and unity and retains our ability to challenge its basic assump-tions. Corporate communications, in this perspective, is the "body" of communication.

The 'Body' of Communication

The word "corporate" derives from the Latin *corpus* which means body. The derived word "incorporate" means to include or integrate, for example to admit someone as a member to a corporation. Often incorporation refers to the processes of becoming united or combined into an organized body as when two organizations are merged into one. Moreover, we talk about "embodiment" when something abstract – for example, a concept, a principle or an image – takes a concrete, material form. Finally, we use the notion of *esprit de corps*, which actually means spirit of the *body,* when we refer to a common spirit of unity, comradeship and devotion amongst members of a group.

Corporate communications is the "body" of communication: a "body" that represents the voice of the corporation by including and integrating its many different dimensions into one unifying expression.

The body metaphor is not a new invention. In western thought, the body is actually an old metaphor for social systems. Traditional society, thus, can be said to represent a body in the sense that the unity and the interpersonal relations are regarded as more important than the individual will. In some tribal societies, for example, there is no word for an individual's identity. To the extent that it is possible to refer to individuality in such societies, it is defined by the whole, through the body of society. The body metaphor reflected the dominant mode of theorizing about political behaviour until the eighteenth century. Plato used the body as a metaphor for society: divided into the head for wisdom, the breast for courage and the lower part of the body for desire. In 1651, the political philosopher Thomas Hobbes (1988/1651) used the biblical image of the monster body, the Leviathan, as a metaphor for the state. And in the seventeenth and eighteenth centuries the king's body was seen as the incarnation of society; the sovereign body. An attack on the king's body was therefore an attack on the sovereignty (Kantorowicz, 1997/1957). For Plato and Hobbes the body was a fairly neutral metaphor for the state. To Plato it was evident that a state must have some "body" that rules, defends and maintains society. He regarded the state as a balanced view of these elements. And while the Leviathan was a monster, the alternative for Hobbes was civil war. In this book, we use the body metaphor in a more challenging mode that allows us to investigate the implications of the idea of an entity orchestrating all dimensions of an organization's communication.

BOX P.3   The Corporation

The notion of the corporation had its forerunner in the regulated professions called "guilds" that flourished in the European Middle Ages, but can be traced back to the ancient world. A guild was an association of people of the

(Continued)

(Continued)

same trade – for example, carpenters, blacksmiths or masons – that formed to protect their mutual interests and to maintain standards of quality, morality and conduct. Guilds are often seen as precursors of modern trade unions and exhibit some aspects of the modern corporation. In the late fourteenth century, when the first corporations emerged, legal theorists in Italy decided that a corporation should be regarded as a legal entity analogous to a legal person. The body corporate would then transcend individuals in time, space and power. Described as a "persona universalis", the corporation was seen as a person composed of many (Turner, 1996). Today a corporation is defined as "a group of people combined into or acting as one body" or, more precisely, as "a body that is granted a charter legally recognising it as a separate legal entity having its own rights, privileges, and liabilities distinct from those of its members"[3] (*The American Heritage Dictionary*). But, we can extend the metaphor to other large organizations that are not literal, legal corporations yet behave as "anonymous societies".

A corporation is a "body of people", a group of people authorized to act as an individual.

What had been solely a metaphor for the organization, the person, became literal in law beginning in 1886 with the US Supreme Court case *Santa Clara County (California)* v. *Southern Pacific Railroad*. From that point in the late nineteenth century, the modern corporation took on rights as a legal or juristic person, and so did many non-corporations enjoy rights to due process and free speech by extension. In the USA especially, but also in many other nations, the organization could eventually argue for itself un bel or participate in quasi-political advertising. The body corporate, thus, took on several new and very powerful senses.

Approaching corporate communications metaphorically as the body of communication has several advantages. It allows us to investigate new dimensions of the corporate body and to ask questions about wholeness, parts, interdependency, balances and imbalances usually not discussed in conventional textbooks on corporate communications:

- What is the relationship between the body and the "soul"?
- How is corporate consciousness, in other words, related to the larger project of corporate communications?

- What is the anatomy of the body: that is, which activities do corporate communications embody?
- What about the corporate face: that is, how does the organization present itself and how is it perceived by others?
- How is the body diagnosed? And what are its relations to its environment?
- What shape is the body in? Is it fragile, disciplined, rigid or adroit?
- Does the body have a message and can the "head" learn to listen to it?
- Can the project of corporate communications, in other words, acknowledge and incorporate the many voices of the corporation?

As a metaphor for the corporation, the "body" allow us to challenge contemporary values and assumptions about professional communication management.

Corporate communications has revived interest in the corporate body in a new and expansive shape. It is this shape – or, if you will, its corporate "anatomy" – that we explore in this book. We take the body metaphor seriously, just as corporations do, by applying it in multiple ways to the organization. At the same time, we are being deliberately playful with these applications so as to interrogate organizations about their own assumptions of totality, control and their ability to orchestrate messages and people. While we accept the power and utility of the bodily metaphor (think of the many ways we use it in everyday thought and talk!), we are also aware of its blind spots. Hence, while using the body metaphor we are also urging organizations – and readers – to think beyond the body corporate and to consider what dynamic, multivocal, and sometimes even incoherent processes of communication sound like. In other words, we want to turn the body metaphor on the organization and at the same time challenge corporate communications specialists to step outside of it. In the chapters that follow, we will in particular focus on these issues and questions:

> Corporate communications is a managerial vision of managing *all* communications that involve the organization as a whole. But who is able to *supervise* such a project?
> As a metaphor for wholeness and unity in communication, does the notion of "corporate communications" not only create insight but also blind spots? Which dimensions does it overlook?
> If "corporate communications" is the body of communication, what type of body does it represent?

Note

1 http: en.wikipedia.org/wiki/Synergy

PART I

The New Corporeal Project

1

The Emergence of Corporate Communications

Rehabilitating the Corporate "Soul"

> The traditional potency of the family, the church, and the local community suddenly seemed dwarfed by the sway of the giant corporations. This momentous shift in the balance of social forces created a crisis of legitimacy for the large corporation.
>
> Roland Marchand (1998: 2)

Introduction

When we talk about current management trends, we often ignore their historical dimension. Some developments, like corporate blogging, are obviously fairly new: they are made possible by the development of digital communication technologies. Most trends, however, have precursors in the history of business enterprise. This is true also for corporate communications. As a field of practice, corporate communications dates back to the second half of the nineteenth century where major corporations felt a growing need to justify their practices to the general public. To do so, they depicted themselves as vital and benevolent institutions of society. A similar trend is visible in today's corporate communications. While the scope of the field, its vocabulary, and the specific techniques of its practice have developed in a number of important respects (see also Chapter 5), most of its basic concerns remain the same. In this chapter, we take our point of departure in the field's historical heritage, but show how it has developed into a multi-disciplinary and strategic discipline concerned with the management of communications at many different levels. In particular, the chapter will address the following issues and questions:

Chapter 1: Points of Challenge

- The driving force behind corporate communications has always been the quest for social legitimacy. How is the issue of legitimacy different in the communication world of today?

- Corporate communications has become a management function with strategic ambitions. How does that ambition change the role of communication?

- By incorporating multiple fields of theory and practice, corporate communications blurs the boundaries between internal and external communication. What are the implications for our notions of senders, receivers and communication purpose?

The Quest for Legitimacy

For more than a century, the driving force behind corporate communications has been the same: *social legitimacy*. In his masterful account of the rise of corporate imagery in the USA, historian Roland Marchand illustrates how the development of corporate communications is a story of an ongoing legitimation crisis for big business. Although public sentiments toward business corporations have shifted many times over the last century, the feeling among large corporations that their social and moral legitimacy is at stake has persisted over the years. From the anti-monopoly sentiment of the late nineteenth century to the expansion and concentration of business during the Second World War and beyond, the size and power of major corporations have been recurrent issues shaping corporate communications in the USA. In spite of its *legal* legitimacy, the growth of the great corporation and its large-scale concentration of capital – often exhibited by extravagant headquarters and massive factory complexes – fostered the feeling that the corporation had become detached from the local community that supported it. Toward the end of the ninenteenth century, a growing number of voices in the USA regarded the big business corporation as a "body" without a soul.

The basic strategy of *corporate* communications has been with us for around 150 years.

Early corporate communications campaigns reflected, in the words of Marchand, a "quest for a corporate soul," (1998: 4) in other words, a desire to restore the social role of the corporation in the eyes of the public. Hoping to fill the vacuum left by traditional institutions of authority, such as family, church and neighbourhood, corporations increasingly depicted themselves as social institutions with responsibilities and aspirations beyond their commercial activities. However, while some corporate leaders undoubtedly had wider social aspirations, the typical corporate communications campaign aimed to make the public understand and, eventually, hold affection for the company. This is what we mean by the corporate quest for social legitimacy: *the pursuit by corporations to be seen as essential and accepted members of the larger community.*

BOX 1.1   Legitimacy

The word legitimacy derives from the Latin *legitimare* and refers to the state or quality of being rightful and justifiable. Legitimacy is considered a basic condition for rule: without a minimal amount of legitimacy, a system of rule will degenerate to a simple coercive system. In political science, the notion of legitimacy is used to refer to the popular acceptance of a governing regime or law. This indicates that legitimacy must be distinguished from legality. An action can be legal without being legitimate (as in the case of an immoral law) just as an action can be seen as legitimate without being legal (as in civil disobedience). Legitimacy has also been applied to

(Continued)

(Continued)

non-political situations, such as the (il)legitimacy of a corporation operating in a developing country, using natural resources and hiring local workers and thus impacting on both natural and social environments.

Legitimacy is linked to questions of consent, whether this is tacit or expressed more explicitly.

Following the works of the sociologists Max Weber (1978) and Talcot Parsons (1960), the notion of legitimacy has attracted considerable attention among organizational scholars addressing the normative and cognitive forces that constrain, construct and empower organizational actors. According to professor of sociology and law Mark C. Suchman "legitimacy is a generalized perception or assumption that the actions of an entity are desirable, proper, or appropriate within some socially constructed system of norms, values, beliefs and definitions" (1995: 574). Based on this definition, Suchman identifies two approaches to legitimacy: a strategic-legitimacy and an institutional-legitimacy approach. In the *strategic-legitimacy approach*, legitimacy serves a function and is designed and controlled by managers to achieve a favourable perception among the organization's stakeholders. In the *institutional-legitimacy approach*, legitimacy is a set of constitutive beliefs constructed by social institutions. It is therefore out of managerial control, but nevertheless permeates the organization entirely. This is the case, for example, when health programmes become a norm for organizations even though they are initiated by health associations to promote people's health or by the state to reduce welfare expenditure caused by obesity and diabetes. So, from a strategic-legitimacy approach, top managers may take a number of initiatives to promote the company's social legitimacy, but if these activities for some reason oppose institutionalized expectations to corporate behaviour, the organization may not be perceived as socially legitimate. From an institutional perspective, social legitimacy extends far beyond managerial decisions and actions.

Organizational legitimacy is a socially constructed set of assumptions about proper corporate behaviour.

Large American companies practised corporate communications long before it became an established discipline. Marchand describes how the US Telephone &

Telegraph Company (AT&T) in 1908 initiated a number of communication campaigns with the aim of explaining and justifying its monopoly status in US society. Hoping to protect the corporation from public ownership or increased regulation, AT&T argued that the company's size reflected its responsibility as a national provider ("Making a Neighborhood of a Nation") and its ability and willingness to deliver a universal service across the country ("In the Public Service"). Simultaneously, the campaigns sought to integrate the associated Bell companies into one unified Bell system. Through the alignment of all advertising to the same style, AT&T's strategy was to create an appearance of national uniformity in all its messages and campaigns. Because the company needed to prove its legitimacy not only to the public but also to itself, internal and external messages were often combined, with the company speaking simultaneously to employees about their indispensable service function in a national network and to customers about their prospective access to a seamless communication "highway". These AT&T campaigns were supplemented by wide-ranging PR material, including books, magazines, newspapers and films, all ostensibly for educational purposes. AT&T's efforts were among the most comprehensive and professional attempts to engage in corporate communications during the first half of the twentieth century. Gradually, other corporations and industries embarked on similar efforts. Among the most prominent industries on this arena were railroads, automobile manufacturers, steel producers, the meatpacking industry and of course oil. The Pennsylvania Railroad, for example, described itself as one big railroad family in which the employees worked as a unified body governed by the head of the family, that is, by top management. As early as the late 1920s, General Motors (GM) launched its first corporate branding campaign. Drawing on metaphors like "neighbourhood" and "family", the campaign was designed to create a higher level of organizational coherence among GM's employees and produce a more clear and distinct image in its surroundings.

Early corporate communications campaigns depicted corporations as tightly knit families or unified bodies with social concerns.

By the end of the nineteenth century, many corporations were involved in extensive corporate communications efforts. At the beginning of the new century, these efforts were expanded considerably. In addition to institutional advertising campaigns, like the ones from AT&T or GM, corporations sought to build and shape their images through the design of urban department stores, through the introduction of corporate welfare programmes, or through their presence at trade fairs, which grew in importance and sophistication during the first half of the twentieth century. Before the end of the Second World War, many of the communication practices associated with *contemporary* corporate communications programmes were already widely known and applied among large business corporations. Thus, corporate branding, integrated communications, social responsibility, sponsoring, image analyses and even storytelling are not nearly as new as we tend to assume. To managers of the 1940s and beyond, they were already regarded as indispensable communication activities, necessary to grant legitimacy to the modern business corporation.

The efforts made by corporations to present themselves as unified bodies have deep historical roots.

Yet, much has changed. Since the Second World War, and particularly during the last few decades, the issue of social legitimacy has intensified dramatically. Under the impact of globalization and new communication technologies, contemporary organizations are facing more critical, outspoken and educated audiences than organizations in the past. In contemporary society, where corporations are expected to play a far more active social role, they often find their "licence to oper-ate" challenged by powerful and well-organized publics. In some towns in the USA, for example, there have been moves to revoke corporate charters. And for many organizations, legitimacy continues to be a salient issue, regardless of what the organization does to improve its moral and social standing in the eyes of the public. TDC, for example, a former state-owned monopoly of Denmark and now one of the largest telecommunications providers in Northern Europe, has for many years been a target of public criticism. The company has initiated many activities within the area of corporate social responsibility, such as the integration of disabled employees, the arrangement of work practices for disadvantaged youth, the inte-gration of ethnic minorities, as well as economic support and collaboration with Welfare for Children, a non-governmental organization working to improve con-ditions for disadvantaged children. Still, the company has great difficulties escaping the type of public attention and scrutiny that surrounded it per its former status. While institutionalized expectations to TDC's societal engagement are high, its social initiatives are often overshadowed by media attention to issues like layoffs, remuneration of top management, shareholder profits and sale of stocks to hedge funds. As an icon of telecommunications, TDC simultaneously finds itself criticized for the shortcomings of the entire industry. Public perception of poor service in the telecommunications industry, for example, often shapes the image of TDC even though the service of other major providers may be just as poor.

In contemporary society, the issue of organizational legitimacy has intensified dramatically.

With the issue of legitimacy reappearing in new and complex ways, the field of cor-porate communications has changed accordingly. During the last decades, the field has been shaped by three central developments: *communicative expansion, disciplinary convergence* and *strategic concentration*. The remainder of this chapter will elaborate on these developments.

Communicative Expansion

Today the scope of corporate communications has expanded to the corporate body *in toto*, encompassing more and more communication functions and activities. Some writers even talk about "total communications" (Åberg, 1990) to describe the tendency for corporate communications to become a pervasive organizational practice that involves both externally and internally directed communication activities. According to mainstream textbooks, corporate communications comprise the following range of communication functions (Dolphin, 1999; Goodman, 1994):

- marketing communication, including advertising and customer relations;
- business-to-business communication;
- image and profiling activities, including sponsorships;
- public affairs, including media relations, government relations and lobbying;
- financial relations, including investor relations;
- financial and non-financial reporting;
- labour relations;
- crisis communication and issues management;
- employee communication, including work instructions and training programmes; and
- technical communication.

The expansion of the field, however, goes further. Organizations of today conceive of virtually *everything* they say and do as potential communication. Thus, in addition to the formal communication activities mentioned above, organizations include a growing amount of organizational dimensions in their communication package, for example: leadership, personnel, architecture and design, accounting practices, investment policies, production methods, resource generation and use, waste disposal, inter-organizational collaboration, product information and so on. Within this expanded communication universe, the question of *integration* becomes urgent: How can the many symbols, messages and behaviours be aligned in order for the organization to retain its credibility and legitimacy vis-à-vis its different audiences? While the integration pursued by AT&T in its early campaigns already involved different audiences inside and outside the corporation, contemporary programmes of corporate communications are more wide-ranging and multi-dimensional, involving the integration of communication at multiple levels across organizational functions (this issue is discussed in more detail in Chapter 2). The latest campaign from

General Electric "Imagination at Work", for example, simultaneously brands the corporation vis-à-vis the consumers and speaks to employees, politicians, media and other opinion leaders about GE's vision for a cleaner planet: "Ecomagination". As such, it simultaneously draws on marketing, public relations and managerial communication to present the corporation as a legitimate player in the market.[1]

The challenge of corporate communications today is defined as an issue of *integration*: the bringing together of messages, images, functions and personnel.

Disciplinary Convergence

As it appears, corporate communications has become a multi-disciplinary vision that involves the expertise and practice of multiple communication disciplines. The identity of the discipline, thus, is shaped by a host of different perspectives that compete for influence and attention. Its most important subfields are public relations, marketing, organizational communication and human resource management. As we shall see below, each of these domains of practice has its own specific agenda, its own assumptions, insights and blind spots, which are imported into the field of corporate communications. Under the umbrella of corporate communications, however, they tend to converge around some of the same concerns.

The field of corporate communications is shaped by disciplinary pluralism and competition.

Originally, most of the activities subsumed under the umbrella of corporate communications were dealt with by *public relations* professionals. Indeed, some managers and consultants still view public relations as synonymous with corporate communications (Dilenschneider, 2000). Public relations arose in the late nineteenth century as a defence-based means of responding to growing public scepticism towards big corporations. Public relations was initially reactive: an "early warning" or "fire fighting" type of activity organized primarily as a response to growing public scrutiny and criticism of industries such as the railroads, the oil companies and the mining and meatpacking businesses. Gradually, the discipline of public relations became more professional and forward-looking, especially through the systematic construction of corporate imagery. By the end of the nineteenth century, the creation of corporate image had established itself as a major function in big business (Cheney and Vibbert, 1987). The primary concern of public relations today is to create and maintain beneficial relations between and among organizations and their various publics or stakeholders, including investors, authorities, politicians, NGOs, neighbours and so forth.

As such, public relations often sees itself dealing with a much broader range of *publics* than other fields of management communication including marketing and organizational communication (Broom et al., 1991; Cheney and Christensen, 2001a). While many public relations activities, such as press releases, media contacts and events, are still handled by journalists, public relations is increasingly seen as a strategic management function. This applies in particular to activities that concern issues of corporate reputation, including questions of ethics, social responsibility and crisis management.

Public relations conceives of itself as the corporate communications discipline *par excellence*.

BOX 1.2   Issues Management

Issues management developed more than 25 years ago as a proactive approach to public relations with a sensitivity to the wider rhetorical enterprise of corporate communications (Heath, 1980). Specifically, a number of large corporations, in particular oil or petroleum companies, began to consider ways to affect broad-based public discourse about issues, some of which did not obviously concern the companies' products or services.

Issues management is a proactive practice of persuading politicians, the media and the general public on issues of corporate interest.

Thus Mobil Oil (now part of Exxon-Mobil) started to publish little essays in US and European magazines called "Observations" on the issues of the day (Crable and Vibbert, 1983). Most of these issue advertisements over the past three decades have had nothing directly to do with Mobil's activities as an energy company. These and similar messages rely on an indirect and circular model of persuasion. That is, the corporation speaks in general terms about values like "freedom" and "common sense", in the hopes of affecting public opinion, even if only in a diffuse, non-measurable way. The strategic hope is that the receptive segments of the corporation's audiences will in turn support political candidates whose policies will be beneficial to the companies and to the larger industry (say, about industry deregulation, privatization of other sectors of the economy or reduced corporate taxes). Ironically, this proactive approach to public relations was triggered in large part by a traditional public relations "crisis": for the oil companies in particular there was a threat of a "windfall" profits tax being

(Continued)

(Continued)

levied by the US federal government following the energy crisis of 1973–1974. In retrospect, we can see how Mobil's change in communication strategy helped to usher in a new era in strategic corporate communications, where organizations of many types would spend more time and money on participating in economic, political and cultural discourses. With attempts at issues management, there is inevitably identity management as well. That is, the organization speaking is setting the stage for a more favourable impression of itself while trying to shape a more favourable treatment of an issue.

Issues management is a strategic management function that helps organizations identify and shape potentially significant issues in their internal and external environments.

Today, we find organizations in all sectors making use of this strategy, and this is true around the world. In the late 1990s and early 2000s, for example, the Chinese government issued a series of television announcements to help "prepare" the public for economic turbulence and specifically for greater unemployment by portraying out of work heads of households as having more time with their families and for leisure. Numerous environmental organizations today are experimenting with different approaches to messaging, hoping to use one campaign, say about rising fuel costs or the increasing frequency of violent storms, as a stepping stone to a larger campaign about global warming.

The field of *marketing*, as we know it today, developed in response to the growing consumer movements after the Second World War. Through their critique of poor products, misleading advertising and questionable production practices, these movements impelled the field of marketing to formulate new visions and standards for how organizations should deal with their markets. These standards are known as *the marketing concept*. The marketing concept is a business "philosophy" that calls for organizations, public as well as private, to focus their activities on the satisfaction of their customers and other relevant publics. Behind the marketing concept we find the conviction that, in order to be profitable, the *whole* organization and not just the marketing department needs to be oriented towards the market

(Drucker, 1954). By integrating and managing marketing intelligence across the organizational setting, the marketing-oriented organization hopes to develop its sensitivity and responsiveness vis-à-vis its external world (Kohli and Jaworski, 1990; Narver and Slater, 1990). As a pervasive managerial norm, the marketing orientation has gradually made its way into all sectors of society to the effect that most organizations today explicitly refer to themselves as "customer-driven" (Gay and Salaman, 1992). Prescribing an organization-wide orientation towards the market, the marketing orientation has been instrumental in the celebration of organizational flexibility and change that has infused contemporary organizations since the 1990s (Zorn et al., 1999). With its focus on external adaptation, however, the marketing discipline has until fairly recently been oblivious about communication processes inside the organizational setting. As a result, marketing has had great difficulties living up to its own ideal of integration.

Although marketing conceives of itself as the master of integration, it has previously been concerned primarily with external communication issues.

The professional field of *organizational communication* arose in the USA of the 1920s where special speech training programmes were developed for corporate executives. Accentuating public speaking in particular, the discipline initially had a clear externally or media-oriented focus. Gradually, however, its emphasis shifted towards internal communication issues, including superior-subordinate communication, communication channels, motivation, socialization, networks and the communication climate (Putnam and Cheney, 1985). While the discipline today has expanded its domain to virtually every aspect of organizational life, it has generally failed to integrate communication issues outside the organizational "container" (Cheney and Christensen, 2001a). Fortunately, organizational communication is beginning to break out of its container, with the help of new technologies, internationalization, the rise of network forms of organization, and blurred boundaries between sectors of the economy and society.

While organizational communication was initially focused on professionalizing externally directed communication, today it is regarded as the field of internal communication studies.

As a field, *human resource management* developed after the Second World War. Human resource management (HRM) builds on the assumption that shared goals, stimulated by openness in communication between superiors and subordinates, promote organizational efficiency (French and Bell, 1984). Approaching employees as collaborators, human resource management regards unrestricted communication between managers and employees as an integrating mechanism (Mayo, 1945; Roethlisberger and Dickson, 1947). And, listening to employees is often proposed as a means to motivate employees (Burke, 1987; French and Bell, 1984) and for example reduce the likelihood of strikes (Imberman, 1979). Indeed, the field of human resource management often considers open communication lines as "a panacea for organizational ills" (Eisenberg and Witten, 1987: 418). However, the privileged form of communication with employees is frequently top-down and largely one way. More recently, the field has developed the idea of mutuality and supportive relationships between superior-subordinates through communication. While the field can be criticized for its simplified notions of commitment, manager–employee relationships and open communication (Gallie et al., 2001; Harley and Hardy, 2004; Watson, 2004), contemporary HRM thinking is still dominated by the ideal of disclosure and exchange of information as a means to achieve consent and consistency on corporate goals.

Human resource management seeks to promote organizational integration and efficiency through open communication.

Today, each of these fields has expanded its outlook and domain beyond its conventional definition. Public relations now encompasses proactive activities such as issues management and identity management. Contemporary marketing includes activities traditionally ascribed to public relations such as fostering and maintaining goodwill among all relevant stakeholders and has now expanded its notion of the "customer" to include families, friends and sometimes even society. Organizational communication has developed an increased interest in how organizations present themselves to the world, for example, through such practices as public relations, marketing and crisis management. Human resource management is increasingly concerned with issues such as public appearance, teamwork with professionals outside the organization, internal branding and how managers and employees construct and present organizational identities that appeal to external audiences, for example potential employees. And corporate communications can be regarded as an attempt to carve out a field of communication that presumes to cover all these dimensions of organizational life.

The major fields of corporate communications are gradually converging to address a growing range of audiences.

Still, there are obstacles to disciplinary integration. Public relations professionals, in particular, have often criticized what they see as imperialistic tendencies on the part of marketing in the expansion of its notion of target audiences (Grunig and Grunig, 1991). And marketers often ignore significant knowledge from organizational communication and human resources when articulating its communication goals and strategies. Across these fields, the tendency to maintain conventional distinctions between different audiences and different situations is remarkably widespread. In the context of corporate communications, however, it makes little sense to maintain such distinctions. Aiming for consistency and integration across different situations and different media (see Chapter 2), corporate communications seek to manage a communication arena on which internal and external messages converge.

BOX 1.3   Auto-communication

The division line between "internal" and "external" communication has never been as clear-cut as we tend to believe. Today, it is widely acknowledged that while employees are important recipients of externally directed communication efforts (Christensen, 1997; Gilly and Wolfinbarger, 1998), external audiences increasingly take interest in matters of internal relevance. The link between these dimensions, however, is more profound than these trends indicate. According to semiologist and linguist Juri Lotman (1977, 1990), a communicator is not only the sender but also, and simultaneously, the recipient of his or her own messages. Any act of communication, therefore, involves a dimension of *auto*-communication. Lotman gives the example of a young poet who reads his own poem in print. As Lotman implies, the poet is probably the most involved receiver of this piece of work and will, accordingly, be inclined to study each poem with more attention to detail than other audiences. A more contemporary example can be found in the fact that many organizations and individuals are the greatest users of their own websites and weblogs.

Auto-communication takes place whenever a sender acts as a receiver of his or her own messages. And this is often the case.

In contrast to conventional notions of communication, auto-communication is not primarily oriented toward sending and receiving messages but toward the display and celebration of codes. Lotman emphasizes that a text is used as a code "when it does not add to the information we already have, but

(Continued)

(Continued)

when it transforms the self-understanding of the person who has engendered the text ..." (1990: 30). In the auto-communication process, communication originally designed for an external audience can be transformed into ideal self-enhancing and self-confirming images. Auto-communication is analogous to what some system theorists call "self-reference". According to Chilean biologists Humberto Maturana and Francisco Varela (1989), all living systems communicate with their environment primarily in order to confirm and maintain themselves as autonomous entities (also see Krippendorf, 1984; Luhman, 1990). Self-reference is a systemic "drive" through which the living system preserves its identity.

Auto-communication is a specific type of organizational self-reference.

A couple of years ago, an advertisement from Ingalls Advertising in Boston said: "When people talk to themselves, it's called insanity. When companies talk to themselves, it's called marketing." While the advertisement addresses a problem, to which we shall return later, that much marketing and communication is narcissistic and self-absorbed, auto-communication is not, necessarily, pathologic. As Lotman puts it: "Addressing oneself in texts, speeches, ruminations – this is a fact not only of psychology, but also of the history of culture" (1990: 21). Auto-communication is an integral aspect of organizational culture, indeed of all cultures. According to leading anthropologists, all cultures communicate with themselves through rituals that help the members share and reinforce, on a frequent basis, their most fundamental values. Whether the ritual involved is a cockfight, an election or a market analysis, the overall purpose of the communication is to express and confirm the specific characteristics of the culture in question. In the process of communicating with itself, the culture defines, rediscovers and reorganizes itself in a way that resembles the constitution of an individual personality (Geertz, 1973).

Auto-communication is vital for the existence and the identity of any social collectivity.

In a globalized world of growing complexity, the similarities between the different domains of communication may well be more significant than the differences. We do not dismiss the relevance of distinguishing between disciplinary orientations. Yet, we observe that the most remarkable development in the current communication environment is the convergence between all the major fields of professional communication. Arguing that different communication perspectives and skills need to come together to solve the challenges facing contemporary organizations, the field of corporate communications has in fact made this convergence and its implied integration of differences in perspectives and practices its particular *raison d'être* (Cornelissen, 2004a). Increasingly, thus, organizations refer to their communication activities as *corporate* communications, hoping that this label will help them force their different practices to work together.

Corporate communications builds on the assumption that management is able to bring different disciplines and fields of practice together to act and speak in unison.

Strategic Concentration

Along with expansion and convergence, we find a proclivity towards concentration in the way contemporary organizations structure their communication activities. Shaped by new and more complex issues of legitimacy, communication has assumed a far more *strategic* role in the organization. Where communication used to refer to a distinct profession or a specific and specialized department, responsible for a limited number of communication parameters, today organizations conceive of communication as a *management* function with strategic responsibilities. One important implication is the tendency to concentrate communication responsibilities at the top of the organizational pyramid (an issue we shall discuss further in Chapter 6). Another implication is the tendency to use communication as an active "driver" in the definition of organizational reality. In the context of corporate communications, strategy is not limited to processes of analyzing and reacting to external contingencies (first-order strategies), but involves conscious attempts on the part of the organization to influence and shape its own environment (second-order strategies). Organizations apply second-order strategies when they seek to define and shape the *conditions* for their strategies. Rather than simply uncovering and recording "what's coming out there" and then designing or prescribing measures to adapt to these changes, scholars and practitioners of corporate communications recognize that in a world of uncertainty, organizations need to set changes in motion themselves that they hope will become true tomorrow (Berg, 1989; Brown and Eisenhardt, 1998; Hamel and Prahalad, 1994). A growing number of organizations in the pharmaceutical industry, for example, have realized that they need to use corporate communications to creatively *enact* realities that are favourable to themselves. Instead of simply adapting their products and practices to current customer demands and political regulations, they participate actively in shaping these dimensions.

Corporate communications has become a vital management function with strategic aspirations.

> ## BOX 1.4   Enactment
>
> Social psychologist and distinguished professor of organization Karl E. Weick has consistently argued and illustrated that organizations to a great extent create their own environments. With his notion of *enactment,* Weick draws our attention to the activities organizational actors set in motion in order to understand their surroundings. In the process of making sense of complex and equivocal situations, organizations do not simply react to a reality "out there", but actively participate in its construction by paying attention to and highlighting certain events, patterns and trends while downplaying or ignoring others:
>
> > *Whenever an organization tries to position itself to "see" the environment better, those actions should be examined from a different standpoint. The question should be, in positioning itself to see the environment, "What is the organization doing that might create the very displays it will see?" (1979: 168)*
>
> Enactment refers to the process of producing (or enacting) the information environment we inhabit. In their attempt to find order and logic in their surroundings, for example, organizations often impose the logic and orderliness they believe they have discovered, thus paving the way for a self-fulfilling prophecy. Enactment is unavoidable: by approaching our surroundings we inevitably "carve out" a relevant world for our subsequent inspections and decisions. Thus, also apparently passive behaviours fall within the frame of enactment, for example the failure of an organization to act in a situation of crisis. Increasingly, however, organizations consciously set out to produce their own environments through *proactive* behaviours, for example when corporations or politicians seek to define situations and values in advance of public attention and demands (Cheney and Christensen, 2001a).
>
> **Organizations enact their own environments by paying attention to certain things in their surroundings and ignoring others.**

Finally, the strategic focus implies a revised notion of the market. While the market originally referred to the ancient Greek *agora*, today it has multiple meanings in public discourse ranging from an understanding of the market as an objective reality to a notion of the market as a story or meta-narrative. To most people, the market is regarded as an exigency or a pressure that forces organizations and other social actors to do certain things and display certain competitive behaviours. And often, the market is seen as an ultimate answer to existential questions about who we are and where we should be heading as human beings and social communities (Cheney, 1998, 2004). With the strategic focus, however, markets are not given in advance, but enacted through proactive corporate behaviours. Consequently, the *outside-in* perspective of the classical marketing concept – by which organizations must adapt to the whims and desires of the market – is replaced by a more complex notion of the market as collective co-creation. In the process of shaping and creating markets, corporations and their members play a significant role, which we will address more fully in the following chapters.

Corporate communications implies a complex notion of the market as collective co-creation.

CASE: The Ongoing Quest for Social Legitimacy

Royal Dutch Shell[2]

Royal Dutch Shell (hereafter Shell) is a global group of oil, gas and petrochemical companies including a portfolio of bio energy and solar interests. Shell operates in more then 140 countries and regions and employs about 109,000 people. This case illustrates how the issue of social legitimacy can continue to haunt a large corporation and impel it to embark on extensive corporate communication campaigns designed to present it as an essential and trustworthy member of the global community. As a highly profiled company within the petrochemical industry, Shell has for many years been used to being an object of frequent and severe criticism. In 1995, however, two major crises shook the company more fundamentally when investors and the general public joined interest groups in their critique of the company's global operations. In addition to public outrage, the company experienced its market value fluctuating dramatically. The case suggests that corporate initiatives to achieve social legitimacy have a tendency to attract attention and produce new social legitimacy challenges in a ongoing cycle.

The Crisis

Shell's *annus horibilis* 1995 began by its decision to sink the floating oil storage and loading buoy, Brent Spar, in the North Sea. Although Shell had made a careful investigation of how to dispose of the 14,500 ton rig in the least environmentally damaging way, Greenpeace activists managed to enact worldwide media coverage, arguing that Shell should consider recycling the rig. Greenpeace questioned the world's most profitable oil

(Continued)

(Continued)

company's motive for sinking the rig as it happened to be the low cost alternative, indicating that Shell was too stingy to dispose decently of its own waste. Greenpeace carefully documented and filmed the "battle" in the Northern Sea between Shell and Greenpeace activists in the small Rainbow Warrior boat, and in the act Greenpeace also managed to reduce complexity by wiping out the "E" on the buoy symbolizing Exxon's 50% ownership of the buoy. Greenpeace was an NGO with a declining membership and staged presumably the first NGO intervention to act as a catalyst of international opinion by demonstrating how big wealthy global corporations seek to occupy not only countries but also territorial waters. Boycotts of European Shell stations led Shell to give up its dumping plans and Brent Spar was disposed of onshore in Norway. Later the same year, Shell was accused of economic and political expediency for engaging with the military junta of Nigeria and for refusing the original Ogoni People a fair share of the oil profits generated from their lands. These incidents, in particular the Brent Spar case, demonstrated to Shell that *legal* compliance was insufficient to retain social legitimacy. While Shell had respected all legal guidelines before making the decision to dump Brent Spar, Greenpeace accused Shell of disregarding environmental concerns. The general perception was, in particular among Europeans, that Shell was *morally* wrong.

The Response

In the wake of these developments, Shell's top management decided to mobilize internal and external stakeholders with the ambition of creating a more favourable corporate image. A small group of Shell executives was assigned to answer the question: "How can Shell become the world's most admired corporation?" Shell's first move after the crisis was to initiate a large self-reflective debate to understand how the company could become more sensitive to its environment in the future. A series of analytical activities was implemented: roundtables, interviews, event studies and surveys. From a number of different countries and regions, opinion leaders such as managers, policy makers, governmental agencies, voluntary organizations, media representatives and academics were invited to discuss the changing perceptions of multinational companies. Shell's conclusion from these meetings was that although people today have considerably higher expectations on matters of corporate social responsibility than companies are able to fulfil, these expectations are real and powerful and need to be addressed as such. Shell's solution was a global campaign launched in 1996 to repair its negative image among the public as well as restore its self-perception. Based on a revision of Shell's "Statement of General Business Principles" and an examination of the company's core purpose, Shell re-introduced itself as an organization in the business of "Helping People Build a Better World".

An internal communication campaign encouraged Shell employees to demonstrate a sense of accountability to non-financial stakeholders. The first annual *non*-financial report was published in 1997 highlighting the company's commitment to human rights, social responsibility and stakeholder dialogue as key features of its values and practices. Among other initiatives, the "Tell Shell" campaign involved an open invitation for stakeholders to comment and critique Shell at its website[3] and a promise from Shell to deliver personal responses. A more recent corporate campaign emphasizes Shell's commitment to protect the environment and improving local communities by focusing on four themes: securing an energy supply, addressing climate change, protecting the environment and working with communities. Each theme features Shell employees concerned about the environment and the local communities in which Shell operates.

The Recurring Issue

Shell has received international awards for its sustainability reports from the United Nations and has managed, in its own words, to change a highly critical and negative public perception of its activities into public admiration with "the highest overall reputation within the energy sector"[4]. While these signs of public recognition are symbolically significant in the process of bolstering Shell's licence to operate, the company is still a major global player in the petrochemical industry traditionally regarded as belonging to the array of "sin stocks" reputed for their exploitation of local environments and indifference to human rights. As Shell has come to realize, social legitimacy is not built overnight. Legitimacy must be carefully developed and nurtured in close collaboration with relevant stakeholders. Today, Shell continues to be one of the most criticized companies in Europe.

While its non-financial reports demonstrate how the company strives to develop sensitivity to the environment and a willingness to listen to its stakeholders, a number of grassroots initiatives systematically test and challenge Shell's statements. For example, while Shell's non-financial report "Lessons Learned 2004" was dedicated to signal transparency by admitting prior faults and demonstrating a willingness and action to improve, it was confronted with a 29 page report "Lessons Not Learned. The Other Shell Report 2004"[5] produced by a number of influential NGOs such as Friends of the Earth and Advocates for Environmental Human Rights. "Lessons Not Learned" is the third in a series of reports having the ambition of documenting "a consistent story of the company pushing forward with business as usual, disregarding the rights of its stakeholders".[6] Interestingly, these reports emulate the format and style of Shell's own reports, but with the explicit ambition of demonstrating that Shell "continues to hold on to an industrial infrastructure that is hazardous to people and the environment".[7]

(Continued)

(Continued)

Many other critical incidents keep reminding Shell that legitimacy is a recurring issue. In 1999, demonstrating Nigerians occupied two Shell helicopters, nine Shell petrol stations and an oil drilling platform, hindering 250,000 barrels of raw oil a day from reaching the market. Frequently protests and demonstrations are organized to remind the general public about the possible links between Shell and the execution of writer Ken Saro-Wiwa and eight other Nigerians in 1995. These anti-Shell activities are not limited to Shell's headquarters in London but take place globally in the Netherlands, Ireland, South Africa, etc., and web-calendars remind their audience about important dates for protesting against Shell on the issues of environmental protection and human rights.

Points of Reflection

1.   Why is legitimacy important for Shell? Globally and locally?

2.   Why and how does Greenpeace enact the Brent Spar incident?

3.   How may Shell safe-guard itself against future critical incidents?

Chapter Summary

In Chapter 1, we have demonstrated that corporate communications is a fairly old practice dating back to the second half of the nineteenth century. Historically, the field of corporate communications has been focused in particular on the issue of legitimacy for large business corporations. Corporate communications programmes were designed and managed to establish and justify the symbolic and social presence of such corporations. While this is still the case today, the salience of legitimacy has intensified dramatically over the last few decades to the effect that a growing number of organizations of all types and sizes embark on extensive corporate communications programmes. During this period, the field of corporate communications has expanded its scope dramatically. Today, corporate communications is a strategic management discipline encompassing virtually all types of communications and straddling formal disciplinary boundaries. In the next chapter, we take a closer look at this expansion process, focusing in particular on how the notion of integrated communications today affects the entire organizational domain.

Notes

1 Examples from this campaign can be found in *Newsweek,* 14 and 17 October 2005.
2 http://www.shell.com. See also, Fombrun and Rindova (2000), Fossgard-Moser (2006) and Klein (2000a).
3 http://www.shell.com/tellshell
4 'The Shell Report 2002', pp. 4 and 17.
5 'Lessons not learned. The other Shell report 2004' (2004) Friends of the Earth and Advocates for Environmental Human Rights, and others. The other two reports are: 'Behind the shine – the other Shell report 2003' and 'Failing the challenge – the other Shell report 2002'. For more information, see http://www.shellfacts.com/
6 'Lessons not learned. The other Shell report 2004' (2004) Friends of the Earth and Advocates for Environmental Human Rights, and others, p. 2.
7 Ibid. p. 3.

2

The Scope of Integrated Communications
Apprehending an Expanding Body

Even though marketing has always regarded itself as an integrative practice ... scholars of integrated marketing communications envision integration in a far more comprehensive sense. ... integrated marketing communications takes seemingly disparate messages, melds them into one, gives them a voice and provides them with a strategically designed persona. The resulting label radiates technical competence as well as confidence.

George Cheney et al. (2004: 91)

Introduction

While corporate communications is the ideal of presenting the organization as one coherent entity, integrated communications may be regarded as the ongoing endeavour to achieve that goal (Riel, 1995). The vision of corporate communication, in other words, is realized through integrated communications. Only through continuous efforts to integrate its symbols, messages and behaviours can an organization, according to the literature, hope to be perceived as a unified corporate entity. Corporate communications, thus, may be described as the epitome of integrated communications (Yeshin, 1998). Interestingly, however, integrated communications has expanded significantly over the years both inside the organization and across its formal boundaries. In this chapter, we shall discuss how the notion and practice of integrated communications have developed from a distinct and specialized activity to an organization-wide issue and concern that permeates and impacts virtually all organizational activities. In particular, the chapter will focus on the following issues and questions:

Chapter 2: Points of Challenge

- Integration may refer to two different things: the ability of the parts to adapt to the whole or the willingness of the whole to encompass differences. What are the implications of these two views for corporate communications?

- In addition to the alignment of formal communication parameters, the ambition of integrated communications is to manage the *informal* dimensions of an organization's communication. What happens to an organization when its informal communication is formalized?

- Managers and scholars often talk about "total communication". Are there any limitations to the integrated communications project?

Integration as Communication

Integrated communications refers to the practice of aligning symbols, messages, procedures and behaviours in order for an organization to communicate with clarity, consistency and continuity within and across formal organizational boundaries (Christensen et al., in press). While integration is essentially another word for organization and, thus, inseparable from any process of organizing, it was not until

the beginning of the twentieth century that integration became explicitly associated with *communication* as a professional discipline and practice. Today, organizations
are becoming increasingly explicit in pursuing integration in their communications.

**Integrated communications can be defined as the efforts to coordi-
nate and align all communications so that the organization speaks
consistently across different audiences and media.**

BOX 2.1   Defining Integration

In everyday usage, integration refers to the bringing together of things:
economies, cultures, religions, ideas, and so on. We also find the notion of
integration used in mathematics and computer science. In the context of
social systems, integration can be defined as the act, the process or the
instance of forming or uniting differences into a whole, of incorporating
parts into a larger unit and thus, eventually, ending or at least managing
segregation. In addition to this focus on unity, we find definitions that highlight the coexistence of *differences* within the larger unit. Integration in this
view refers to the process of assembling a multiplicity of differences
(people, perspectives or expressions) into equal association, as for example in an organization. The first definition stresses the ability of the system
to envelop its parts and make them adapt to the whole: for example, in the
case of immigrants learning and adopting the norms of the host culture. In
situations where such adaptation involves the absorption into an established order and a loss of the distinct characteristics of the parts, we talk
about assimilation. By contrast, the second definition emphasizes the system's tolerance toward its parts and its willingness to acknowledge and
bend toward their individual qualities.[1]

**Depending on the perspective, integration emphasizes the system or
the parts, the unity or the differences within the whole.**

Recognizing this dual property of integration, sociologist Niklas Luhmann
(1995) points out that integration not only implies the notion of inclusion but
also presupposes *exclusion*. Talk about integration characterizes something else as differentiated or fragmented. At the same time, messages
about integration suggest that the talk originates from a position that is

(Continued)

(Continued)

already integrated itself. By inference, then, we can say that integration is implicitly related to the notion of control. Moreover, we find that integration suggests at once openness and closure. On the one hand, integration is assumed to open the system towards something new, something beyond the system as it has been defined previously. On the other hand, integration is expected to circumscribe this "new" into the system, to "identify" the new with the integrating unit. When this is a two-way process, the incorporated part will be able to modify the incorporating system. Integration, in other words, is a process that, ideally speaking, redefines both the parts and the whole. The derived notions of *integrity* and *integral* mirror this tension between the whole and the parts. While integrity designates the quality or condition of being whole, consistent or undivided, to be integral means to constitute a vital part within some complete unit or whole, that is, a part that retains relative autonomy within that unity. Integration, thus, is about the identity of both the whole and its parts.

Talk about integration assumes a privileged perspective from where similarities, differences and fragmentations can be observed and articulated.

Syncretism refers to a specific type of integration characterized by reconciliation or fusion of different or opposing systems of belief. Syncretism is particularly used to characterize situations where success is partial and does not fully support one or the other belief system.[2] As opposed to eclecticism that *draws upon* different theories or perspectives, syncretism *reconciles and finds new agreement* between those perspectives. While syncretism is often used to describe the blending of two or more religious belief systems into a new system, the idea resonates well with theories of innovation in which incorporation into one tradition of beliefs from unrelated traditions is known to stimulate the development of new ideas.

Integrated communications presents a number of immediate advantages to an organization: corporate messages become mutually aligned, which makes it easier for the organization to claim consistency across different audiences. Integrated messages also make it is easier to brief the communication agency, to make sure that media budgets are spent more efficiently, to obtain a higher degree of precision in campaigns, and, consequently, to assure that economic resources are employed optimally. Conversely, non-integrated or disintegrated communications sends disjointed messages that weaken the impact and confuse, frustrate or irritate the organization's audiences (Smith, 1996). Because consistency of meaning is crucial in today's world, the orchestration of organizational messages is regarded as necessary for organizations to survive and prosper (Drobis, 1997). With the notion of integrated communications, this conviction is spelt out in elaborate details that claim to encompass both formal and informal dimensions of organizational life. In the remainder of this chapter, we shall address the many aspects of integrated communications as the practice has developed from formal to informal domains within and across organizational boundaries.

Integrating Formal Communication

The concern for unified and integrated corporate images was, as we have seen, already evident in mid-to-late nineteenth century corporate communications. The systematic application of integrated communications programmes, however, is often attributed to the introduction of house style manuals in the 1930s (Riel, 1995). With such manuals, specialists of corporate design sought to implement clear and consistent guidelines for the use of corporate symbols in order to maximize exposure and create a clear and distinct impression of the organization in its surroundings. Today such design manuals are used both in public, private, and third sector organizations. They often prescribe in minute detail the correct use of corporate symbols and insignia and may include even buildings, vehicles, letterheads, logos, signs, uniforms, packaging, etc (Olins, 1989). Still, the integration associated with corporate design is a fairly simple exercise involving invention, implementation and regulation. In some cases, however, the desire to express the organization consistently through a logo and other design features takes on an aura of significance not unlike that of national and religious symbols. For example, the State Farm Insurance Company specifies the proper display and treatment of the logo and associated materials in all its offices (Cheney, 1983).

Corporate design confines integrated communications to the coordination of visual signifiers.

In *marketing*, the notion of integrated communications dates back to the classical marketing mix of the 1950s. With its 4Ps, the marketing mix emphasized the importance of aligning *product, price, place* and *promotion* within a coherent plan designed to reach the organization's target audiences (McCarthy, 1960). Underneath the umbrella of this general coordination, a more detailed integration was supposed to take place *within* each of the 4Ps. Thus, integration within promotion could take place at the level of messages, campaigns or media. Also, integration could be approached from both a synchronic and a diachronic perspective. Today, the pool of marketing Ps has expanded to include *people*, *processes*, *principles*, and so forth. While integration within the context of the marketing mix can be rather time consuming, it rarely moves beyond the level of coordinating a limited set of well-defined parameters (messages, publications, outlets) to ensure maximum exposure and impact in a clearly specified target group.

Within the context of the marketing mix, integrated communications refers primarily to maximal exposure.

While the trend toward integrated communications has been evident in many areas of marketing, including logistics, information systems, distribution and networks (Blackwell, 1987), today the notion is used most consistently within the relatively young subfield of integrated *marketing* communications. The American Association of Advertising Agencies defined integrated marketing communications (IMC) as:

> A concept of marketing communication planning that recognizes the added value of a comprehensive plan that evaluates the strategic roles of a variety of communication disciplines and combines them to provide clarity, consistency and maximum communication impact through the seamless integration of discrete messages. (Yeshin, 1998: 68)

Stressing comprehensiveness, consistency and strategic planning, this definition presented IMC as a fairly simple and logical idea concerned primarily with communication *efficiency*. That is, IMC was seen as a way for managers to increase the behavioural effects of corporate messages.

In its early days, the field of IMC was focused primarily on increasing communication impact.

The classical marketing concept, however, prescribes a broader view on integrated communications than are represented by notions of exposure and communication efficiency. With its notion of putting the customer's wants and needs in the centre of the firm's activities, the marketing concept calls for communication that stimulates organization-wide openness and responsiveness vis-à-vis the market. Without abandoning its focus on impact, scholars of IMC have over the years sought to compensate for the definition's lack of attention to the receiver end of the communication process. In 1994, marketing professor Tom Duncan suggested that IMC is "the process of strategically controlling or influencing all messages and encouraging purposeful dialogue to create and nourish profitable relationships with customers and other stakeholders" (Duncan and Caywood, 1996: 18). While still oriented toward sender control, this definition promoted a broader understanding of IMC that acknowledged factors like multiple audiences, sources of information, consumer behaviour, stakeholder relationships and brand loyalty. Following Duncan's perspective, IMC is increasingly regarded as a corporate perspective that includes employees and the media along with other external audiences (Gronstedt, 1996b).

Today, IMC has a vision of nourishing relationships with a growing range of audiences.

In spite of its broader ambitions, integrated marketing communication is often confined to programmes of branding or customer retention. Among leading scholars we find IMC defined as "the philosophy and practice of carefully coordinating a brand's sundry marketing communications elements" (Shimp, 2003: 6) or "a process for planning, executing, and monitoring brand messages that create customer relationships" (Duncan, 2005: 17). While IMC proponents regard the brand as the natural locus for coordinating communications and as the quintessence of integrated marketing communications, (Schultz and Kitchen, 2000), they often further this idea to thinking of the *corporation* as a brand thus extending the logic to the whole organization (Schultz and Schultz, 2004). As such, IMC proponents are in line with scholars of corporate branding who argue that contemporary organizations need to brand themselves as total or monolithic entities (see Chapter 3) (Balmer, 1995; Harris and de Chernatony, 2001; Ind, 1997; Mitchell, 1997). According to this understanding of integrated marketing communications, a corporation such as Apple needs to focus its branding efforts on itself as an *organization* rather than on its individual products. Obviously, an extremely successful product like the iPod challenges the logic of such a practice.

The brand is often thought of as the embodiment of integrated communications and thus as a convenient label for directing concerted marketing efforts.

Integrated communications has moved beyond IMC, which tends to assume that integration takes place, or should take place, within the realm of marketing. Including internal dimensions of the organization's communication and claiming to address a broader range of audiences than customers, integrated communications is now an expansive discipline that links marketing with the fields of public relations, organizational communication and HRM. Management consultant, Anders Gronstedt, describes the expansion this way:

> *Integrating the work of everyone in the company, not only of communication professionals, is necessary because companies communicate with everything they do. The performance of the products and services, accuracy of the billing, and treatment of employees, are all communicating powerful messages to the stakeholders. (1996a: 39f)*

Gronstedt has even suggested that integrated communications is equivalent to total quality management in its focus on optimization of the whole through synergy. He argues that integrated communications, just like total quality management, is a holistic approach to managing the entire business. Such management, according to Gronstedt, is facilitated through the cultivation of long-term relationships between an organization and its various stakeholders, including their communication agencies. Finding traces of such perspective in both public relations and marketing, Gronstedt (1996b) posits that marketing and public relations have more in common than is usually believed by representatives from either discipline (Hutton, 1996). Integrated communications, according to his perspective, has the potential to facilitate collaboration, trust and commitment among customers, employees and other audiences inside and outside the corporation. When organizations, for example, align their internal and external messages they have a greater chance of creating understanding and involvement among their employees: something which in turn breeds trust among external audiences (Scholes and Clutterbuck, 1998).

Inspired by total quality management, integrated communications is envisioned as a holistic practice that stimulates coherence, collaboration and commitment.

Integrating the Informal Organization

With a few exceptions, scholars of integrated communications have focused primarily on the organization's *formal* communication: on those communication parameters that can easily be identified, planned, and circumscribed by the techniques of marketing and related disciplines. However, with organizational culture that has shaped the management literature since the late 1970s, the notion of integrated communications has gradually moved outside the realm of formal communication to include *informal* dimensions as well. As another metaphor for an organization's totality, "culture" became a point of reference in discussions and analyses of organizational integration. Thus, studies of organizational culture have demonstrated in various ways how organizational discourses, narratives, rituals, myths and ceremonies can be important sources of coherence and integration – as well as fragmentation (Young, 1989). Although there is disagreement as to *if* and *how* culture can be managed (cf. Deal and Kennedy, 1982; Martin, 1992), the notion of culture continues to be a central focus of managers in their pursuit of a coherent corporate spirit. In their famous study of the Fortune 500 corporations, for example, Thomas Peters and Robert Waterman (1982) came to the conclusion that excellent companies were able to cultivate the shared meaning of the organization, that is, to nurture the organizational culture and steer it in the right direction. This way, ironically, the informal organization is formalized.

With the notion of organizational culture, integrated communications has been extended to include the *informal* dimensions of the organization, albeit in a formalized version.

Crossing Organizational Boundaries

Integrated communications is not confined to the symbols, messages and behaviours of the *individual* organization. Today, the ambition of integrated communications has expanded significantly to include the organization's network of other organizational actors. In this expansive shape, integrated communications push and traverse and challenge formal organizational boundaries. Here we find a source of increased organizational complexity.

BOX 2.2   Boundaries and their Multiple Senses

The idea of boundaries is as important for organizations as it is for individuals and for nations. In fact, the very notion of a boundary is inescapable, as anthropologist Mary Douglas (1996) describes so well in her book *Natural Symbols*. The inevitable use of language to determine categories of "what's in" and "what's out" – as shown in the mundane example of defining "dirt" – reveals the pervasiveness of boundaries in our lives. At the individual level, our sense of self depends to a great extent on a concept of "where I end and the environment and others begin". In fact, some forms of schizophrenia are characterized by a failure to make this distinction. Of course, we use the term "boundaries" to refer to our personal space as well, with the importance and extent of this varying across cultures. For a nation or a region boundaries are extremely important: they determine the arena in which a particular state or governing body has jurisdiction or legitimate authority. Nation states have never been very comfortable with fuzzy boundaries when it comes to their dominions, which is evident in cases of disputes over borderlands such as Kashmir or divided islands such as Cyprus. Perhaps one of the most interesting aspects of corporate globalization is the fact that corporations today are simultaneously appealing to and disregarding national boundaries.

Although boundaries are inescapable, they are often defied in today's globalized world.

(Continued)

(Continued)

While this book challenges the idea of an organizational self as a persistent and "essential" core of an organization, we need to recognize the importance of boundaries for organizations. Dimensions of these borders are geographic, physical, economic, social, political and communicative (Hirschhorn and Gilmore, 1992). Still, many developments in today's society are eroding the notions of well defined organizational boundaries: some of these trends include public–private partnerships, joint ventures, flexible manufacturing networks and virtual teams/organizations. From the standpoint of identity and corporate communications, one of the most important questions to ask is when does an organization become so diffuse that it cannot effectively speak with one voice, or even try any longer to do so? From the point of view of members, we should at the same time ask in what ways might it actually be beneficial to shatter the illusion of organizational voice and unity?

Contemporary programmes of integrated communications urge organizations to conceive of their communication in a larger inter-organizational context. What, for example, are the images of the organization's suppliers? Do they deliver quality products? Do they treat their employees decently? What do their production processes look like? Are they considered environmentally sound? If these and similar questions cannot be answered satisfactorily, it may be difficult for the core organization to maintain its own image. Today, we find that a growing number of organizations seek to integrate their communications with other organizations, including suppliers, distributors and advertising agencies. These collaborators are found both upstream and downstream in their value chain (Gronstedt, 1996b). Some organizations, thus, set explicit standards for their partners in terms of their expected social, political and environmental conduct. For instance, an important dimension of relationship management today deals with how to set and comply with such standards within areas like manufacturing, engineering, human resources, finance and accounting (Gummesson, 1999; Morgan and Hunt, 1994). While such practice challenges formal organizational boundaries, its primary impetus is to secure legitimacy and maintain a positive image across the organization's many different constituencies.

Including the messages and behaviours of other players in the value chain, integrated communications becomes an expanding field of activity without clear organizational boundaries.

CASE: The Drive Toward Standardization

Theodore Levitt's globalization thesis

With frequent mergers and acquisitions, the practice of integrated communications has moved far beyond traditional organizational boundaries, often to include companies and departments in distant geographical locations. With globalization, this process has intensified dramatically. As a consequence, the question of whether to standardize corporate messages or adapt to local markets attracts renewed attention and interest. Can organizations pursue coherence, consistency and unity in their messages while retaining a sensitivity and adaptiveness to cultural differences? This is a practical as well as a socio-political and philosophical question. In his now classic article "The Globalization of Markets," published in 1983 in *Harvard Business Review,* marketing Professor Theodore Levitt claimed that standardization is an essential condition for corporations operating in a global world. Levitt argued that business firms, in order to survive in a competitive environment, need to operate as if the world were one large market, ignoring what he called "superficial regional and national differences". Although some regional differences persist, the world, according to Levitt, is generally moving towards a converging commonality in terms of tastes, preferences and life styles:

> *The global corporation operates with resolute constancy – at low relative cost – as if the entire world (or major regions of it) were a single entity; it sells the same things in the same way everywhere ... Ancient differences in national tastes or modes of doing business disappear ... The global competitor will constantly seek to standardize its offering everywhere. ... It will never assume that the customer is a king who knows his own wishes. ... The global corporation ... actively seeks and vigorously works toward global convergence. (1983: 92, 94, 95)*

Stimulated by media and technology, people all over the globe seem to want the same products and brands, including McDonald's, Coca-Cola, Revlon, Sony and Levi's. In line with Levitt's perspective, other writers have added that the Internet is now speeding up the globalization process by making products and services instantaneously available to customers around the globe thus augmenting the tendency toward convergence and homogenization (Hennessey, 1999). Interestingly, Levitt's analysis did not end with this diagnosis. Based on his observations, he urged organizations to abandon the usual practice of adjusting their products and practices to each individual country in which they operate in favour of one standardized approach. His description of an increasingly globalized world, thus, is accompanied by a *prescription* for organizations to actively seek and enact global convergence.

Under the impact of globalization, integrated communications is often reduced to a question of standardized soluvtions for diverse situations.

(Continued)

(Continued)

Levitt's article stirred up considerable controversy, inside as well as outside the marketing community. Critics claimed that Levitt's analysis was impervious to significant cultural differences, ignoring the fact that few marketing ideas have a universal appeal, that consumer preferences always are local, that there are serious translation problems associated with standardization, that differences in legislation prevent marketers from pursuing fully standardized global approaches, and that few people *outside* the organization have an eye for let alone an interest in standardized campaigns (Vardar, 1992). As Onkvisit and Shaw put it: "… until the world is ready to adopt a single language, a single currency and a single political ideology, it is premature to accept the standardized approach and its sweeping generalization" (Onkvisit and Shaw, 1987: 54). In addition, some marketing scholars argued that greater returns could be achieved by adapting products and marketing strategies to the specifics of individual markets (Kotler, 1985). In spite of an extensive critique of standardized solutions, we experience in these years a resurgence of Levitt's vision of a standardized approach to corporate communications. In line with Levitt's prescriptions it is now argued fervently by corporate communications theorists and practitioners that organizations should aim for a unified, consistent voice across different markets and different audiences. The communication strategy of Bang & Olufsen, for example, stresses *a unified global presence* above anything else. With the slogan "A life less ordinary", accompanied by colourful and rather unusual images of trendy consumers (e.g. a weirdly dressed couple with a Bang & Olufson television on a leash or a young man with an trendy haircut shouting), the campaign addresses the hip, postmodern consumer of the western metropolis. This campaign, however, has been implemented in all major cities in the world, irrespective of cultural differences. Although managers at Bang & Olufsen are aware that their campaign may be seen as offensive in some cultures (for example in South-East Asia), their desire to project one global image in all markets is so strong that they decided to ignore such differences. Years back, the same was the case for the LEGO Corporation. Rather than adapting to local differences, the LEGO Corporation took for many years the position that LEGO *is a global product* and that it, accordingly, should be available, in more or less the same form, all over the world. While LEGO managers recognized differences between markets, their global ambition made them focus systematically on similarities across markets – similarities consistently confirmed by their own market research (Cheney and Christensen, 2001a).

The "globalization thesis" is frequently used to justify corporate communication programmes.

Integrating the Customer

Interestingly, the trend toward standardization runs parallel to a growing emphasis on customer-adapted solutions. Integrated (marketing) communications, thus, increasingly refer to the application of data-driven communication programmes designed to facilitate interactivity and dialogue and support *product customization*. In setting up systems that record individual wants and needs and allow the customer to co-design his or her own product or service, such organizations practise integrated communications at a highly sophisticated level. Here integrated communications refers to the combined practice of integrating the voice of the customer fairly early in the production process, of translating specific customer choices to internal practices and procedures across functional departments and of responding swiftly with the desired product or service (Schultz et al., 1994; Rogers, 1993 and Peppers). Such practice has been reported in the production of personal pagers where the application of computerized design procedures allows producers to offer a huge amount of combinations of distinct features for their pagers (Pine et al., 1993). In a similar manner, some automobile production systems allow the customer to design his or her own car (from a set of available options) in the dealer showroom on a computer linked directly to the factory production line (Achrol, 1991). Where the early conceptions of integrated communications merely looked at the coordination of marketing parameters in order to provide message clarity and message consistency, this latter kind of integration involves the organization more substantially by, ostensibly, putting the customer at the centre of all its activities. For that reason, integrated communications has been presented as a true realization or even radicalization of the classical marketing concept (Schultz, 1993). With its focus on the wants and needs of the consumer, the marketing concept claims to serve the interests of the individual as well as society as a whole. Not only is that assumption questionable, however, it is also debatable whether the integrated communications practice is able to move production beyond its orientation toward standardization.

Integrated communications is often celebrated as the ultimate realization of the marketing concept and its notion of the responsive organization.

BOX 2.3   The Consumer Society

We are so used to hearing media, politicians and CEOs speak about our countries as "nations of consumers" that we barely notice when, for example, the *New York Times* refers to mainland China not as a people or a country but as an emerging market of 1.25 billion *consumers*. In fact, this has become the typical way of describing a country's inhabitants. In 1900,

(Continued)

(Continued)

"consumption" referred to waste and to tuberculosis. With the birth of lifestyle advertising in the 1920s, advances in mass production in the middle of the century, and the infusion of marketing into all domains of society in the 1990s, consumption became not simply something we do to live but what we do and *who we are.* While the consumer movements of the 1960s–1970s brought increased awareness and critiquing of business corporations and the products and services they were manufacturing and marketing, the overall trend of the past several decades has been to elevate consumption to the main goal of our society.

Influenced by the media, politicians and corporations, most people today define themselves primarily as consumers.

Not so long ago, most people thought about themselves as *citizens.* To be a citizen implies being a member of a political community, which originally was (in ancient Greece, for example) a city but today is usually a country. In contrast to the notion of the consumer, citizenship carries with it a right (and, to some extent, an obligation) to political participation. Citizens, in other words, are expected to be actively engaged in the public realm beyond the self and the moment. While consumers certainly have rights, these rights do seldom translate into responsibilities. Thus, when people "vote" through their patterns of consumption, they rarely take the larger "good" of society into consideration (Cheney, 2004).

Although mass customization arrangements allow organizations to respond more rapidly and efficiently to perceived changes in their markets, such arrangements are not the radical departures from standardization they may first seem to be. Customization, in fact, can only work if the company has defined its flexible parameters proactively, that is, delineated its adaptive responses *in advance* of specific wants and demands in the market. The car producer, for example, that allows the customer to design his or her "own" car can only be responsive on dimensions determined *a priori*, allowing the customer to choose between a *preset* range of colours, seats, steering wheels, headlights, rims, and so forth. Other dimensions, like the name or the logo of the car, are fixed. Product customization, thus, co-exists with standardization.

As a proactive strategy, integrated communications enables the corporation to be responsive without surrendering its ability to predict and standardize its responses.

Integrating and Shaping the Wider Environment

A similar type of integrated communications is at play in the efforts of contemporary corporations to build elaborate stakeholder databases and organize *strategic dialogues* with select stakeholders. This practice is increasingly found in embattled industries such as chemicals, oil and tobacco, but other organizations host such dialogues as well (Cheney and Christensen, 2001b). By inviting stakeholders such as environmental groups, health care organizations, insurance companies or neighbours to participate in the articulation and, sometimes, resolution of imminent corporate issues, such corporations seek to transform integrated communications from a mainly sender-oriented exercise to a two-way practice. In such practice, the desired outcome of integration is not so much message consistency as beneficial relations between the organization and its various interest groups. A well-known example is Royal Dutch Shell's meetings and deliberations with Greenpeace in the aftermath of the Brent Spar crisis of 1995 (see Chapter 1). In line with the notion of two-way symmetrical communication (Grunig, 1992), Shell and other corporations seek to implement a listening orientation and a more responsive posture towards their relevant surroundings. Through the organization of such dialogues, corporations integrate the voices of powerful stakeholders and in this way hope to achieve the necessary societal endorsement of their plans and decisions.

Strategic dialogues allow corporations to integrate critical stakeholder in their decision processes, thus enhancing social acceptance and legitimacy.

Increasingly, organizations incorporate the role of *the media* in their integrated communications programmes. This is not only the case when companies host press conferences, but also when media relations are handled more proactively. While some organizations produce their own journalistic material for the electronic media, including films, CDs or scientific studies, other organizations *stage* media events with the strategic intent of shaping the news agenda. During the Brent Spar crisis, for example, Greenpeace produced a film describing its conflict with Royal Dutch Shell in the North Sea. The film, which was released on CD-ROM and sent to a large number of television stations, portrayed the conflict as a clash between David and Goliath: between ordinary people and big corporations, between good and evil. In this way, Greenpeace managed to define the Brent Spar-agenda for months while attracting many new members and sympathizers (Wätzold, 1996). Most companies, however, work more discretely with the media delivering, for example, stories to business sections of newspapers.

Proactive corporations increasingly incorporate the media in their integrated communications programmes.

In addition, integrated communications regularly includes the integration of *the political system*. This type of integration finds its most familiar expression in traditional lobbying activities where corporate representatives seek to influence the opinions of legislators and other public officials for or against a specific cause. More indirect and sophisticated forms of political integration are found when political initiatives are shaped by proactive or visionary corporations. Thus, when politicians formulate principles within the area of environmental protections they often listen to prominent companies that impose stricter environmental standards on themselves than are required by law. The steps taken by the pharmaceutical corporation Novo Nordisk, for example, have often served as inspiration for politicians when suggesting new standards in the area of environmental protection (for further details on Novo Nordisk see the case discussion at the end of this chapter) (Cheney and Christensen, 2001a). In cases where companies have experience in setting political standards and where this influence is employed strategically, politicians indirectly become players in the integrated communications project of the corporation. This practice is not limited to the environmental field, but takes place also in the area of food production, insurance and other business areas where politicians consult corporations in their process of developing new political agendas and proposals.

Integrated communications increasingly implies the integration of various actors in the political system.

Digitialization as Integration

Finally, the practice of integrated communications is dramatically shaped by new digital media. On the one hand, digitization has created a shared language that allows employees, without technical skills, to exchange and share information (numbers, text and images) across different functions and geographical locations. Known as the XML (the Extensible Markup Language) this language is capable of describing many different kinds of data and, consequently, to facilitate the sharing of data across different systems, particularly systems connected via the Internet. This language, thus, is essentially integrating. On the other hand, the digitization of information makes it faster and easier to compare messages across different media and different audiences. This way, the new information technologies allow organizations to identify inconsistencies in their messages and symbols and, accordingly, support their insistence on coherence in everything the organization says and does. Contemporary information technologies, thus, have accentuated the call for integration within and across the organization's formal boundaries.

The digitization of information has become a key "driver" of integrated communications.

An Expanding Project

As it appears, integrated communications has come to mean many different things: from the coordination of corporate design or the strategic alignment of marketing parameters to the pursuit of a coherent and shared corporate culture or the vertical integration of business partners, customers and NGOs. Integrated communications, thus, has moved from a fairly bounded and specialized activity to an organization-wide issue and concern. Adding to this the organizational challenges associated with the new communication technologies, integrated communications has become an increasingly expansive ideal much in line with the Finnish communication scholar Leif Åberg's (1990) notion of "total communication". Such an all-inclusive notion of integrated communications may appear overtly ambitious and unrealistic: as a fantasy in the head of a few communication managers. However, as evidenced by the growing number of business conferences on the topic, many organizations today would claim that they pursue, or wish to pursue, corporate communications in this broad sense. Corporate managers are increasingly using the language of integration when they approach the expanding field of market-related communication. Although the growing managerial endorsement of integrated communications does not match its actual implementation in practice, managers have gradually come to share the language of integration and its implied notion of aligning and coordinating all com-munications (Cornelissen, 2001, 2003). Integrated communications, thus, is a power-ful indication of the resurgence of the corporate body in a new and expansive shape. If we accept the proposition, introduced in the Preface of this book, that communi-cation *does things* or has "organizing properties" that inevitably shape and generate our organizations (Cooren, 1999), we need to pay careful attention to how organiza-tions formulate visions and ideals for communication purposes. Such visions and ideals are not only prescriptions for how to handle communication but also defini-tions of organization that guide the behaviours of managers and employees far beyond message creation and message handling per se (Putnam et al., 1996).

BOX 2.4   Communication is Organization

In everyday usage, and typically within the fields of marketing and man-agement, we tend to think of an organization's *communication* as some-thing distinct from the organization itself. Organizations, according to this perspective, *produce* communication, not as their general way of being or existence but as something distinct and separate from their organizing

(Continued)

(Continued)

practices. Against this perspective, professor of organizational communication James Taylor and sociologist Elisabeth van Every argue "it is equally true to say that organizations emerge in communication" (2000: 4). Communication and organization, they claim, are *equivalent* terms. Inspired by, for example, phenomenology, speech-action theory and conversational analysis, Taylor and van Every show how an organization comes into being through the ways its leaders and members speak about and account for its actions and activities. Speech, in other words, *is* action just as our acts simultaneously speak. Accordingly, it is not possible to distinguish in a meaningful way between what an organization says and what it does. This is not to suggest a simple one-to-one correspondence between what an organization says and what it is. Obviously, an organization that describes its marketing communication activities in terms of, for example, "dialogue" does not emerge as an excellent communicator simply by talking this way. This perspective implies that the ways organizations talk about themselves and their communication practices are not neutral undertakings, but are activities that contribute to the articulation of beliefs, values and horizons – and thus to the creation of organizational reality. Rather than being something distinct and separate from the organizational practice, communication, thus, is the "essential modality", as Taylor and van Every put it, for organizational life.

Our organizations are created and shaped by the communication ideals they acclaim. This also applies to the notion of corporate communications and its ideal of integration.

Some readers may find that the discussion above carries the notion of integrated communications a bit too far. After all, they might claim, integrated communications only means to speak consistently and coherently across different audiences and different media. The point here, however, is not to legislate terminology or to determine a priori what *counts* as truly integrated communications but to explore the corporate extensiveness of the term and its organizational implications. As this text is being written, integrated communications expands to still more areas of organizational practice. The fact, for example, that many organizations pay their top managers huge salaries, sometimes in the form of stock options, has become an important communication to the public about corporate practice. Since something always escapes the formalization of corporate communication, organizations are continuously induced to update and expand their notion and practice of integrated communications.

Today integrated communications potentially embraces all aspects of the organizing process.

CASE: *Aligning and integrating communications within a framework of sustainability*

NOVO NORDISK[3]

Novo Nordisk is a world leader in diabetes care, but it also holds a leading position in the areas of hemostasis management, growth hormone therapy and hormone replacement therapy. The company headquarter is located in the outskirts of Copenhagen. Novo Nordisk employs approximately 22,000 people in 78 countries. Its products are marketed in 179 countries. The corporate communications challenge of Novo Nordisk is primarily to raise positive awareness of its activities and initiatives within social and environmental responsibility. The case exemplifies how a medical corporation seeks to achieve international recognition and legitimacy by integrating all communications into a coherent and consistent message across a broad range of audiences and markets.

The Issue

Like other companies in the pharmaceutical industry, Novo Nordisk operates under increased public scrutiny. And like other companies within that industry, Novo Nordisk is frequently challenged by external stakeholders on issues like GMOs, animal testing and global health. At the same time, Novo Nordisk has managed to maintain and in some cases strengthen its social legitimacy. For a number of years, Novo Nordisk has been internationally renowned for its proactive stance on sustainability. Novo Nordisk's participation in a large number of international initiatives on the promotion of corporate social responsibility has not only led to admiration and a positive media reputation but also to a number of prizes and awards as recognition of its engagement in social issues. Novo Nordisk is being cited widely as a responsible company concerned about not only its customers, but also about its employees, the local community, and the environment in general. Recently its former Chair Mads Øvlisen was appointed as one of two European business representatives to join the prestigious board of the United Nation's Global Compact initiative that works to improve business–society relations. Nationally, the company is a corporate icon of environmental and social responsibility. For a number of years it has achieved top positions on national image rankings as the most admired corporation. And among MBA students, Novo Nordisk is often labelled as the preferred place to work. This position is rare in an industry that is increasingly subjected to public scrutiny.

(Continued)

(Continued)

Yet, the issue of how to craft and maintain an image for itself at the global level, especially in the USA, remains a continuous challenge.

The Organization of Corporate Communications

Novo Nordisk's longstanding tradition for excellence in sustainability was organization-ally consolidated in 2002 when its department of Stakeholder Relations (including Corporate Communications) was included in Executive Management. Under the leadership of executive vice-president Ms Lise Kingo, the department expanded in 2004 into the department of "People, Reputation and Relations" (PRR). PRR, which currently has approximately 200 employees, serves as the locus of integrating all communication activities. The PRR department drives, challenges and monitors the strategic focus on sustainability strategies and helps individual business units implement new activities in relation to sustainability by:

- Spotting trends that may affect future business.
- Identifying and reconciling dilemmas with stakeholders.
- Building stakeholder relationships locally and globally.
- Embedding the Triple Bottom Line mindset throughout the company.
- Accounting and conveying Novo Nordisk's performance, positions and goals.

In addition, the task of PRR is to ensure that strategic goals and results are communicated consistently and coherently at all organizational levels. Only a decade ago, Novo Nordisk relied on locally developed marketing strategies adapted to local demands and individual managerial preferences. Today, Novo Nordisk seeks to align all marketing activities under the aegis of one corporate logo and one corporate culture, called The Novo Nordisk Way of Management. The Novo Nordisk Way of Management extends beyond individual products and manufacturing operations to include the management of social activities. As such it sets the tone and standards amongst managers and employees in the entire organization.

Stakeholder Integration

To realize its goals on sustainability, Novo Nordisk carefully nurtures its relations with many different publics. The integration of external stakeholders had begun already, in the late 1960s in the form of occasional dialogues with critical environmentalists. Today, it involves more formalized dialogues with a variety of stakeholders, including the European Union, consumer associations, NGOs, neighbours, journalists, investors and politicians. And today, the dialogues involve deliberations on both *social* and environmental issues. Novo Nordisk claims that these dialogues, accounted for in its non-financial reports, have served on multiple occasions to stimulate new goals for future sustainability practices. Recently, for example, Novo Nordisk collaborated with the World Wildlife Foundation (WWF) to reduce its CO_2 outlet within 10 per cent by 2014. Without such collaboration and commitment, the company foresaw its CO_2 outlet to increase considerably. In addition to favourable media attention, such proactive change measures allow Novo Nordisk to define for itself the standards it needs to adapt to. Novo Nordisk's proactive strategies have previously be able to influence industry standards on corporate social responsibility. Novo Nordisk not only monitors its own standards and behaviours, its suppliers are frequently evaluated on issues such as salaries, working hours, child labour, assembly rights, discrimination and privacy. Sport Direct, a supplier of "corporate gifts and gadgets", for example, has subjected itself to a thorough scrutiny of all its business practices and its *suppliers'* practices in order to remain in business with Novo Nordisk. While Sport Direct's engagement in sustainable business practices was not compulsory, it was strongly recommended by Novo Nordisk.

Integrated reporting

Novo Nordisk's ambition of integrating all activities within one coherent communication framework was symbolically marked in 2004 by the integration of the financial report and the sustainability report into one comprehensive "economic, social and environmental report". While the first sustainability report published in 1993 was an experimental grassroots level of publication, the sustainability report has now achieved its status as the company's most important corporate communication document. The 2003 report was released via 20,000 copies. The 2004 report was released via 70,000 copies. With the integrated report, the responsibility for communicating the financial results is now in the hands of the PRR department.

While non-financial or integrated reports are most often seen as communication tools for external consumption, at Novo Nordisk the reports are used deliberately to educate employees in sustainable business practices. The sustainability report 2002, for example, was named "TakeAction!" and was dedicated to promote the idea of involving employees voluntarily in projects of social responsibility. A number of employees have initiated TakeAction! projects, ranging from small local projects with only a few people involved to large annual events. Among such activities are a flea market where the profits are donated to a home for people with diabetes, book sales and the collection of clothes for diabetes clinics in less developed countries as well as, information and prevention campaigns about diabetes – one of these being the development of a cookbook with recipes for promoting healthier eating habits among employees, etc. In addition to these local initiatives Novo Nordisk offers the NovoHealthy programme, with paid stop-smoking courses for all employees, a fitness centre, stress management and an annual diabetes check-up to support a healthier lifestyle and prevent diabetes among employees. These initiatives along with a

(Continued)

(Continued)

number of other employees-oriented activities (day care for NovoNordisk employees' children, health insurance, and so on) all seek to make each employee part of an integrated relationship. Again – while participation is not compulsory, it is strongly encouraged by management.

Points of Reflection

1. What does Novo Nordisk hope to achieve by aligning all its communication, marketing and human resource activities under one logo and one message?

2. What are the limits to integrating employees in the corporate communications programme?

3. Do you see any ethical challenges to Novo Nordisk's endeavour to align also its external stakeholders under its "corporate umbrella"?

Chapter Summary

In Chapter 2, we have shown how the project of corporate communications operates through the practice of integrated communications. Integrated communications refers to the ongoing endeavour to coordinate and align all communications in order for an organization to speak consistently across different audiences and different media. This endeavour embraces still more aspects of the organizing process. In particular, we have discussed how the practice of integrated communications has expanded from an emphasis on tangible design and marketing parameters, over branding, to an organization-wide focus on everything organizations say and do. In its early days, integrated communications was concerned primarily about message exposure and communication impact vis-à-vis a few external audiences. Today, its ambition goes further to include also *informal* dimensions of an organization's communication and to implicate the voices and behaviours of employees, collaborators, the media and politicians. As the project of corporate communications is expanding from a distinct, delimited and clearly demarcated set of activities to a broader, all-encompassing communication ideal, it has wide-ranging implications for organizational life. In the next chapter, we unfold some of these implications as they manifest themselves through corporate branding.

Notes

1   See *The American Heritage Dictionary* – electronic version.
2   http://en.wikipedia.org/wiki/Syncretism
3   http://www.novonordisk.com. See also, Morsing and Oswald (2006) and Schultz et al. (n.d.). To order copies contact sales@dardenpublishing.com

3

Corporate Branding and Identity

The Body is Marked

The skin figures. It is what we see and know of others and ourselves. We show ourselves in our skins, and our skins figure out the things we are and mean: our health, youth, beauty, power, enjoyment, fear, fatigue, embarrassment or suffering. The skin is always written: it is legendary. More than the means we happen voluntarily or involuntarily to disclose to sight, it has become the proof of our exposure to visibility itself.

Steven Connor (2004: 51)

Introduction

Corporate communications today subsumes still more aspects of organizational life. Yet, the expansion of the corporeal domain that we are witnessing these days is not an unregulated or uncontrolled process. On the contrary. The corporate body is nurtured, trimmed, profiled and staged. In short, it is *branded*. The ultimate ambition of corporate communications is to develop and present the organization as one unified brand: a corporate brand. While branding is usually associated with products, today we often find it applied to organizations as well. Corporate branding can be defined as the attempt to brand the organization as one coherent entity, one integrated body (Ind, 1997). As such, it builds on principles of product branding, but extends these principles through a systematic reflection on the organization's identity, including questions about the role of the employee. The aim of this chapter is to discuss how branding is permeating the organizational domain to the effect that the organization, its culture and its members, becomes the primary focus of attention. In particular, the chapter will address the following issues and questions:

Chapter 3: Points of Challenge

- The ambition of corporate communications is to present the organization as a unified corporate brand. Can such a brand provide the organization with clear and stable points of differentiation?

- Corporate branding is founded on the assumption that consumers increasingly "buy" the companies *behind* the products. To what extent is that assumption realistic?

- Corporate branding assumes a strong coherence between the corporate brand promise, the image and the organizational culture. Is consistency necessary to build a strong corporate brand? And what is the role of the employee in all of this?

Product Branding

Originally, the word branding referred to the process of burning an identifiable mark into the hide of livestock animals, so as to establish ownership and prevent theft. In the western USA and Canada, the unique mark made it possible for cattle to graze freely among other cattle until the time they were driven to market. Since the 1950s, branding has developed into a sophisticated marketing practice that equally helps identify the owners or producers of products (Gardner and Levy, 1955). Unlike the branding of cattle, however, contemporary branding serves to *accentuate* and draw attention to the distinction of products in order to help them stand out in a competitive marketplace. When physical product differences are easily copied by competitors or eroded by technological developments, organizations use branding to imbue their mass produced products with additional meaning and thus endow them with more stable identities (Schultz and de Chernatony, 2002). In some cases, the added meaning is more important than the product's physical qualities. In fact, in recent years, branding has even extended to career workshops and websites, explicitly urging people to rebrand themselves in the face of job loss, uncertainty or crisis (Lair et al., 2005).

Contemporary branding practices have intensified the social significance of differentiation.

According to branding expert Wally Olins (1989), the idea of branding the same product to different consumers had already been developed in the late nineteenth century. By dressing up products such as tea and soap in different types of packaging, thus suggesting different identities, it was possible to sell the same tea or soap to diverse customer segments. Today, of course, branding goes far beyond packaging. Contemporary products, thus, are "wrapped" in design, status, sex, lifestyles and other symbolic constructs through which producers hope to create more stable product identities, stimulate customer loyalty and justify premium prices.

The assumption behind branding is that added and crystallized meanings provide products with better marks of distinctiveness than their physical product qualities.

According to professor of branding David Aaker (1996), a brand is a *promise* to the consumer regarding the product's social, emotional or aesthetic qualities. The typical brand promise is that the product (for example, Ray-Ban sunglasses, Audi cars, Nokia telephones or Nike running shoes) will make the consumer appear more attractive to his or her surroundings: look younger or better, signal membership of a particular social class, or indicate affiliation with an aesthetic subculture. In today's advertising, however, where products are often branded through the use of humour (for example, Toyota or Camel) or sophisticated symbolism (for example, Absolute Vodka or Silk Cut cigarettes), it is impossible to spot the exact brand promise. Still, brands provide consumers with a pool of symbols to use when constructing their personal identities. Watches and cars are classic examples of brands that offer identities to the people who buy them: Rolex, Timex or Swatch? Rover, Citroën or Skoda? Likewise, producers of cosmetics are highly aware of the identities associated with their product lines: Elisabeth Arden, Clinique or Body Shop?

In their quest for individual identities, consumers become dependent on the identity of branded products.

BOX 3.1   Identity at Issue

Identity is one of the most salient issues for contemporary individuals and organizations. The fixation on identity that we find in modern (especially Western societies), however, is only a fairly recent phenomenon. As Emile Durkheim and other social theorists have observed, for essentially tribal societies, identity does not regularly come into question for a person. In such societies, one's "identity" is immersed in the body social; in cases of extreme cultural collectivism, it is not even possible to speak in a language about one's "own personal identity". In any case, with tribal cultures, the individual is not understood as something to be continually highlighted and even celebrated.

The notion of a distinct personal identity is largely absent in traditional or tribal societies.

In the modern world, things are different. Freed up from some of the traditional moorings of the self, many people find themselves struggling over identities that are given (for example, by their families, religious upbringing, neighbourhood, ethnicity and nation), coping with the tension between "local" and "global" identities, and trying to "find themselves" in adolescence or during a so-called "mid-life crisis". This means ironically that identity crises become social issues as well. Thus, we are by now accustomed to reading about and hearing discussions of "German identity" after reunification of the country in 1990, "threats to Western culture" by immigration from the Middle East or North Africa, or the maintenance of "hybrid" identities by Mexicans who have moved to the USA.

In modern society, identity is an ongoing issue, both desired and contested at many different levels.

Despite the importance of identity in modern society, we have a hard time settling on what identity is. On the one hand we tend to think of identity as essence, as something solid and continuous. In the context of organization, for example, identity is often referred to as dimensions that are "central", "distinctive" and "enduring" (Albert and Whetten, 1985). On the other hand, we frequently talk about identity as something to be created or shaped. Thus, in addition to "having" identities, individuals and organizations speak of shaping identities, expressing identities and sometimes changing identities. Through various forms of communications, organizations try to express "who they are", and consultants in corporate identity try to help organizations communicate their "essences". While psychological research has found that people perceive of organizations in corporeal terms and as having identities (Cohen and Basu, 1987), critical analysis has argued that powerful corporations throughout history have abused this notion of corporations as persons to obscure, in both law and public opinion, the fact that they exercise more power than the rest of us (Bakan, 2004). Identity is clearly an elusive concept.

The notion of identity at once expresses surface and depth, skin and soul. This is also true for corporate identity.

Some consumers shape their identities by avoiding certain brands. Corporations like Phillip Morris, Coca-Cola, Pepsi, Marlboro and Shell, for example, frequently face critical consumers or consumer associations that advice their fellow consumers to buy alternative brands. Blackspot shoes made from vegetarian materials, including hemp and recycled tires, appeal to people who are cynical about consumerism. Referring to Nike's famous logo the "swoosh", Blackspot has called one of its shoes the "Unswoosher" (Walker, 2006). A number of websites have been created to support anti-brand campaigns and to protest against the power of the global corporations (Klein, 2000). One of the most popular targets for anti-websites and blogs is Wal-Mart,[1] but Nike,[2] McDonalds[3] and Starbucks[4] have also attracted the attention of dedicated activists who in serious but also creative and humorous ways declare their resentfulness against the corporate activities. Often these sites and blogs are illustrated by video-clips, quotes, photos, posters, t-shirts and lengthy reports as well as encouragements to boycott.

The identities of individuals, groups and societies are shaped by and reflected in brands as well as anti-brands.

Sometimes, the sentiments associated with anti-brands appear stronger and more focused than the emotions attached to regular brands. Perhaps, anti-brands influence consumer choice more strongly than product brands? A study reports that 18 per cent of the US population at some point have been involved in a consumer boycott, with the ambition to either affect policies or to communicate disapproval (Miller and Friday, 1992). Today, boycotts are professionally organized and do not only target particular product brands but also sometimes entire industries, for example boycotts against disposable diapers, detergents with phosphates or the fur-trade (Jackson and Schantz, 1993). More recently, the National Boycott News has listed 17 cosmetic companies that have announced to end the use of animal testing (Gelb, 1995). With *corporate* branding, the focus on such issues becomes even more accentuated. As we shall see in the remainder of this chapter, corporate branding drives corporations themselves to draw attention to the organization "behind" the product.

Branding the Corporate Body

In a 2001 *Harvard Business Review* article, professors of organization Mary Jo Hatch and Majken Schultz declared that successful companies of today "promote a corporate brand – a single umbrella image that casts one glow over a panoply of products" (2001: 3–4). To support their claim, they listed a range of corporations, including McDonald's, Disney, Nokia and the LEGO Group, that all have managed to develop a corporate-level position across different markets and business areas. Drawing on a set of values, a distinctive design, a shared story or other organizational symbols, the aim of corporate branding is to provide the organization with an aura of tradition, aesthetics and credibility that adds distinction to the organization relatively independent of its specific products and markets. According to this perspective, corporate branding relies on the organization's identity as a "nest" from which to develop and express distinctive features of the organization. The notion of "corporate brand" encapsulates those dimensions of organizational identity, that are highlighted and staged vis-à-vis the surrounding world (Schultz, 2005). While corporate branding has been applied most extensively to private companies, today non-governmental organizations, political parties, cultural institutions, municipalities, cities and even countries are striving to be recognized as unique brands.

Corporate branding is the systematic effort to develop and present the organization as one unified brand.

Underlying this endeavour is the conviction that consumers increasingly "buy" the company *behind* the products or the branded goods. "Consumers want to know about the company, not just the products," says Proctor & Gamble's one-time CEO Ed Artz (Swasy, 1991). Similarly, a Starbucks' webpage tells us: "Consumers are expecting more than a "product" from their favourite brands. Employees are choosing to work for companies with strong values. Shareholders are more inclined to invest in businesses with outstanding corporate reputations. Quite simply, being socially responsible is not only the right thing to do; it can distinguish a company from its industry peers."[5] The title of marketing professors John M.T. Balmer and Stephen A. Greyser's (2003) book *Revealing the Corporation* expresses the same idea: since the company behind the products has become the focus of growing public attention, organizations need to learn how to reveal themselves in favourable ways to their many different stakeholders.

Corporate branding is founded on the assumption that consumers increasingly "buy" the companies *behind* the products.

Following this line of thought, it may be argued that corporate branding is not simply an option available to managers but a necessity for contemporary organizations facing many critical and inquisitive stakeholders. When organizations chose to brand only their products, consumers and other stakeholders may still evaluate and make judgments about the company behind thus forcing the organization to take charge of the corporate branding process itself. Even for companies with strong product brands, the pressure to brand the entire organization is more pronounced than ever before. Proctor & Gamble, for example, that used to brand only its individual products (Pampers, Tide, Fairy Liquid, and so on) has now embarked on an extensive corporate branding project. This is true for other organizations as well. Consequently, the sharp distinctions between "monolithic", "endorsed" and "branded" identity strategies that we often find reproduced in conventional textbooks (Olins, 1989; also Wright, 1989) may no longer be as relevant as they used to seem. Many organizations initiate corporate branding programmes, even when their product brands are strong and respected. Indeed, some corporate brands have emerged from the success of single product brands. Virgin and Caterpillar, for example, have stretched their names from airlines and trucks respectively to business areas such as music, soft drinks and clothes. Others have been strong corporate brands for ages (e.g. Disney, Shell and IBM). Thus, we have to realize that different branding and identity strategies are complementary rather than mutually exclusive. While some dimensions of branding provide the organization with points of differentiation and uniqueness, others are more focused on establishing goodwill and legitimacy.

An essential dimension of corporate branding is the pursuit of legitimacy through socially accepted behaviour.

BOX 3.2   Uniqueness and Legitimacy

The tension between standing out and being accepted is a basic one for organizations as for individuals. A stress on uniqueness is partly a matter of separation from the larger community (of people, organizations or whatever). A stress on legitimacy appeals to "the common grounds" – in Aristotle's terms, the *topoi*, or commonplaces – that form the reservoir of meanings from which an entire community or society draws. This distinction strikes at the heart of "the identity problem" as conceived especially in the modern western world: how to be sufficiently different to stand out in the crowd yet how to blend in such that one is not seen as being weird or too different.

Identity-work brings out a fundamental tension between being unique and being legitimate.

This issue relates to the body, literally and figuratively, to identity in all its aspects, and to communication in relationships. Relying upon a common set of value terms, for instance, organizations speak the language of their times, their national culture(s) and their industries. This is one route to rhetorical legitimacy and indeed persuasiveness: finding the symbolic levers for getting the attention and perhaps the allegiance of others. But a communication strategy must be more than this: In fact, to speak too much in the language of others can make the organization seem to be merely pandering, to be superficial or even to have inauthentic commitments. Thus, the organization must try to find its "own voice" or at least sound as if it has one. So, distinctiveness may involve using accustomed slogans in unaccustomed ways, inverting meanings, creating neologisms or directly insisting on the fact that "We're different". The balance between legitimacy and distinctiveness therefore parallels the relationship between sameness and difference, with inevitable ironies, contradictions, and paradoxes – as we discuss throughout this book (see Martin et al., 1983).

As we saw in Chapter 1, the field of corporate communications is shaped by disciplinary convergence. While product branding takes its point of departure in the discipline of marketing, corporate branding calls for a much broader disciplinary engagement, including stragegic management, human resources, public relations, issues management, logistics, accounting and even finance. All these functions, it is argued, need to support the messages of the corporate brand (Schultz and Kitchen, 2004). And where product branding is most often guided by specific marketing objectives such as positioning and targeting, corporate branding, we are told, is inspired by broader goals such as legitimacy, trust and credibility among a wider range of stakeholders (de Chernatony, 2002). In spite of its intentions to embrace a variety of disciplines and address a multiplicity of stakeholders, however, corporate branding is typically limited to issues of visual identity or consumer seduction. This is much like product branding. In fact, principles of product branding are often applied to corporate branding projects. Consequently, the difference between product branding and corporate branding is often indiscernible. The Coca-Cola Company is one of the world's most recognized brands. But is it a product brand or a corporate brand? The Coca Cola Company owns and manages about 400 products in over 200 countries and many of them are quite strong product brands such as Fanta, Sprite, TAB, and Ciel. Does that position Coca Cola as a corporate brand or rather as a giant-product brand? And what about Rolex, LEGO, or 3M? How can we distinguish between product and corporate? And what is the significant difference?

In practice, it is often difficult to distinguish clearly between a product brand and a corporate brand. Yet, the organizational differences are significant.

According to the corporate communication literature, corporate branding has many advantages. Strong corporate brands, we are told, are able to communicate quality, safety and credibility in a world where other symbols are being eroded. Because a strong corporate brand provides a promotional platform for several products, corporate branding may simultaneously help the organization reduce its advertising and marketing expenses. Also, it has been suggested that a strong corporate brand has the potential to attract, maintain and engage the brightest brains (Fombrun and van Riel, 2004). In addition to these conventional explanations, scholars claim that corporate brands offer customers a sense of community and belonging. For example, Apple's rainbow coloured logo may appeal to customers who are willing to pay more for a badge of identification that makes them feel part of a legitimate and respected community. Moreover, corporate branding may help an organization defend itself in cases of outside assault. Finally, corporate brands "create common ground" in the sense that they develop a symbolism that is robust enough to promote a feeling of togetherness across cultures (Hatch and Schultz, 2001).

Corporate brands are expected to communicate quality, credibility, tradition and assurance and therefore provide meaning and community across cultures.

Research seems to indicate that organizations with strong corporate brands often have market values that are more than twice their book values (Hatch and Schultz, 2001). Based on this immaterial value, corporate branding can stimulate rapid growth on new markets. Once an organization has firmly established its corporate brand, like Virgin did in the air travel business, it is easier to expand to new business areas such as trains, music, soft drinks, cellular telephones and even wedding gowns. Thus, Disney's strong international brand leads parents across the world to trustfully buy the latest Disney movie because it represents a certain quality with certain values, views and narrative structures. Being a strong brand for more than 100 years has made it relatively easy for Disney to transfer its success to amusement parks and children's clothing. Customer loyalty, it is assumed, follows the brand and reputation gained on one product arena can safely be transferred to another. This potential has convinced international companies about the immense advantages of corporate branding. Such "brand stretch", however, is not always logical. Why should a transportation company be particularly good at providing soft drinks and mobile services? And why should a company that is best known for its motorcycles be *trusted* when it decides to produce musical instruments?

The theory seems to suggest that corporate brands develop a life of their own, disconnected or 'autonomized' from material substance.

Incorporating the Employee

Corporate branding, however, implies strong links between organizations and their employees. When organizations are investing their corporate brands with emotional, cultural and social significance, they are engaging in an exercise which is far more binding for their members than traditional product branding. In contrast to product brands, the corporate brand makes a promise, which employees are expected to support. When Microsoft says "We See", it commits its members to see innovative ideas that members of other organizations do not envision – just as Avis's classical "We try harder" slogan called for employees to work harder every time they faced a consumer. Likewise, when the tabloid press promises to be tougher or bolder than other newspapers, it puts their managers, journalists and other organizational members under pressure to enact the promise. Employees, thus, are expected to translate promises, visions and aesthetics into day-to-day actions that ultimately provide flesh and blood to the corporate brand (Ind, 2004; see also de Chernatony, 1999; Ind, 1998; Karmark, 2005). Increasingly, thus, organizational members are referred to as embodiments of the corporate brand.

BOX 3.3   A Fractal Vision

The notion that the employee must represent the organization and its corporate brand bears resemblance to the structure of fractals. A fractal is a geometric pattern that is repeated at ever smaller scales to produce irregular shapes and surfaces that cannot be explained or represented easily by classical geometry. More importantly in this context, fractals are defined as "images that can be divided into parts, each of which is similar to the original object".[6]

Fractals are perfect embodiments of the whole; versions of totality repeated again and again.

By analogy, the corporate branding project conceives of the employee as a 'walking-around fragment' of the organization, that is, as a perfect version of the whole. Corporate branding can be described as a fractal vision, a vision of a totality represented entirely by its parts. For example, since the late 1990s BP has re-branded itself from British Petroleum to Beyond Petroleum, and this move is reflected in aspects of the company from its copyrighted "BP green" colour to its advertisements linking the firm to environmental concerns and the exploration of non-fossil fuels, to featured testimonials by employees, to pronouncements about the culture of the organization. Whereas the original brand only had a limited organizational scope, involving primarily marketing and production, the new version implicates the employees as essential constituents of the brand or, put differently, as indispensable fragments of the whole.

When the principles of branding are extended to the organization as a whole, employee identification becomes a prominent issue. While we have known for quite some time that organizations represent a significant source of individual identity (Burke, 1973; Cheney and Tompkins, 1987), today identification has become an explicit and strategic dimension of corporate branding. Managers are advised "to ensure that on-brand behavior becomes instinctive" and "to convince employees of the brand power" (Mitchell, 2002). Arguing that the success of a corporate brand depends on "the extent to which there is harmony between the managerially defined values, effective implementation of values by staff and appreciation of these values among customers," professor of marketing Leslie de Chernatony urges organizations to develop strong cultures that motivate employees to support these values without supervision (de Chernatony, 2002: 116, 122; see also Ho, 2001–02). Organizational members, in other words, are expected to align their personal values with the identity of the corporate brand. It is an open question, however, as to what happens to loyalty and identification when such feelings become managerial projects of "internal branding".

BOX 3.4   Identification

The term "identification" was first used by psychologist Sigmund Freud in the late nineteenth century to refer to one kind of defense mechanism whereby a person would, say, attach himself to a workplace boss in the same way he might have done with his mother or father. In other words, Freud saw identification as a means of confusing relationships and in being led astray by misplaced loyalties and emotional connections. In the first half of the twentieth century, theorists such as psychologist-philosopher William James, political scientist Harold Lasswell, and literary and rhetorical critic Kenneth Burke saw in the concept of identification much wider applications. For all of them, identification represented not only an emotional or even a rational bond between one person and another (including a group) but a fundamental way of answering questions such as "Who am I?" or "Why did I do that?" In the past 100 years or so, answers to those questions have increasingly become groups and organizations. Thus, when asked to fill out the blank in the following sentence "I am __," (Kuhn and McPartland, 1954) many people not only list personal characteristics but also quite a few groupings of people, including employing organization, political party, religious affiliation, sports club, and so on. In such cases, one's identification with an employer, a brand, a profession, or a nation becomes a key point of reference.

Organizational identification refers to situations where people define themselves in terms of an organization, including its products, its missions and its values.

Identification becomes a social, political and ethical issue when loyalties come into conflict. Since the 1970s, research has demonstrated that some employees will choose a "professional" identification over their attachment to the organization and perhaps choose to "blow the whistle" on policies or practices they find to be morally wrong or simply wrong-headed. Identification, thus, is as much communication-based as it is psychological and sociological. How we answer those basic questions – "Who?" "Why?" and "What for?" – not only to help to "fix" or solidify our points of identification but also to become parts of the ongoing stories we tell about ourselves. Once we answer those questions in patterned ways, that pattern becomes a certain part of our identity, even when we do not entirely internalize it.

Identification is embedded in and shaped by the narratives we construct about ourselves.

Obviously, organizations hope to play a role in shaping these narratives. Through various forms of communications, organizations try to express "who they are" in ways that invite us to join the community. In this process, consultants and other architects of corporate identity try to help organizations identify and communicate their "essences". Identifications, however, are hard to invent. In a world saturated with symbols, where identity itself is more urgent yet more elusive, what does it mean not to identify with an employing organization, or brands or organizations? Is organizational loyalty a thing of the past? Or is it taking new forms? And, what about *over*-identification with an organization's image, its goals or its practices? These are important practical questions to ask. In fact, they remind us of the relationships between trends at work and those of the larger society; communication managers would do well to pay attention to them.

While employees are regarded by management as walking-around embodiments of the company brand, they in turn expect the organization to provide *them* with attractive points of identification. In fact, it has been suggested that for employees to maintain an acceptable level of self-esteem, it is important for them to regard their workplace as legitimate and to be highly motivated to enhance its construed external image (Humphreys and Brown, 2002). Yet, while people may identify strongly with their workplace, they may identify more strongly with the business unit, the department or the project team they are affiliated with, than with the entire organization (Ashforth and Mael, 1989; Brown, 1969).

Communicating through the Employee

To have competent employees who understand and support the vision of their workplace cannot be taken for granted. Professor de Chernatony, therefore, talks about the "orchestration of staff", arguing that staff need to "be genuinely committed to delivering the [brand] promise" if the corporate brand is to be successfully implemented (2002: 114; see also Barrett, 1998). Likewise, in a *Harvard Business*

Review article, Colin Mitchell from Ogilvy & Mathers calls for organizations to "sell the brand" to the employees: "Just as in a consumer advertising campaign, you need to surprise and charm your audience. This is a task of persuasion, not information" (2002: 104). The question is, of course, if such a "selling" approach is the route to employee identification.

In corporate branding, the primary audience for corporate messages is often the employees.

Following Lotman's notion of auto-communication (see Chapter 1), it may be argued that much corporate communications is directed primarily to the senders themselves. Strategic plans and annual reports, for example, may be regarded as auto-communicative devices by way of which corporations tell themselves and their members what they would like to be in the future. As organizational scholars Henri Broms and Henrik Gahmberg suggest "A strategic plan is made partly for the element of hope and belief, the element of myth, inherent in it – an element the organization needs badly" (1983: 490; see also Berg, 1985). Through their articulations of long-term plans, managers tell themselves who they are and how their organization ought to look. Although many plans and strategies are never implemented, this type of communication is essential for the self-perception of the organization. Likewise, we find numerous examples of auto-communication in mission statements, corporate values, annual reports, job advertisements, corporate design and architecture, etc. in which senders are attracted, moved, or in some way seduced by their own messages. A similar potential can be found in advertising (Christensen, 1997). Organizational communication scholar George Barnett says:

> *Advertisements in the mass media, both print and electronic, provide cultural information as an organization communicates to the environment; it reveals its values and style to those outside the organization, as well as, to its members. How it conducts its public relations, announcements, or services and speeches by its officers tells the public what it would be like to be part of the organization ... In other words, the external communication feeds back to impact upon its internal culture.* (1988: 104ff)

Instead of hiring professional models or having third parties endorsing the corporate messages, increasingly we see organizations use their own managers and employees to speak positively about the organization in corporate communications messages. A number of years ago, Chemical Bank, for example, addressed its own members in advertisements showing a smiling employee, her signature and the slogan "Expect more from us". Likewise, airline companies such as Lufthansa and Thai Airways have over the years used advertisements in external magazines to remind their employees about responsibilities and duties. In a more recent advertisement featured in *The Economist* (1 October 2005), Toyota presents one of its employees with an infant on his arm. Under the headline "Respect" the ad says: "Meet Romain Tissot Charlod, father of a newborn son and one of our 55,000 employees in Europe. Romain is a team member at Toyota Motor Manufacturing France in Valenciennes, just one of our eight plants in Europe". To underscore the theme of 'respect', Romain says: "I earn respect in my role as a trainer for young people; they ask me for advice, we exchange knowledge and discover who we are. It's really rewarding …" Along the same lines, a series of advertisements from Shell feature employees who work hard to meet the growing demand for energy while showing concern for the environment. One of the adverts, showing a picture of a Shell employee, says: "Can market forces help cut carbon emissions? This trader thinks they can. Garth Edward is a trader in carbon emissions. He believes that his work can help companies meet the objectives set by governments to reduce carbon output …" By presenting and/or giving a voice to select employees or close key stakeholders in expensive external media, these companies hope to enhance their external communication objectives by stimulating pride and belongingness amongst their employees. The strategic and organizational implications of this observation will be unfolded in Chapter 8.

To augment internal and external communication goals, corporate communicators increasingly employ employees in auto-communicative messages.

Auto-communicational messages, such as those above, address an important concern of corporate communicators: to combine the expectations and demands of external constituencies with a growing sensitivity to the internal need for identification and work gratification. Public relations scholars Eileen Scholes and David Clutterbuck (1998) cite studies that show how employees who speak positively about their workplace have a stronger influence on would-be customers than other factors, like advertising or distribution. As a consequence, they predict that internal and external communication will become so closely aligned in the future that they will be carried out by the same people, sometimes even with the internal side as the most significant dimension. Scholes and Clutterbuck cite British Airways' Director of Communication for saying that he plans to let 90 per cent of his communication budget be focused on employees. Conceptualizing integrated communications in terms of relationships, Scholes and Clutterbuck point out that an integrated approach to stakeholder communication implies placing the responsibility of employee communication on the same footing in the organization as public relations, investor relations and government relations.

Auto-communicative messages are central to corporate branding because they integrate the concerns of internal and external audiences.

The logic of auto-communication does not rule out the possibility that corporate messages *simultaneously* communicate to external audiences. In fact, these two dimensions are closely related (Christensen, 2004). However, in a cluttered communication environment filled with symbols, slogans and identity claims, corporate messages are more likely to stimulate interest among organizational members than outside the organization's formal boundaries. As illustrated by the examples above, companies that understand the principles behind auto-communication can use external media for the promotion of messages of internal significance and in this way enhance the corporate brand. The status and authority of the external medium endow the message with a trenchancy that can usually not be attained through the use of traditional internal media. By using external media to present, praise or press their staff, organizations hope to foster reactions not possible through the use of traditional internal media, that is, instil pride among employees, enhance an internal *esprit de corps* and perhaps even stimulate motivation and productivity – developments which, in turn, may produce significant secondary effects such as enhanced goodwill, investments and perhaps even sales. When an organization communicates in an external medium, it draws on that medium's prominence to simultaneously tell itself and its employees that it has a certain status and is capable of expressing this status professionally and authoritatively. In a sense, thus, external media may help organizations seduce themselves and their own members. This may well be the most fundamental dimension of corporate identity and corporate branding.

The external medium is crucial when organizations address their own employees; it seduces them by endowing corporate messages with status and authority.

BOX 3.5   Seduction and Self-Seduction

Seduction is usually thought of as the process through which a person deliberately entices another person into doing something he or she would not have done otherwise. As such, lots of corporate communications activities, including most advertising, can be regarded as seductive practices. This, at least, is the typical viewpoint of the marketing critic. However, the Danish philosopher Søren Kierkegaard (1997) has emphasized that a seducer can only seduce if he or she is already – in some sense – seduced in advance. All seduction, in other words, is equivocal and circular in nature. Drawing on Kierkegaard's notion of seduction, the French sociologist Jean Baudrillard remarks:

> *Doesn't the seducer end up losing himself [sic!] in the strategy, as in an emotional labyrinth? Doesn't he invent that strategy in order to lose himself in it? And he, who believes himself [sic!] the game's master, isn't he the first victim of strategy's tragic myth?* (1990a: 98)

Does the notion of *self*-seduction apply to corporate communication as well? As professors of organizational communication Lars Thøger Christensen and George Cheney have argued, there is great potential for self-seduction within the realm of identity management where organizations have a propensity to overestimate the external interest and involvement in corporate identity markers such as logos, slogans, design and architecture. The combination of external indifference and corporate vanity implies that corporate senders often get caught in their own communications to the effect that they loose touch with their relevance and impact outside the organization's formal boundaries – and sometimes even within (see also Christensen and Cheney, 2000).

Like auto-communication, corporate communications programmes potentially involve a circular dimension of self-seduction.

Although employees are expected to lend support to the corporate brand, their status in the corporate branding project is still rather unclear. Are they true participants in the exercise or simply another target for marketing seduction? In both cases, organizations may find that employees are more critical readers of corporate messages than other audiences. In an interesting study of how organizational members perceive advertising campaigns from their workplace, marketing professors Mary Gilly and Mary Wolfinbarger (1998) showed that accuracy in advertising messages was crucial in order to maintain pride and loyalty. In one of the companies they studied, employees were used in the corporate branding campaign to demonstrate publicly that the organization valued its workers, while the company simultaneously was laying off linemen. Understandably, organizational members found that corporate messages were inaccurate and that the campaign did not reflect the culture of the company. Similarly, United Airlines launched a brand campaign as a response to customers' increasing resentment against the airline industry (Mitchell, 2002: 102–3). The campaign labeled "Rising" was meant to signal that United Airlines acknowledged room for improvement on the quality of their services. Finding that the campaign indirectly discredited their prior efforts, however, employees were not able to support the promise of "Rising". Eventually United Airlines withdrew the campaign. In other cases, it may not always be possible for employees to live up to the promises of the corporate brand. In the case of Holiday Inn's "No Surprises" campaign, staff could not live up to the promise because of the high frequency of surprises that appear in complex service organizations (Gilly and Wolfinbarger, 1998).

When employees are subjected to corporate auto-communication, it becomes increasingly relevant to ask if they "buy" the message.

The Quest for the True Organization

When employees are expected to emotionally and socially "live" the corporate brand, the question of its organizational validity becomes salient. With its emphasis on the organization "behind" the communication, the project of corporate branding calls for managers to focus attention on discrepancies between different organizational dimensions of the corporate brand. Hatch and Schultz (2001), for example, have developed a so-called "corporate branding tool kit" that allows managers to identify the nature of the corporate vision, the corporate culture and the corporate image and, most importantly, to expose the gaps between these dimensions. Such gaps, according to Hatch and Schultz, reflect key organizational problems and need to be eliminated to create and maintain a strong corporate brand. To ensure trustworthy communication, Hatch and Schultz claim, organizations must avoid "breach[es] between rhetoric and reality" (2001: 4) primarily because such breaches result in cynicism, suspicion and dispirited employees. Similarly, professors Charles Fombrun and Cees van Riel (2003) argue that organizations should express themselves as authentic and transparent as part of their corporate appeal to multiple audiences. In line with this view, other scholars recommend organizations to embark on "soul-searching" exercises to discover their true values and ideologies (Cornelissen, 2004; Barrett, 1998). Prominent writings within the field, thus, suggest that if a corporate brand promise is to be trusted, it must build on an authentic culture of "deeply rooted" and "shared" values (de Chernatony, 2002). In fact, it is emphasized that "[a]n inauthentic organizational culture can jeopardize a corporate brand" (Hatch and Schultz, 2001: 6). The project of corporate branding, thus, reproduces an essentialist philosophy.

Corporate branding calls for the organization to uncover and present its true corporate soul.

BOX 3.6   Essentialism and the Discourse of Authenticity

Essentialism is the idea that objects and phenomena contain an innate essence independent of time and space. The essence cannot be negotiated, constructed or reconstructed. It is what it is. This idea can be traced back to Aristotle, but is also found among contemporary philosophers. In contrast, the French philosopher and existentialist Jean-Paul Sartre claimed that existence precedes essence. What a "Thing" or a person *is* – its essence – has to be produced and therefore may be changed continuously. An individual's life, according to Sartre, is never destined to be some fatal journey but is constantly created through the choices one makes.

Essentialism and existentialism are contrasting perspectives on the question of existence.

Since the essence of Things, according to the essentialist perspective, is without change or decay, essentialism represents an *a*historical perspective. As the British philosopher Karl R. Popper pointed out, an essentialist perspective calls for science to "discover and to describe the true nature of things, that is their hidden reality or essence" (1945: 31). People, who have access to this privileged perspective such as managers, administrators or consultants, often have a feeling of superiority: they believe strongly that they are able to see what others cannot see. Essentialism, thus, has suggestions of authoritarianism and conservatism within the world view associated with its very definition.

Essentialism favours an elitist perspective on reality; a perspective based on a privileged access to the world as it "really" is.

In the field of corporate communications, essentialism is often expressed as a quest for *authenticity*. In today's world where the search for truth, meaning and happiness has intensified, the urge for authenticity is a recurrent theme in the workplace. Authenticity has several dimensions. Nominal authenticity is defined by philosopher Denis Dutton (2003) as the correct identification of the origins, authorship, or provenance of an object, ensuring, as the term implies, that an object of aesthetic experience is properly named. Expressive authenticity refers to an object's *character* as an expression of an individual's or a society's values and beliefs. In postmodern writings, the notion of authenticity is often challenged by the observation that an image does not always mirror or reflect reality, but sometimes also *masks* or perverts a reality, masks the *absence* of a reality, *simulates* a reality, or bears *no relation* to a reality whatsoever. In the latter case, the image refers exclusively to itself. Such an autonomized and self-referential image is sometimes called a "simulacrum" (Baudrillard, 1994; Perniola, 1980).

The copy or the fake may often be regarded as being as authentic or genuine as that which it imitates.

The corporate brand is assumed to reflect shared and authentic values. The literature on branding, thus, seems to suggest that values are of an essential nature. With its notion of "core values", this literature reproduces the dream of finding the "true soul" of the organization – sometimes referred to as its "platform". Thus defined, values are irreplaceable and beyond discussion. Although some scholars have suggested a distinction between, for example, "generic values" and "more authentic and deeper values" (Cornelissen, 2004), they still adhere to an essentialist perspective, assuming that some values are more basic than others. Such a distinction, however, is somewhat arbitrary: who defines which values are generic and which values are authentic?

The notion of "true" and "authentic" corporate values becomes a managerial means of unifying and integrating the organization.

Although the corporate brand is presumed to reflect shared and "authentic" corporate values, those values still need to be "sold" or explained to the organization's members. This contradiction is sharpened when the same organizations announce that "we at Acme all believe in ..." and top management has not even asked the employees what they think or care about. In fact, writers on corporate branding often suggest that values proclaimed by the CEO or by corporate organs must "trickle down" to all employees and insist that management must provide ongoing guidance as to how the values should be understood and internalized (Cornelissen, 2004: 76; de Chernatony, 2002: 119). Thus, presenting "true" corporate values is not enough to assure their vibrancy in the organization. In some cases, we find that employees will ignore such proclaimed values or even talk about them cynically (Fairhurst et al., 1997; Jordan, 2003).

While corporate values are assumed to be true and authentic, their organizational existence still depends heavily on internal marketing efforts.

Authenticity is as much a creative construction as an inherent quality of the organization itself. We should always ask: Whose authenticity? Where do we find it? How do we know it? This problem is exacerbated by current employment practices in much of the industrialized world. Lifetime employment with the same organization is now a rarity in any sector. Whereas corporate branding and its notion that consumers buy the company behind the product presuppose a stable workforce able to develop and internalize a feeling of sharedness and ownership, we are increasingly experiencing a flexible work market where many employees are "contingent" (Smith, 1997; Smith, 2001). This means that many organizational members are now hired (and let go) on a contract, seasonal and part-time basis. In fact, the vaulted "social contract" between individuals and organizations has largely gone in many industries and fields, and for employees in highly mobile professions such as new technologies, this is not a bad thing. Overall, however, we find diminished loyalty to the organization, along with greater instability in the workforce in any given situation, making it very difficult for an organization to say anything with confidence about its "We" (Gossett, 2002).

CASE: Decoupling the Corporate Brand from the Corporation?

NIKE[7]

Nike is presumably the world's most well known corporate brand within the sports and fitness industry. The company operates on six continents and employs 24,300 people. In addition, its suppliers, shippers, retailers and service providers employ close to one million people. Today, Nike is primarily a design and marketing organization. This case challenges the assumption that a strong corporate brand is necessarily tightly coupled to the organization "behind". Put differently, strong corporate brands are not always rooted in organizational cultures that enact the brand promise. As the case of Nike illustrates, a corporate brand may be perceived as globally strong and unique even when detached from organizational reality.

The Challenge

While Nike's "swoosh" represents one of today's strongest corporate brands, it has also become the symbol of sweatshops, low salaries and child labour. When it was publicly revealed that Nike's sportswear and apparel was manufactured in sweatshops under extremely poor working conditions, the company became the focus of one of the most comprehensive and persistent anti-corporate movements in the world. Nike has been critiqued and exposed publicly in television programmes, documentary films, social research, Doonesbury cartoons, protest rap songs, anti-corporate websites and blogs, and in thousands of protest letters.

Nike's decision in the 1980s to devote itself to design and marketing implied the outsourcing of most manufacturing to contract factories in developing countries such as Vietnam, Malaysia, Thailand, Pakistan and China. In a strictly legal sense, the conditions in the sweatshops are not the responsibility of a design and marketing company. Still, Nike was held *morally* responsible by the public, including the organizations in its supply-chain. One of the more severe cases for Nike was the first revelation of child labour in the production of hand-stitched balls in Pakistan in 1995. Nine years later this issue remains highly critical to Nike. In the Corporate Responsibility Report of 2004, Nike presents the case like this: "By far our worst experience and biggest mistake was in Pakistan, where we blew it" (Nike, 2004). Nike responded with a number of initiatives

(Continued)

(Continued)

to control and monitor contractors in order to improve working conditions and not to have any workers under the age of 18. Yet, as Nike states: "But the damage was done. A June 1996 *Life* magazine article branded Nike as "a child labor company", and "... the label sticks nonetheless" (Nike, 2004).

The Company "Behind"?

CEO Phil Knight and his top management team expected that criticism would vanish with Nike's support of local activities to improve conditions for people in sweatshops in Pakistan. Criticism, however, continued and increased. Since the mid 1990s, Nike has been the focus of public criticism for its labour law violations, wages, working conditions, health and safety practices, child labour and sexual harassment. Studies have systematically investigated and compared Nike's corporate brand promise with local realities contrasting, for example, what Nike told American consumers about its labour practices with what an NGO, Vietnam Labor Watch, found at factories in Vietnam. The studies demonstrated a huge gap between the *claimed* corporate brand and the *lived* corporate brand.

Nike's marketing messages have intensified the critique. Presenting itself as a supporter of societal well-being has produced numerous counter-statements. The "Just do it" slogan, for example – a slogan reflecting the American dream of freedom and "anything is possible" – has been described as hollow and in sharp contrast to Nike's disregard for human rights. Various activist groups and individuals have suggested "Just don't do it", "Nike, Do it Just" and "Justice. Do it, Nike". A target audience for Nike sportswear is inner-city youth, often living in high unemployment areas, willing to sell drugs, steal or mug to afford fancy brands such as Nike. The fact that Nike not only charged premium prices in poor US areas, but also exploited children and underpaid labour in developing countries, added to the strong discontent. "Nike continues to treat its labour problem as a matter of public relations", protests an anti-Nike website.[8] Interestingly, reactions were particularly strong in Nike's home state of Oregon, where many people had benefited from Nike's success. A donation from Nike to a local school became controversial, as people started to question if the money was given to local children at the expense of poor and underpaid children in developing countries. In an editorial, the local newspaper *The Oregonian* expressed deep concerns about Nike's influence on Oregon as a brand, urging CEO Phil Knight to demonstrate decent behaviour: "Spare us the added humiliation of being known as the home of the most exploitative capitalist in the free world" (Zuman, 1996).

The Decoupling

At the same time as Nike has experienced severe attacks on its corporate legitimacy, it has managed to improve its social standing, as represented by business ethics rankings. Right now, as the anti-Nike movement continues, Nike is climbing the ladder (from 31 in 2005 to 13 in 2006) in the Business Ethics Magazine list of 100 Best Corporate Citizens.[9] Nike's new position on the list is based largely on the perceived strength of its community and environmental programmes. Moreover, the company's increased emphasis on environmental programmes earned it the No. 1 ranking in that category the same year. Also, on the Human Rights Campaign Foundation's Corporate Equality Index, in 2006 Nike received a favourable score for the fifth consecutive year.[10] Thus, Nike's corporate brand seems to have developed a life of its own, detached from organizational decisions, values and practices. Simultaneously, the case suggests that some critical images, when these are held by non-dominant, non-visible stakeholders, may not have a significant impact on the overall global brand. While it may seem that Nike is currently in safe waters, the company needs to continuously monitor the range and significance of critical images. When non-visible and non-powerful voices combine into a critical mass (as we have seen in the case of Wal-Mart) they may turn out to have a significant impact on a company's reputation and global brand.

There are signs, however, of Nike pursuing a stronger coherence between the corporate brand promise and the brand. In November 2005, Phil Knight left the position as CEO to Bill Perez who has a strong track record within corporate responsibility. Perez's philosophy is presumably that companies must invest in and improve their communities. Responding to criticism from activists, Nike now has 90 full-time employees monitoring overseas factory conditions, and its focus on stakeholder concerns is reflected on the corporate website:

> *An earlier mission statement pushed us to be the best sports company in the world. While it may have been a worthy ambition, it was focused only on the company; it was entirely about us. Our current mission pushes our sights outwards. Focusing on the needs of athletes – particularly given our broad understanding of athletes – leads directly to a consideration of the needs of communities around the world [...] Our hope, over time, is to demonstrate that social and environmental innovations can help add an important dimension to our brand.[11]*

Obviously, a corporate brand may never be a perfect reflection of organizational practice. It remains an open question, however, to what extent a corporate brand can maintain its legitimacy if organizational practices are perceived to conflict with it. Time will tell whether Nike's top managerial generation shift will lead to a change in public perceptions and lead to a stronger coherence between the corporate brand and the organization "behind" or whether the decoupling between the corporate brand and organizational practice will persist. For now, it remains to be repeated that Nike is one of contemporary society's strongest global brands.

Points of Reflection:

1. What are the main reasons for the development of Nike's corporate brand?
2. To what extent does Nike's identity influence its corporate brand – and vice versa?
3. Are there any risks or ethical limits to a decoupling of the corporate brand from the corporate identity, as we have seen in the Nike case?

Chapter Summary

In Chapter 3, we have discussed how branding today is permeating the organizational domain to the effect that the organization, its culture and its members, becomes the primary focus of attention. To grow and prosper in global markets, scholars, consultants and managers increasingly advise organizations to initiate extensive corporate branding projects. Corporate branding is the systematic effort to develop and present the organization as one unified brand. Building on the assumption that consumers increasingly "buy" the companies *behind* the products, corporate branding posits employees as integral dimensions to the brand. More specifically, employees are expected to blend their personal identities with the corporate identity and to identify with the corporate brand. The logic put forward is that if the brand is to be trusted, it must build on a "true" identity constantly enacted and lived by employees. Thus, prominent journals encourage managers to induce employees to identify with the corporate brand. While identity and identification have always been central organizational issues, today they have turned into explicit and strategic dimensions of the corporate branding process. In the next chapter, the notion of the organization "behind" will be elaborated through a critical examination of corporate reputation management.

Notes

1 Examples on anti-Walmart websites: http://www.hel-mart.com/links.php, http://walmartwatch.com/,http://www.wakeupwalmart.com/. http://walmartvswomen.com/, http://reclaimdemocracy.org/walmart/links.php

2 Examples on anti-Nike websites: http://www.saigon.com/~nike/ – Boycott Nike, http://www.geocities.com/Athens/Acropolis/5232 – Canada Boycott, http://www.globalexchange.org/corpacct/nike/index.html – Global Exchange, http://www.oeonline.com/~chevy/nike_sucks.html – Nike Sucks, http://www.harborside.com/home/s/stevenm/public_html/antinike.html – Anti-Nike, http://www.caa.org.au/campaigns/nike/ index.html – Nike Watch, Big One, http://www.dogeatdogfilms.com/mikenike.html – Phil & M. Moore

3 Examples on anti-McDonalds websites: http://billboardom.blogspot.com/2005/12/anti-mcdonalds-billboards.html, http://c.webring.com/hub?ring=antimcdonaldsrin, http://www.mcspotlight.org/, http://www.petitionspot.com/petitions/antimcdonalds, http://craigtr.tripod.com/, http://www.mypage.tsn.cc/c_richardson/maccas.htm

4 Examples on anti-Starbucks websites: http://www.organicconsumers.org/Starbucks/081403_starbucks.cfm, http://www.epublicrelations.ca/Starbucks.html, http://gallery.future-i.com/comedy/pic:starbucks/, http://www.starfuckz.com/

5 http://www.starbucks.com/aboutus/CSR_FY01_AR.pdf

6 http://en.wikipedia.org/wiki/Fractal

7 http://www.nike.com/nike.bizz. See also: http://www.geocities.com/athens/acropolis/5232/ http://www.saigon.com/nike and Klein (2000).

8 http://www.saigon.com/nike/

9 http://www.nike.com/nikebiz/nikebiz.jhtml?page=59&iten=tppr&year =2006&release=05a

10 http://www.hrc.org/Template.cfm?Section=Get_Informed2&COTETID=31668& TEMPLATE=/ContentDisplay.cfm

11 http://www.nike.com/nikebiz/nikebiz.jhtml?page=54

4

Corporate Reputation and Stakeholder Communication

The Body in the Eyes of the "Other"

> Whereas I cannot apprehend my body as an object but only as a body-for-itself, I apprehend the body of the other as an object about which I take a point of view and realize that my body as an object is the body-for-others ... Being seen and observed by the other results in a recognition of my facticity, that I am an object to the other.
>
> Bryan Turner (1996: 77)

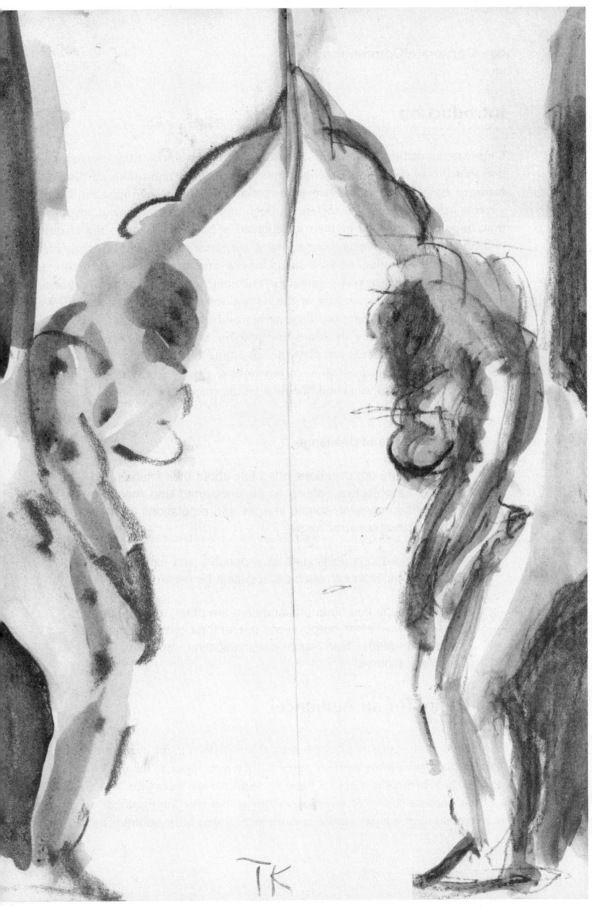

Introduction

Corporate reputation has become an essential building block in the communication strategies of contemporary organizations. Increasingly, reputations are planned, managed and staged by corporate actors seeking to establish and maintain themselves as legitimate players in society. Through reputational management, organizations hope to be regarded by their stakeholders as *bodies with souls*. In this chapter we will discuss and challenge the notions of corporate reputation and stakeholder communications focusing in particular on how organizations actively participate in the construction of their own reputations. Following an introduction to corporate reputation, we take a closer look at the institutions that measure reputations. We argue that such institutions contribute to a world of "communicational politics" in which the management of images and opinions is sometimes more important than the solving of material issues. At the same time, however, the professionalization of communications may allow corporations to experiment with new ways of organizing. The central issues and questions of the chapter are outlined below:

Chapter 4: Points of Challenge

- Contemporary organizations often talk about their images and reputations as objective entities to be uncovered and measured. In what sense, however, should images and reputations be regarded as ambiguous constructions?

- Many corporations participate in expensive and extensive reputation analyses. How can such participation be regarded as a ritual?

- Interest groups and other stakeholders are often, and for good reasons, skeptical when corporations praise their own social and environmental deeds. Can such communication, however, produce positive outcomes?

The Desire for an Audience

The identity of the corporate body is seen and confirmed in the eyes of the "other". Organizations have always been interested in their reputations, in the images and perceptions their surroundings hold of them. In organizational theory, the "environment" is usually seen to consist of other organizations, but also "unorganized" audiences such as consumers are part of the environment. Today, an organization's interest in what others think has become professionalized and institutionalized. In fact, organizations of all types now speak of their *reputation* as a fundamental dimension of their existence. One could argue that the growing interest in corporate reputation simply reflects the self-absorption of our time, the social need for recognition and admiration that also affects organizations (Berg and Gagliardi, 1985). Vanity of course requires an audience. The need for social accreditation, however, goes deeper than just vanity. The body can be nurtured, sculpted and posed, but it is not until it is regarded through the eyes of a specific or a "generalized other" that its identity develops and unfolds to its full potential.

Organizations are increasingly concerned about their appearance in the eyes of the "other".

BOX 4.1   The Eyes of the "Other"

In the social sciences, the notion of the "other" or "the generalized other" refers to the general image that a person has of the expectations that *other* people hold about appropriate actions and thoughts in his or her society. The notion of the (generalized) other, thus, does not refer to any actual group of people, but to a *conception of people in general* – a conception that guides and regulates a person's opinions and behaviours. Whenever people try to imagine what is expected of them, they are taking on the perspective of the generalized other.

The generalized other is the conception we have of other people's expectations of us.

The social psychologist Charles Horton Cooley (1983) coined the notion of "the looking-glass self" to describe the fact that we develop our self-image on the basis of the messages we receive from others, as we understand them. We look at others looking at us, trying to figure out what they see. And we develop our self-feeling out of our assessment of their judgment. In line with Cooley, symbolic interactionist George Herbert Mead (1934) argued that the ability to assume the roles of others, that is, to see situations from another person's perspective, is vital for the development of a child. From its very first moments, a child's dependency on strong eye contact with its surroundings defines

(Continued)

(Continued)

the basis for its continual development as a mature person. This dependency gradually becomes internalized so that the child learns to imagine the thoughts (intentions and expectations) of others – including the ways it is perceived by them. Obviously, some people are more important to our personal development than others. Such people are sometimes referred to as "significant others".

Our self-image is shaped and developed by the fact that other people observe and judge us.

The sociologist Erving Goffman (1969) used the metaphor of the theatre to describe a person's dependency on an audience in the process of constructing his or her identity. The fact that we stage ourselves as actors does not in itself create our identity. The identity or the "self" emerges when the actor experiences the effect of his or her performance, that is, by observing the reactions of the audience.

The individual experiences him or herself through the gaze of other people and organizations.

Delineating Corporate Reputation

We usually think of corporate reputation as a specific character or trait ascribed to an organization by outsiders based on their observations of its products, decisions and actions. A reputation may be based on personal experiences, but is often provided by other sources including the organization itself, its competitors, its stakeholders or the media. The fact that an organization believes it has a reputation indicates that it is concerned about the way it is being perceived by others (Thyssen, 2003). When such evaluations become formalized in managerial programmes and activities, they are referred to as corporate reputations. Professor of management and Director of the Reputation Institute, Charles Fombrun has defined corporate reputation this way:

> [Corporate reputation is] a perceptual representation of a company's past actions and future prospects that describe the firm's overall appeal to all of its key constituents when compared to other leading rivals. (1996: 72)

In *Fame & Fortune* (2003) Charles Fombrun and professor of corporate communications Cees van Riel argue that a strong reputation leads to growth, high market value and high earnings. Fombrun and van Riel suggest that a strong reputation is like a magnet, because it attracts and affects all organizational stakeholders. People, they claim, are more inclined to appreciate, respect and associate with organizations they remember and recognize – for something positive, of course. Put differently, a strong corporate reputation casts a "halo" over the products, the services and even the members of the organization, as it extends the corporate identity to everything associated with the organization. While the "halo effect" is conspicuous when it comes to celebrities, such as footballer David Beckham and the energizing effect his presence has had on his team, his audiences, his groupies and his businesses, it may also play an important role for organizations. A strong "halo effect" can even overshadow negative publicity and poor service. This was the conclusion by *The Wall Street Journal* in their assessment of Richard Branson's success in giving Virgin the best reputation among Britain's most visible companies during the same period where Virgin faced severe public criticism for the unreliability of Virgin Rail, the flop of Virgin Cola and the losses of Virgin Megastore (*Wall Street Journal*, 2004). While reputation scholars and managers argue that a positive "reputation is the product of years of superior performance" (Hall, 1993: 616), it appears that a strong corporate reputation may be somewhat divorced from actual business performance.

A strong corporate reputation is not necessarily tightly coupled to economic performance.

In addition to growth and profits, a strong corporate reputation can help an organization in its efforts to differentiate itself from its competitors and, eventually, charge premium-prices for its products (Fombrun, 1996). Also, a strong corporate reputation can guide consumers when shopping for products that are almost identical in terms of price, quality and aesthetics such as mobile phones and detergents (de Chernatony, 2002; Harris and de Chernatony, 2001; van Riel, 1995). By simplifying the shopping experience, a strong reputation makes it easier to choose, especially in cases where the product is complex, information is insufficient or overwhelming, or when time is limited. The competition for talented employees has also been used as an argument for building strong reputations, as people take pride in working for companies that are positively evaluated within the general public (Boyle, 2001). Moreover, in spite of well-documented measurement problems, it is generally assumed that there is a strong *causal* link between strong reputations and high stock market earnings (McMillan and Joshi, 1997; Srivastava et al., 1997). As Fombrun, puts it: "Corporate reputations have bottom-line effects. A good reputation enhances profitability because it attracts customers to the company's products, investors to its securities, and employees to its jobs" (1996: 81).

A strong corporate reputation holds similar promises to the organization as a powerful corporate brand: identification, differentiation and profitability.

Fombrun and van Riel suggest five principles for building and maintaining a strong corporate reputation: "be visible", "be distinctive", "be authentic", "be transparent", and "be consistent" (Fombrun and van Riel, 2003). As the observant reader may notice, the principles and advantages of a strong reputation are difficult to distinguish from those of corporate branding. Yet, Fombrun and van Riel maintain that there *is* a difference between branding and reputation. A strong corporate brand may have a poor public reputation, as for example is the case for companies like Nike, Bridgestone/ Firestone and Phillip Morris. The same authors argue that while branding "describes the set of associations that customers have with the company's products", reputation "involves the assessments that multiple stakeholders make about the company's ability to fulfill their expectations" (2003: 4). While branding, in their view, is targeted to influence customer behaviour, reputation is constructed in the interaction between many stakeholders. Consequently, Fombrun and van Riel conclude, branding is a subset of reputation management. It is questionable, however, whether this distinction is sustainable in a world where strong corporate brands, as we have seen in Chapter 2, are designed to appeal to *multiple* stakeholders.

Managing Corporate Reputations

Reputation is not a passive thing, which the company waits for to emerge once it has communicated its messages. Reputation must be created, managed and sustained. Defining corporate reputation as a *representation,* as we saw in Professor Fombrun's definition above, draws attention to its constructed nature. Corporate reputation is a specific *account* or interpretation of an organization's history, its accomplishments and its potential future. Typically, however, there are many competing descriptions of an organization. When Wal-Mart is described by its customers as cheap and reliable, by its suppliers as a tough negotiation partner, by the media as an old-fashioned employer, by employees as a hierarchical, efficient and brutal workplace, by the local community as an arrogant capitalist, and by Fortune's "Most Admired Corporations" as a top-performing company, Wal-Mart's reputation is anything but obvious and by no means a clear-cut thing that can be unequivocally deduced from these different descriptions. An organization, thus, does not have one and only one reputation. Even the most universally known companies, such as Coca-Cola and Microsoft, or global icons such as Madonna, Yumi Matsutoya or Björk, will have different reputations depending on the context, the expectations and the information available. There will always be competing views of how to regard the organization (or the person). And these different views do not necessarily support each other. Referring to *the* corporate reputation therefore means referring to an *authoritative account* or interpretation of the organization where certain descriptions have more weight than others.

Corporate reputation is a formalized and authoritative description of an organization.

But even the authoritative description is ambiguous. On the one hand, organizations talk about reputation as an entity with a life of its own, which can be studied through the use of proper analytical methods (much like a butterfly captured with a net and studied for its colours and its anatomical features). On the other hand, organizations talk about *creating* their reputations, about projecting and maintaining favourable corporate images in their surroundings. In practice, the two perspectives often co-exist within the same discourse, such that the organization simultaneously talks about its reputation "out there", as an objective reality which it has to understand and measure, *and* as something it shapes itself by planning, aligning and controlling its corporate messages.

Corporate reputation is an image of an organization, an image that at once suggests reality and construction, depth and surface, signified and signifier.

BOX 4.2   Image and Corporate Image

In common usage, image (from the Latin *imago*) refers to an impression that an audience is forming of a public person or a well-known organization (Ind, 1997: 48). The image may be more or less accurate or fair, but is often taken to represent, or at least indicate, reality. Sometimes images are only short-lived – for example, the image of a television-host; in other instances, they are enduring and difficult to get rid of, for example the negative image of large corporations such as Royal Dutch Shell, Nestlé or ExxonMobil. Semiotically[1] speaking, an image is a mental picture created or stimulated by a sign or a set of signs: for example, a gesture, an event, a rumour, a photograph, a graph, a statue or a painting. While the subject of an image need not be real, human beings form images of everything around them.

An image is an impression of a person or an organization created in the mind of an audience.

(Continued)

(Continued)

We talk about a *corporate* image when we refer to some kind of collective or partly shared impression of an organization. Yet, we need to distinguish between corporate image in this general sense and the more specific and well-defined impression that decision-makers deliberately hope to develop in the public. This preferred impression we can call the organization's "official self-image". The official self-image sometimes contrasts considerably with the general impression or estimation of the organization as formed by the public (Christensen and Askegaard, 2001).

A corporate image has at least two dimensions: the organization's official self-image and its reception within the general public.

Professor of corporate identity John Balmer distinguishes between corporate image and corporate reputation in terms of their endurance in the eyes of the public. Whereas corporate image, according to Balmer (1999), refers as to how the organization is perceived *now,* corporate reputation refers as to how it is regarded over time (see also Fombrun, 1996; Fombrun and van Riel, 1997). Yet, images and reputations are not independent features of the environment that pop out all by themselves. Unavoidably, they are shaped and created by organizations (Christensen and Askegaard, 2001). In the organizational literature, we find numerous definitions of corporate image that illustrate its complex nature and indicate the difficulties of determining *whose* image we are talking about. Notions such as "construed external image," "projected image" and "desired future image," for example, imply that a corporate image, in a sense, is a construct of the organization *itself* based on its *own* reading(s) of "external" impressions (Dukerich and Carter, 1998; Dutton et al., 1994; Gioia et al., 2000).

The Reputational Institution

With the growing focus on corporate legitimacy, the interest in shaping the formation of corporate reputations has increased dramatically. Corporate reputations are managed primarily through formalized assessment programmes. John Graham, Fleishman-Hillard's chairman and CEO, states: "The reputation of a company and its products used to be regarded as an intangible asset that was very hard to quantify. Now it is clear that reputation is a vital component of a company's value and is becoming a key measure of a company's performance".[2]

Corporate reputations are shaped, managed and measured by specialized institutions.

The field of reputation management is driven by the idea of recording and comparing long term assessments of intangible assets, so-called "reputational capital" (Fombrun, 1996: 28). Increasingly corporate reputations are benchmarked and ranked on dimensions such as leadership, vision, quality, environment, service and workplace environment. Private companies, public institutions, actors, politicians and business schools are assessed and ranked according to public perceptions of their performance on a number of areas. Even within the United Nations Environmental Program we find rankings conducted on for example "Corporate Sustainability Reporting". Often, lots of publicity and recognition follow the winners of the reputation rankings. And a top-end position is said to foster an "upward spiral of achievement" (Fombrun, 1996: 28). *Business Week's* annual reputation rankings of US B-business schools, for example, were immediately felt as an increase in the number of student applications among the schools rated at the top end of the scale (Elsbach and Kramer, 1996). Reputations may also affect funding patterns. While, for example, central funding for universities in the United Kingdom depends on numbers of students, a certain proportion of the annual Research Assessment Exercise (RAE) depends on non-quantifiable data such as "strategy" and "facilities."[3] The assessment of these dimensions eventually influences reputation – and, thus, the flow of funds.

Reputation rankings have become an influential dimension in the game for money, growth and legitimacy.

Corporate reputation management is a major business in itself. Among the most prominent ranking institutions we find PriceWaterhouseCoopers, MORI (Market and Opinion Research International), the Reputation Institute and the BBDO advertising agency. Often, these institutions develop the entire survey apparatus, that is, define the parameters to be measured, select the companies to be ranked, choose the respondents and interpret the results – often in collaboration with the business press. In fact, some of the most influential rankings have been established by or in close collaboration with newspapers or business magazines, for example the *Financial Times* with PriceWaterhourseCoopers ("Most Respected Companies") and the *Wall Street Journal* with the Reputation Institute. The ranking results are typically followed up by offers from reputation management consultants and agencies that hope to assist organizations in their efforts to improve their position on the ranking ladder. Interestingly, the parameters measured are often remarkably close to the core business competencies of those management consultancies. For example the Reputation Institute (RI) states that the mission of its Consulting Group "is to assist RI members and other clients to develop reputation strategies and programs by implementing the findings of reputation research, analysis and change".[4] As an obvious business strategy, the ranking institution has defined the assessment criteria within areas where the institution itself can act as an expert. This may seem a logical business development, but one of the implications is that *only measured activities count*. An organization's sponsorship of cultural events or efforts to integrate ethnic minorities, for example, will not contribute to its corporate reputation if the agencies behind the ranking system have decided not to include such types of sponsorship or integration practices in its analysis. Ranking agencies, thus, have become powerful institutions shaping the types of reputation activities organizations embark on. In this sense, the reputational institution may be described as a closed circuit in which the analysis primarily serves as a ritual able to confirm established practices.

Corporate reputation is a business practice in which consultancy firms not only assess and diagnose the corporate body but also prescribe and provide appropriate treatments.

BOX 4.3   The Analysis as Ritual

Although contemporary organizations devote huge amounts of resources to external analyses, they are typically less interested in new information than they claim to be (Thompson and Wildavsky, 1986). It is well documented that organizations, in spite of their preoccupation with data from outside sources, tend to handle such data in ways that confirm and justify established perspectives and practices. More specifically, studies have shown that organizations collect data more or less automatically (Aguilar, 1967), that the data thus accumulated are handled to fit established preconceptions, decisions or routines, (Feldman and March, 1981; Manning, 1986; Weick, 1979) and that information which conflicts with what is well-known, practical, desirable or cheap is often rejected as irrelevant, incompatible or unsupported by other sources of "evidence" (Ference, 1970; Fornell and Westbrook, 1984; Rogers and Shoemaker, 1971). Professors of organization Martha Feldman and James March explain such behaviour by reference to the modern conception of rationality. Because information is an important symbol of rationality in modern society, there is a constant pressure on managers to collect and use information. Most organizations, however, primarily use information as a ritual to demonstrate rationality and justify decisions already made.

Organizations rarely participate in external analyses in order to obtain new information.

When organizations use external analyses ritualistically, as a mirror in which they recognize their own assumptions, values and concerns, they engage in auto-communication. The use of reputational analyses, for example, to confirm and justify relative positions in an institutional ranking game demonstrates the closed nature of such analyses. Sociologists have argued that external respondents in such analyses are often reduced to a passive role of "regurgitating" answers to survey questions, answers that are often given in advance by the media or former analyses (Baudrillard, 1983; Laufer and Paradeise, 1990).

Not all organizations participate in reputation analyses. While some ranking institutions select organizations based on size (Fortune 500), others invite organizations to nominate themselves (or other organizations) to participate, for example *Business Week*'s annual B–Business School's Ratings. Still others charge a fee. RI, for example, charges participant organizations an annual fee to appear in its reputation ranking. In addition to money, participating organizations often have to invest time and personnel in registering and reporting the required information. And, preparing for awards or prize nominations is time-consuming as well. Interestingly, if an organization chooses *not* to participate in an analysis, ranking or award, it will not officially *have* a reputation. At least not one that is registered, comparable and collectively admired. Although monopolies like the army and national taxation authorities all have a need for legitimacy, they do not participate in the reputation rankings. Their need for justifying their existence is apparently not urgent. For different reasons small- and medium-sized enterprises such as Rice, Boda, and the local mechanic do not have official reputations. They cannot afford a corporate communications department to manage their participation in the rankings. The reputation ranking, thus, is a game reserved for large competitive organizations and ranking institutions. In the process of developing, maintaining and protecting their own reputations, organizations uphold the ranking institution itself.

Organizations have official reputations only if they subscribe to the ranking institution itself.

Typically, reputation rankings are based on surveys or interviews where respondents are asked to express their *perceptions* of select corporations. And often, reputation analyses are organized by consultancy firms in exclusive set-ups where managers are invited to evaluate managers of other organizations. For example, *Financial Times'* and *Fortune's* surveys are based on compiled ratings on surveys of executives, directors and analysts. Respondents are asked to rate attributes such as "quality of management", "quality of products and services", "innovativeness", "long-term investment value", "financial soundness", "ability to attract, and keep, talented people", "responsibility to the community and the environment", "wise use of corporate assets" and "global acumen". Rankings are rarely based on the opinions of consumers, but on perceptions among a crowd of peers in other companies – peers who typically attend the same networks and conferences as the managers of the organizations that are being assessed. The "controller" and the "controlled," thus, are often closely linked in reputation assessments. Acknowledging the bias of having managers assessing managers, however, some reputation analyses now take in additional respondents, including citizens, opinion leaders, students, and so on.

Reputation rankings are often fairly closed systems of business peers assessing each other's organizations.

As more stakeholders are invited to assess the reputations of organizations, the task of influencing the opinion of the general public becomes vital to reputation management. In that process, the media play a central role. This is true also for the opinion of internal audiences. As an interesting study of the Port Authority of New York and New Jersey demonstrated, the representation of companies in the media influences the way organizational members come to see themselves. More specifically, the study showed how the organization's handling of growing homelessness affected the self-perception of employees when the organization was associated with the issue in the media (Dutton and Dukerich, 1991). The influence of media coverage on public perception has been well-known for many decades (Ader, 1995; Behr and Iyengar, 1985). Based on this insight, professor of management David Deephouse (2000) has suggested that media reputation, defined as the overall evaluation of an organization in the media, should be regarded as a strategic resource that needs to be cultivated carefully (see also Ind, 1997). Such practice is sometimes referred to as "spin".

BOX 4.4   Spin

In the context of communication, spin means to provide an interpretation or a depiction of a statement or an event in a way that influences public opinion. Writings on public relations often use the notion of spin in a pejorative manner, implying deceit and the manipulation of facts or at least a heavily biased portrayal in the sender's own favour. In a more neutral sense, spin refers to the design of a message or a situation in order to bring about the most positive result possible for the sender. Being traditionally a strategy for politicians, organizations increasingly seek to stage themselves with the purpose of creating public attention. In this game, spin has become a strategic way of spurring potential employees, consumers and investors to assess an event or a crisis – not so much based on facts but on information created and disseminated by the company itself. In this process the media plays a central role.[6]

Spin is increasingly accepted as a strategic and necessary means of impression management.

The word "spin" offers a slightly different take on more familiar terms like "persuasion", "manipulation" and even "propaganda". While all these terms are contested and can never be defined in any absolute way, they point to the way influence happens and to the degree of legitimacy it is seen to have. The word "spin" helps to realize that there is no such thing as *pure* information or completely value-neutral messages. On the other hand, the term can make us cynical in thinking that everyone is pursuing narrow self-interests when they are crafting messages. "Spin" and "spin doctors" are here to stay – that is, at least until we start calling them something else. "Sophists", perhaps.

The notion of spin draws our attention to the persuasive dimensions of corporate messages.

In his book *The Image: A Guide to Pseudo-Events in America*, from 1964, historian Daniel Boorstin described how the reproduction or simulation of actual events, a process stimulated by advertising, was becoming even more important than the event itself. Anticipating the work of the early postmodern writers, Boorstin argued that modern citizens had become accustomed to spin. A growing proportion of what we read, see and hear, Boorstin claimed, consists of "pseudo-events":

> *In competition for prestige it seems only sensible to try to perfect our image rather than ourselves. That seems the most economical, direct way to produce the desired result. Accustomed to live in a world of pseudo-events, celebrities, dissolving forms, and shadowy but overshadowing images, we mistake our shadow for ourselves. To us they seem more real than the reality. Why should they not seem so to others?* (in Collier and Horowitz, 1976: 152).

Communicating Responsibly with Stakeholders

External audiences rely on the reputation of an organization to judge the quality of its products, its employment practices, its prospects for growth, its socially responsible behaviour, and so on. And while it is important to monitor and shape such perceptions, it becomes increasingly vital for organizations to understand and be influenced by them. In addition to spin and other short-term communications, corporate reputation management involves the manufacturing of lasting and beneficial stakeholder relationships (Andriof et al., 2003).

BOX 4.5   Stakeholders

The notion of a stakeholder[7] is an old concept in law where it originally referred to a person who held the values (money or property) while it was determined who the right owner was. Along the same lines, a stakeholder can also refer to a person who holds the bets in a game or a contest. Today, stakeholders are most usually described as "interest groups". In the mid-1980s, professor of strategy Edward Freeman introduced the notion of the stakeholder to management, the defining it as "any group or individual who can affect or who is affected by the achievement of the firm's objectives" (1984: 25). Among such groups and individuals we find managers, consumers, investors, suppliers, grass roots organizations, employees and their families, host communities, local governments, state and national governments, general society, and sometimes even foreign governments. While employees, for example, are affected by issues like working conditions, salaries, and security of employment, the local community holds stakes in the natural environment, taxes and jobs. In his analysis of stakeholders, Freeman (1984) emphasized *the urgency of ethics*, arguing that an ethical decision is one that takes into consideration the implications of the corporate decision on *all* relevant stakeholders (see also Freeman and Gilbert, 1988; Freeman and Velamuri, 2006). In practice, however, most stakeholder analyses focus on *strategic* stakeholders, that is the groups and individuals who have sufficient power or media attention to seriously affect corporate decisions.

While a stakeholder is any group or person with stakes in organizational decisions and outcomes, in practice it most often refers to interest groups with the power to shape corporate reality.

The management of stakeholder relations has become an integrated dimension of an organization's responsibility towards the local and the global community. In its mission statement the Body Shop, for example, declares that one of its reasons for existing is "To creatively balance the financial and human needs of our stakeholders: employees, customers, franchisees, suppliers and shareholders", and "To courageously ensure that our business is ecologically sustainable: meeting the needs of the present without compromising the future"(The Body Shop, 1996: 7). The official name for such efforts is *Corporate Social Responsibility* (CSR). While different definitions abound, corporate social responsibility usually refers to "a concept whereby companies integrate social and environmental concerns in their business operations and in their interaction with their stakeholders on a voluntary basis".[8] Prevalent in CSR theory and practice is the involvement of those affected by the corporate decisions and practices: the stakeholders (Smith, 2003). Professor of management Archie Carroll (1979) talks about four types of corporate responsibilities to stakeholders: economic, juridical, ethical and philanthropic. While the economic and the juridical responsibilities already reside within business logic, the ethical and philanthropic responsibilities seem to appeal to moral obligations beyond, and perhaps even against, business interests. Recently CSR has been gaining a foothold within a business logic: where CSR used to be considered out of a desire to do good in the sense of ethical and philanthropic responsibilities ("the normative case"), today CSR reflects what is called an "enlightened self-interest" embracing all four responsibilities ("the business case") (Smith, 2003).

Increasingly, corporate social responsibility is considered part of normal business practice.

Interestingly, strong criticism against CSR is voiced from separate ends of the political spectrum. Based on neo-liberal thinkers such as professor of economics and Nobel Prize winner Milton Friedman, the Right argues that social responsibility works against the interests of the corporation's primary responsibility: profits. Critics within this camp argue that CSR is like imposing an additional tax or spending other people's money. Social responsibility, in this view, is disingenious window-dressing, an unnecessary distraction, or a hint of socialism (Friedman, 1970). Drawing on arguments from Friedman and Adam Smith, *The Economist* has claimed that CSR is a waste of corporate resources: it distracts companies from their core roles of producing goods and services and making profits. From the Left, it is frequently argued that corporations are incapable of anything like true responsibility and that CSR, as a consequence, is an oxymoron (McMillan, 2007). That is to say that an organization based in certain private interests is structurally incapable of assuming the position of the larger public good. In his book and film *The Corporation*, Joel Bakan depicts CSR as window dressing that enables companies to continue unethical practices and to resist government regulation.

Corporate social responsibility is producing suspicion at both ends of the political spectrum.

Due to the social significance of corporate social responsibility, however, the corporate landscape has produced a marked increase in messages and reports about environmental behaviour. "Imagination at Work", the campaign by General Electric (GE) mentioned earlier, depicts GE's major products as being naturally and essentially connected to the environment. While the mirror image of the GEnx airplane is illustrated as a bird, the Evolution Series locomotive is reflected as a flock of zebras (*Newsweek*, 2005). Besides delivering power, GE dramatizes its concern for the environment. In addition to green advertising, the number of non-financial reports and corporate statements on values and social responsibility has grown conspicuously over the last decade. According to the Association of Chartered Certified Accountants, in 1993 less than 100 companies produced reports disclosing other issues than financial results. In 2003, more than 1500 non-financial reports on environmental and social issues were published.[9] Because the production of non-financial reports is not compulsory, there is no set of national or international criteria on which companies are expected to measure and report their CSR efforts.[10] Yet, these reports play a significant role in corporate self-presentations. Imitating the format of the annual financial report, many non-financial reports present quantitative data on all CSR issues, for example women in management, animals in laboratories, accidents in production, satisfaction in the workforce, cleanliness of waste water, and even the number of stakeholder partnerships. Although the non-financial reports often subscribe to a neutral, fact-presenting design, they are still expressions of one-way corporate communications: designed, staged and communicated from company to stakeholders for the purpose of corporate self-presentation. Still, the non-financial reports serve as an important brick in corporate reputation building, as they are compared, assessed, ranked and awarded by accounting firms and management consultants (PriceWaterhouseCoopers, 2005).

Stakeholder management has become a question of managing sophisticated communications to stakeholders.

BOX 4.6   Communicational Politics

According to professor of sociology Graham Knight (2007), the increased investment in communication has given rise to a world of "communicational politics" where the focus on opinion management is more pronounced than the interest in resolving material problems. This tendency, according to

Knight, is influencing both corporations and their adversaries. Communicational politics is manifested, for example, in "blame management" which plays a key role in the efforts of social movements to attribute causes and responsibilities for a particular problem. Using risk as argument, resource-poor social movements are able to challenge the legitimacy and performance of powerful corporations and governments and force them to rethink and redefine their practices even when no specific problems are present. Highlighting well-known corporate brands, social movements are able to generate events discursively in ways that mobilize the interest of the media and public opinion and potentially amplify existing problems and define new precedents. Documentary films such as Michael Moore's *Fahrenheit 9/11*, Morgan Spurlock's *Super Size Me*, and Al Gore's *An Inconvenient Truth* are increasingly employed as an influential means of creating political attention.

Both corporations and their adversaries employ sophisticated communication practices.

Professor Knight mentions two discursive strategies that companies may employ in their response to criticism: multilateralism and proceduralism. *Multilateralism*, in the words of Knight, is "a strategy for dispersing causal and remedial responsibility for problems" (2007: 314). Implying that problems are systemic and collective rather than specific to a particular corporation, this strategy seeks to spread the blame to more than one corporate actor. This has been a common strategy by oil and automobile companies, when they are under criticism for insufficient support of energy conservation efforts, clean-air standards, and the development of non-fossil fuels. Basically, the excuse is: "Everyone's doing it". This is precisely what professors of organizational communication Juliet Roper and George Cheney (2003) found in an examination of New Zealand businesses' responses to the Kyoto Protocol and the national commitment to reduce greenhouse emissions. The most common defense was: "We can't make the change unless everyone else is doing it". *Proceduralism* refers to the practice of establishing institutional mechanisms for dealing with problems, for example investigations, assessments, verifications, reporting and so forth. Such practices reduce real problems to issues of procedures and semantics. In this way, statements such as "we are in dialogue with our stakeholders" may deflate criticism from social movements: a disagreement is acknowledged and action is taken in the form of "dialogue".

Society is clearly ambivalent about CSR-related communications. Although we see more CSR messages in corporate advertisements today, many organizations still hesitate to announce their CSR efforts directly (Morsing and Schultz, 2006). Anita Roddick, then CEO of Body Shop, commented: "We went into the social audit with a sense of "damned if we do, damned if we don't" (The Body Shop, 1996: 3). Research supports such concerns: while stakeholders encourage companies to engage in CSR, they do not unambiguously encourage glaring corporate communications about CSR activities (Morsing and Schultz, 2006). It has been argued that the more organizations expose their ethical and social ambitions, the more likely they are to attract critical stakeholder attention (Ashforth and Gibbs, 1990). As some marketing scholars have pointed out, "if a company focuses too intently on communicating CSR associations, is it possible that consumers may believe that the company is trying to hide something?" (Brown and Dacin, 1997: 81). CSR, thus, presents a subtle challenge to corporate communications: how to achieve a positive reputation for being socially responsible, without communicating "too much" about it? In spite of these difficulties, organizations are rarely silent about their efforts to be responsible corporate citizens. In 2002 Philip Morris spent $US75 million on social activities. The same year, the company spent $US100 million *telling the world* about these activities (Porter and Kramer, 2002).

Corporate messages about CSR initiatives have a tendency to attract critical attention.

The general public has good reasons to be skeptical of what corporations say about themselves, including their values and their social and environmental deeds. Corporate messages about such matters are often blatantly unrealistic and self-celebratory. The attempts, for example, by many auto manufactures to present their cars as environmentally sound (for example, Toyota "Aim: Zero Emissions" (*The Economist*, 2005) and General Motor "See how GM vehicles save resources and energy"[11]) call for immediate objections and counter arguments. Yet, our propensity to criticize or reject such types of corporate communications has its limitations. Professors of management and geography Sharon Livesey and Julie Graham argue that corporate communications has the potential to influence an organization to change it behaviours to become more socially or environmentally responsible. Studying how eco-talk emerged in the Royal Dutch/Shell Group after years of stakeholder criticism, Livesey and Graham demonstrate how such talk became a creative force in pushing the corporation toward more sustainable practices. Interestingly, Shell's adoption of a new way of talking about sustainability influenced the wider array of choices made by the corporation. Livesey and Graham (2007) insist that what we think and say about sustainability and other dimensions of social responsibility, even when the utterances are contradictory, matters in the process of shaping and adapting to new situations in our social and natural environments. Although we should continue to be critical of what organizations say or do with respect to social responsibility and sustainability, we may need to allow organizations to experiment with the ways they communicate about these and related issues. Such latitude not only allows them to find new solutions for themselves and their own organizational practices, but also helps society at large discover new ideals, goals and healthy practices (see also Chapter 8).

CASE: Challenging the Monolithic Reputation

BP[12]

BP (former British Petroleum) is one of the world's largest oil producers. On Fortune 500's list of the largest US corporations in 2006, BP is No. 4. Because of its size, BP is regarded as a so-called "barometer company" in the UK, as BP's successes and failures are likely to be mirrored in the UK economy as a whole. BP employs around 96,000 people. More than 70 per cent of its profits are generated in Europe and the USA. This case demonstrates that many descriptions of a company compete when we talk about an organization's reputation. As such, the case challenges the idea that an organization has one authoritative reputation.

Staging a New Reputation

Being a visible and highly influential player in the global oil industry, BP recognizes the importance of a favourable reputation. David Walton, head of public relations, says BP's reputation is "a major commercial and political asset. Like any asset, it has to be managed and looked after" (quoted in Rawstorne, 1989: 5). In 1989 British Petroleum decided to change its name to simply 'BP'. The company redesigned its logo and refurbished its petrol stations to promote a greener and more environmental and socially responsible image. In 2000 BP rebranded itself again, this time as 'bp: Beyond Petroleum'. The ambition was to present BP as an energy company, not just an oil company, by drawing attention to its efforts within the field of solar energy. BP replaced its logo with a green–white–and–yellow sunburst named after Helios, the ancient Greek sun god, supporting the new corporate brand's commitment to the environment and solar power. The lower-case letters were chosen "because focus groups say bp is friendlier than the old imperialistic BP" (Hale, 2000). The process of rebranding cost BP around 600 million US dollars (Noor-Drugan, 2000).

Competing Reputations

In 2006, BP was ranked no. 76 at Best Global Brand Report by Interbrand (the same year Nike was 31 and Shell 89). However, when the media portrays the corporation, it is often

(Continued)

(Continued)

in a critical tone. On 16 October 2005, for example, *Fortune Magazine* reported three serious problems in the company's operations: a refinery explosion in BP's Texas City refinery that killed 15 people and injured 170, a serious leak and corrosion of the pipelines running from wells to the Trans-Alaska Pipeline, and an accusation from government regulators claiming that BP's US trading unit was cornering the market for propane in 2003 and 2004, artificially driving up prices.[13] The *Magazine* said:

> *"How could BP, a company that has made being green a core part of its identity, even rebranding itself as "Beyond Petroleum," suffer within one year both the worst oil spill in the history of the North Slope and the worst U.S. refinery accident in more than a decade? And how did CEO John Browne, the energy visionary who publicly broke with his industry to acknowledge a possible link between emissions and global warming, earning a prominent spot in* Vanity Fair's *recent green issue, become a scapegoat for Big Oil?"*[14]

The damaged Alaska pipeline seriously hurt BP's image in the USA. In March 2006, 200,000 gallons of crude oil leaked onto the Arctic tundra because of a damaged pipeline, leading USA regulators to question the company's corrosion prevention practices, according to Reuters. After the spill, the government allowed BP to continue operations but warned it could force a shutdown if leaks continued.[15] BP was forced to close its operations a few months later.

Among human rights organizations, BP holds a reputation for focusing on profits at the expense of democracy. In addition to many accusations of violating human rights, BP has been in the limelight for allegedly backing up a military coup that overthrew the democratically elected government of Azerbaijan in 1993. One year later BP signed the "Contract of the Century" as it was granted large oil drilling rights in Azerbaijan.[16] Also BP's oil operations in Colombia have been linked to protect BP's interests against the local guerrillas, who believe the oil industry should be nationalized, by installing a special brigade of 3,000 soldiers from the Colombian army for preventative protection for BP's staff and installations (Beder, 2005).

Among environmentalists, BP holds a mixed reputation. In the late 1980s, its commitment to the environment was ridiculed at the sight of BP clearing large areas of rainforest in Brazil. More recently, in March 1999, BP launched its "Plug in the Sun" programme based on its investment in solar energy and the installation of solar panels on petrol stations around the world. While consumers were still pouring petrol into their cars, the ads said, "We can fill you up by sunshine". For this programme BP "earned" a Greenwash Award by Corporate Watch. In a similar satirical vein, Greenpeace USA gave CEO John Browne an award for the "Best Impression of an Environmentalist". In 1992 Greenpeace International named it one of Scotland's two largest polluters. And in 1991 BP was cited by the state as the most polluting company in the USA based on Environmental Protection Agency toxic release data.

Even BP employees have criticized the corporation publicly. An anonymous BP employee reported to *Fortune Magazine* that BP is driven by a sense of being untouchable and a "it can't happen here" mentality.[17] The managerial focus on the bottom line shows no concern for the environment.

Reputation Management

In response to a growing critique, BP has taken a number of initiatives to defend its reputation. For example, the company has proactively engaged with Oxfam and Friends of the Earth.[18] BP also sponsors cultural institutions including parts of the British Museum, the Tate Gallery, Edinburgh's Festival Fringe, the Museum of Mankind and the National Portrait Gallery. In 1997, BP made its strongest effort to demonstrate environmental consciousness. CEO John Browne decided to leave the Global Climate Coalition (GCC). This group of 50 corporations and trade associations had consistently claimed that global warming was unproven and action to prevent it was therefore unwarranted. John Browne argued it was time to act to prevent greenhouse warming rather than continue to debate whether it would occur. With this new stance on climate change, BP earned a reputation as an environmental progressive corporation in an industry that largely refused to accept the likelihood of global warming. Browne received praise also from environmental groups, including Greenpeace. More recently, an initiative from BP has caused the UK's first mainstream scheme to "neutralise" the CO_2 emissions caused by driving. The scheme has been developed in consultation with leading NGOs and reputation ranking institutions. Time will tell if these efforts will earn BP an more unambiguously positive reputation or if its operations in the Nigerian Delta, Iran, Kuwait, Iraq, Papua New Guinea, Algeria, Libya, Somalia, Yemen, Aden and elsewhere will continue to produce negative counter-images of this large corporation.

Points of reflection

1. What are BP's interests in participating in international reputation analyses?
2. To what extent does reputation management at BP reflect Fombrun and van Riel's advice for companies to be visible, distinctive, authentic, transparent and consistent?
3. In spite of its endeavour in reputational management, BP does not have one reputation but many. Will BP ever be able to achieve one favourable reputation?

Chapter Summary

In Chapter 4, we showed how the desire to appear legitimate and attractive in the eyes of stakeholders drives organizations to carefully trim, train and pose their reputations. We argue that reputations are not simply registered; they are continuously constructed and managed. While corporate reputation has become an important dimension of economic performance, reputational management has developed into an influential and lucrative business. Increasingly, thus, corporate reputations are shaped, managed and measured by specialized institutions. Providing formalized and authoritative descriptions of an organization, such institutions help organizations stage their willingness to become transparent, authentic, visible, consistent and distinctive institutions that are part of society. Challenging this practice, we demonstrated that the images of companies with favourable reputations may not be as clear-cut, transparent or authentic as they claim to be. By contrast, we argued that the reputational game creates a world of communicational politics in which the desire for information and insight is often overshadowed by a power play in the arena of communication. Indeed, the desire for global recognition drives corporate talk to become self-congratulatory and sometimes disparate from corporate action. Yet, the chapter concluded by emphasizing that such talk may allow organizations to discover new ideals and to find new solutions. So far we have only hinted at some of the difficulties and limitations of the corporate communications project. In the second part of the book, we shall explore our critique even further.

Notes

1 Semiotics, or semiology, is the theory and study of signs and symbols and their lives in society.
2 'Corporate brand reputation outranks financial performance as most important measure of success' (http://www.prinfluences.com.au/index.php?artId=393).
3 For more information in the UK Resaerch Assessment Exercise, see: http://www.hero.ac.uk/rae/ For a concrete example see Cranfield University: http://www.som.cranfield.ac.uk/ som/ research/ building/index.asp
4 http://www.reputationinstitute.com/main/index.php?=cons&box=cons01
5 http://money.cnn.com/magazines/fortune/fortune500/
6 http://en.wikipedia.org/wiki/Spin_(politics)
7 http://en.wikipedia.org/wiki/Stakeholder
8 http://www.emcc.eurofond.eu.int/source/eu02002s.html?p1=topic&p2
9 This number is reported by Association of Chartered Certified Accountants, http://www. CorporateRegistar.com, 'Towards transparency: progress on global sustainability reporting', p. 8.
10 While the Global Reporting Initiative (http://www.globalreporting.org) and the United Nations' Global Compact (http://www.unglobalcompact.org) have proposed a set of guidelines for companies to follow, these are articulated in rather abstract and general terms. Furthermore, so far only around 1000 companies are registered to follow the GRI guidelines for reporting and around 2500 companies have signed up to the Global Compact.
11 http://www.gm.com/company/gmability/environment/index.html
12 http://www.bp.com. See also, Beder (2002) and Marsden (2006).
13 http://money.cnn.com/magazines/fortune/fortune_archive/2006/10/16/8388595/index. htm?postversion=2006100210
14 Fortune Magazine (2005) 16 October, see: http://web.ebscohost.com/ehost/ external?vid= 2&hid=13&sid=6736ca5b-3e20-4abb-b45e-14184ea637f9%40SRCSM2
15 http://www.pbs.org/newshour/updates/business/july-dec06/oil_08-07.html
16 http://www.moles.org/ProjectUnderground/drillbits/5_06/1.html
17 Fortune Magazine (2005) October 16, see: http://web.ebscohost.com/ehost/detail?vid=1 &hid=13&sid=6736ca5b-3e20-4abb-b45e-14184ea637f9%40SRCSM2
18 http://www.corporatewatch.org/?lid=289#pr

Interlude

From Total to Wholesome Bodies

In the first part of this book, we introduced the reader to the field of corporate communications as a specific *mindset* that claims to encompass all communications within one coherent perspective. Conceptualizing corporate communications as the "body" of communications, we have demonstrated how contemporary organizations, in their pursuit of identity and legitimacy, are increasingly preoccupied with the management of total images of organizations. The ambition of corporate communications is to integrate all symbols, messages and behaviours in order for the organization to speak consistently across different audiences and media. In its quest for integration, corporate communications has become an expansive managerial project that permeates the entire organizational domain and shapes its outlook, its culture and its members. With corporate branding and the notion that consumers "buy" the company behind the product, these organizational dimensions have taken centre stage in efforts to present contemporary corporations as legitimate players in the world. And, through reputational management, such efforts have become professionalized with the effect that the organization "behind" is now a formalized and institutionalized image.

In the second part of the book, we will challenge this perspective with regard to corporate communications. We will argue that the emphasis on totality prevents organizations from developing healthy practices to operate in complex environments. More specifically, we will deconstruct the basic assumptions behind corporate communications, arguing that the diagnosis, which guides theory and practice within the field, is limited and flawed. In spite of its limitations, the diagnosis impels organizations to strictly manage and control all communications in ways that intensify and expand corporate discipline at all organizational levels. This way, the project of corporate communications potentially clashes with other organizational concerns, such as diversity, flexibility and responsiveness. We argue that organizations need to respond to a complex world by increasing their sensitivity to both internal and external environments: this means that corporate communications can be regarded as the (ironic) management of polyphony.

PART II

Behind the Corporeal Project

5

Justifying Corporate Communications
Diagnosing the Fragile Body

> ... social texts do not merely reflect or mirror objects, events and categories pre-existing in the social and natural world. Rather, they actively construct a version of those things. They do not just describe things; they do things. And being active, they have social and political implications.
>
> Jonathan Potter and Margaret Wetherell (1987: 6)

Introduction

The literature tells us that that the growing emphasis on the corporate body in professional communications is unavoidable. In a world saturated with signs and images, it seems necessary to unify, align and coordinate all communications to ensure consistency in corporate messages and behaviours – in other words, to integrate the many dimensions of the organization's communication. After all, what is the alternative? Equally, the efforts to brand the organization as a whole rather than branding individual products seem logical in a world where product differences are rapidly eroded. These arguments are well known to contemporary communication professionals. In fact, they are often reproduced without much reflection. In this chapter, we ask how contemporary organizations justify their engagement with corporate communications. In other words, what is the rationality behind the "bodily" pursuit in today's communication? And how does management explain its renewed interest in integration? Chapter 5 examines the conventional diagnosis behind corporate communications in order to challenge and deconstruct its most basic assumptions. In particular, the chapter will address the following issues and questions:

Chapter 5: Points of Challenge

- The call for organizations to integrate all their communications is based on a description of the market as "cluttered" and fragmented, filled with symbols, messages and media. Is it possible, however, that integrated communications itself precipitates this condition?

- The corporate communications discourse seems to assume that integration endows organizations with more stable points of differentiation than their tangible products. How can corporate messages themselves erode differences between organizations?

- The practice of corporate communications takes for granted that organizations are able to become transparent to both themselves and their surroundings. What does it imply to say that such transparency is often enacted and staged?

Diagnosing as Framing

When we ask what type of environmental diagnosis is brought forth to inform and justify managerial preoccupation with corporate communications, we take our point of departure in the philosophy that guides this book: communication is consequential and the "reading" of a situation has implications for the solutions we are able to envision. The diagnosis behind corporate communications should be made explicit for a number of reasons. First, since assumptions are rarely discussed openly, decision makers may not be fully aware of the explanations and trends they subscribe to. This is evident, for instance, in western notions of identity as one's "uniqueness". When explanations are taken for granted, organizations easily become victims to management fashions and fads, believing that they are doing something unique while in fact they are moving in the same direction as everybody else. Second, approval of an idea is often based on a *lack* of clarification. People frequently endorse an idea until the arguments behind the idea are spelt out in detail. Third, an organizational diagnosis is not a passive or neutral reflection of reality. An organizational diagnosis is a description of reality that actively frames, and thus constructs, a *version* of the organization and its surroundings – often with an implied cure (Levinson et al., 1972).

BOX 5.1   What's in a "Frame"?

The idea and term "framing" has recently been popularized by linguist George Lakoff. During the 2004 US presidential election, Lakoff (2004) argued that the Republican party had become more effective than the Democratic party in attaching catchy labels and images to issues such as substituting "death tax" for "inheritance tax" or helping to make the word "liberal" seem both outdated and threatening. A very good example of reframing in North America, Europe and elsewhere was the 1980s-era shift from associating "revolution" with left-wing politics to linking it with conservatism. This is a good example of a *reappropriation* of a symbol for reframing which in this case helped to brand and shape an entire movement. Prior to about 1980, conservatism was associated more with tradition and with the "conservation" of the status quo. So, what *is* framing? According to Lakoff, framing represents a symbolic and cognitive way to handle and address a complex issue. Thus, for example, a problem such as poverty can be "framed" as mainly an individual issue, as chiefly a social problem, or as a mixture of the two.

Framing refers to the way we think about, approach, and talk about an issue, acknowledging that these are not neutral undertakings because they help shape perception of the issue.

(Continued)

(Continued)

Consider the global debate today over what counts as "torture". Ultimately, we decide what acts to put under the symbolic umbrella of torture and which to classify in other ways: for example as "appropriate means of interrogation". This debate has enormous implications: legally, politically, practically, and of course morally. In the context of work and social relationships, what is going on when a friend or a family member tells a young person "Get a real job!" (Clair, 1996). With this simple phrase, the work being done is downgraded, and cultural assumptions are marshaled to persuade the person that their pursuits are not worthwhile (or not worth enough money). Some frames are powerful because of their specific allusions: for example, how we describe the opposition forces in any particular country may make historical allusions that are tough to beat, persuasively speaking. Other frames, like words, are potent because of their ambiguity: this is true for the term "democracy" around the world because only a handful of countries actually make no claim to be democratic. So, what are some ways to *re*frame?

- We can use new labels for old ideas. (Business trends are a good example of this.)
- We can put new ideas under old labels (as is the case with the ways we talk about some new electronic media, using familiar mechanical terms).
- We can make striking new comparisons or contrasts (say between corporate globalization and the colonial era of western European nations).
- We can create new pictures for unfamiliar issues such as ethnobotanist Wade Davis's use of the term "ethnosphere" to help people understand the disappearance of many cultures around the world (Davis, 1997).

In an interesting dissertation analyzing the use of communication consultants by Norwegian public sector organizations, political scientist Arild Wæraas demonstrated how communication agencies tend to use standard and "off-the-shelf" vocabulary when diagnosing corporate communications problems. Wæraas (2004) illustrated how various communication agencies employ almost identical expressions when characterizing the communication material of their customers. In addition to descriptions such as "fragmented communication", "unclear identity" and "poor reputation", the diagnoses were phrased in *negative* terms, stressing the need for the organization to unify its messages in order for the organization to speak consistently or with "one voice". While some of these diagnoses may lead to sound advice, much more is going on. Too many economic, human and societal resources are invested in "bodily" projects today for us to accept the conventional diagnosis at face value.

Embedded in the organizational diagnosis is a managerial ideal. Making the diagnosis explicit allows us to openly discuss its premises.

The Diagnosis

Prevailing explanations of the current interest in corporate communications emphasize in particular issues of message "clutter", audience fragmentation, media multiplication, parity marketplace, retailer power, critical stakeholders, and new communication technologies. These issues can be summarized by the following three propositions:

- A communication effects thesis.
- A differentiation thesis.
- A transparency thesis.

The communication effects thesis observes that the market is saturated with signs and images, all insisting on being heard and taken seriously. As a result, contemporary organizations struggle to break through "the clutter". Simultaneously, the communication environment is described as fragmented or "splintered" into a multitude of media options competing for our time and attention. Such fragmentation is illustrated by the growing number of available television channels: the advent of smaller, targeted media alternatives like direct mail, event sponsorships and telemarketing; and the emergence of communication vehicles in digital applications that allow for more points of exposure. In addition to message "clutter" and media fragmentation, the communication effects thesis observes a general disintegration or demassification of audiences into individual lifestyles, subcultures or tribes with distinct modes of perception and interpretation (Schultz et al., 1994). Young members of the US rap culture, for example, not only live different lives to those of suburban middle-class families, they also have a distinctly different language. Across their differences, however, many audiences exhibit a growing indifference or disinterest in what organizations have to say about themselves. Consequently, it is argued, corporations find it increasingly difficult for their messages to reach and impact consumers and other relevant target groups. With a plethora of media alternatives and with the explosive growth in the number of audiences in the communication project, the task of putting forth a clear, consistent image at once becomes more difficult yet more urgent. Professor of marketing M. Joseph Sirgy articulates the diagnosis this way:

The increased emphasis on marketing communications has brought with it increased marketing communications clutter, decreased message credibility, database marketing, increased cost and decreased effectiveness of mass-media communications, mergers and acquisitions of marketing communications agencies, increased media and audience fragmentation, and a shift of information technology. These, in turn, have made marketers very cognizant of the need and power of IMC [Integrated Marketing Communications]. (1998: 10)

The communication effects thesis states that communication clutter, along with media and audience fragmentation, have made it increasingly difficult to *influence* target audiences.

According to the differentiation thesis, the quest for visibility and credibility in a cluttered and challenging environment has made differentiation a salient issue for organizations in most sectors of society. The availability of new technologies implies that most forms of product differentiation can quickly and easily be offset or copied by competitors. Consequently, it is argued, the current marketplace is flooded by an increasing number of "me too products" where differences between brands are negligible. Marketing scholars talk about a "parity marketplace in which the only differentiating features are logistics and communication" (Schultz et al., 1994: 44; see also Schultz and Kitchen, 2004). To counter the erosion of differences, we are told, corporations need to create alternative and more stable points of differentiation centered on communication. Because mobile phones, for example, are increasingly similar in terms of their physical features, producers seek to differentiate themselves through branding. Simultaneously, organizations face significant changes in the power of retailers. The consolidation in the retail industry implies a power shift from manufacturers to retailers. In contrast to small local retailers, large retail chains have a growing influence on the presence, organization and visibility of brands in the retail outlet, for example, in deciding which products are highlighted and given a special attention in their stores. This influence accentuates the need for manufacturers to play the differentiation game, that is, to make sure that their products are so well-known and distinct that the chains cannot afford to ignore them. The chances of a new brand of toothpaste attracting attention in a supermarket are slim if the producer is not able to establish and defend some clear points of differentiation vis-à-vis other toothpaste brands. By establishing and maintaining clear points of distinction and communicating these points consistently across different audiences, producers hope to influence retail chains – sometimes through the demands of the customers – to carry and highlight their brands (Belch and Belch, 1998). Without a clear identity, constructed around a distinct corporate profile, the diagnosis argues, producers can no longer expect that their products will receive the necessary space, attention and support in the stores.

The differentiation thesis asserts that while traditional product differ-ences are eroded, new points of differentiation must be established through integrated communications.

The transparency Argenti thesis addresses the emergence of new critical stakehold-ers and their growing propensity to examine and question organizational products, norms and behaviours. As we saw in Chapter 1, public confidence in big business has been challenged many times during the twentieth century (Argenti, 1998). Today, however, organizations on a broader scale are exposed to an intensified level of public awareness and scepticism. While business practices are inspected by media and business analysts, organizations are increasingly held accountable for their strate-gic choices (Deephouse, 2000). Investment policies of pension funds, for instance, are regularly scrutinized by investors and other citizens. Being exposed to the crit-ical gaze of pressure groups, media, legislators, business analysts and other inquisi-tive stakeholders, it is not surprising to find that the organizations of today feel more vulnerable and transparent than ever before (Backer, 2001; Christensen, 2002). At the same time, organizations are expected to contribute to transparency themselves by sharing relevant information with their surroundings – a trend driven by the new communication technologies, especially the Internet. While internal and external stakeholders expect to have unrestricted access to corporate information, legal restrictions force organizations to disclose information about their actions and plans, including the publication of annual reports (van Riel, 2000). A large producer of food ingredients like Danisco, for example, has previously been known as a silent organization with little emphasis on external communication. Today it is not only scrutinized intensively by interest groups but is strongly encouraged to provide information to the general public about the quality and contents of its products.

The transparency thesis holds that contemporary organizations have become increasingly transparent to the critical gaze of inquisitive stakeholders.

Together, these three theses recount a story of an increasingly complex world in which organizations are led to align and integrate their communications, both to ensure the impact of their messages and the efficiency of their media spending and to stand out as distinct, recognizable and legitimate players in the market (Argenti, 1998; Fombrun and Rindova, 2000; van Riel, 2000). Depicting organizations as fragile "bodies", whose communication is constantly exposed to a complex mix of indiffer-ence, fragmentation, critique and competition, the diagnosis underlying corporate communications promotes *a clear managerial prescription*. While corporate communica-tions is presented as the ultimate ideal, the practice of integrated communications is prescribed as a compelling and necessary cure for these problems. Rather than simply adding more signs and images to an already cluttered and fragmented communication environment, the promise of integrated communications is to coordinate all communication activities in order to secure consistency, clarity, continuity and, thus, maximum legitimacy, meaning, and impact inside and outside the organization (Pickton and Broderick, 2001; Schultz et al., 1994; Sirgy, 1998). In this way, we are told, the organization can overcome the limitations of the communication environment.

Corporate communications has become a central management discourse in which the diagnosis and the cure fit neatly together.

BOX 5.2   Discourse and the Construction of Reality

In semantics, a discourse is understood as a linguistic unit composed of several sentences making up conversations, arguments and speeches. Discourses cohere around a theme, story, and list of ideas. People who use or share a particular discourse are referred to as a speech community. In the social sciences, the notion of discourse is used in a broader sense referring to an institutionalized way of thinking that shapes what can possibly be said about a certain topic. In modern society, for example, most organizational choices are talked about and evaluated in terms of rationality, growth, and of course profit. Modern managers, thus, need to phrase and justify their decisions in terms of how they contribute logically to the general betterment of the organization or the larger society. A discourse, thus, not only describes the world as it is but takes active part in its continuous (re)production (Grant et al., 1998). By defining what is acceptable or true, discourse is inseparable from issues of power.

A discourse shapes and defines possible ways of perceiving and talking about a specific topic.

Professors of organization David Knights and Gareth Morgan (1991) describe discourse as a dominant configuration of ideas and talk that define and structure organizational "problems" and the proper ways of dealing with these problems. In this sense, popular management programmes like Total Quality Management or Business Process Reengineering are discourses that at once help managers identify barriers or limitations to rational organizational practice and prescribe the action necessary to overcome the limitations. Once a discourse is established as "common sense", participants in discussion find themselves either needing to adopt or refute it; in any case, they have to refer to it.

Corporate communications can be described as a managerial discourse, a specific way of talking about market-related communication phenomena that sensitizes the attention of managers to certain characteristics of the market while justifying the (momentary) ignorance of others. On the one hand, corporate communications advances a diagnosis of the market as cluttered, fragmented, critical, etc.; a diagnosis that depicts the conventional way of managing communications as unfocused, disjointed and inefficient (Schultz et al., 1994; Sirgy, 1998). Based on this diagnosis, corporate communications, on the other hand, emphasizes the importance of bringing together and orchestrating all corporate media and messages in order for the organization to project a clear, consistent and coherent image in its surroundings. By framing, classifying, labelling and suggesting specific readings of the market, corporate communications has, in other words, produced what professors of organization Robert Cooper and Gibson Burrell call a "subtle and covert prior structuring" of the problems that the discourse itself claims to handle (1988: 102). Within the universe of corporate communications, solutions are not only implicated in the diagnosis produced by the discourse, they are promoted as necessary, logical and inevitable steps for contemporary organizations to become professional communicators. In the remainder of this chapter, we will discuss these theses with a critical eye as to how the environmental diagnosis not simply identifies important trends to which organizations need to respond but itself perpetuates the inclination for contemporary organizations to embark on corporate communications programmes.

Challenging the Communication Effects Thesis

Considering the growing abundance of messages and images striving to be heard in today's world, it is difficult to dispute the observation that the market is cluttered. Yet, while the communication effects thesis observes too much communication, it still expects the communication discipline to deliver the cure. "Clutter", however, is not a separate property of the surroundings, but typically a byproduct of intensified engagement with communication: the more organizations communicate, the more messages they will find in their surroundings. Although corporate communications claims to be a different *type* of communication, it is not entirely clear how communication programmes labelled "corporate" or "integrated" are able to escape the problem of clutter. The classical marketing emphasis on "share-of-voice" is outdated – even in its integrated version – by the fact that everybody communicates everywhere, all the time. Under such circumstances, "share-of-voice" is often reduced to "share-of-noise". Instead of seeing integration as a panacea, corporate communicators need to ask themselves what happens when all or most players in the market integrate their communications? How, in other words, does clutter or noise manifest itself in such a universe? And is it possible that the growing emphasis on communication, stimulated by the corporate communications discourse, may precipitate the condition of clutter that contemporary organizations hope to escape? In more practical terms, corporate communicators not only need to communicate in more focused and integrated ways, they also need to be more parsimonious. Lots of communication resources are wasted because organizations define their voice and symbolic presence in quantitative terms. Less is often more, and this is true both for each individual organization focusing on a few corporate signifiers and for society as a whole relieved from the attention "drought" caused by too much communication.

The corporate communications perspective ignores the possibility that the practice of integrating all communications may *itself* become a source of noise and clutter.

Simultaneously, the notion of media fragmentation tends to reproduce a narrow understanding of human communication. The ability of organizations to convey clear and consistent messages across different audiences seems to be reduced by the growing number of media options. Yet, this observation conceptualizes the communication process exclusively in terms of media *reach* and *exposure*. While these dimensions are essential in any mass communication situation, they only capture a minor part of corporate communications. That is, media reach and exposure are only the first steps in a mass communication process – steps that do not automatically lead to understanding and acceptance by the audience. Even in a *non*-fragmented world of few media options, the ability of organizations to build and sustain a distinct and unambiguous "presence" in the marketplace is frequently challenged by alternative and creative readings of corporate messages.

BOX 5.3   Reception as a Source of Integration – and Fragmentation

Rather than simply receiving corporate messages and images in a passive and receptive mode, receivers actively participate in the construction of meaning. In line with reception theory (Isar, 1974; Jauss, 1982), communication scholar Allessandro Duranti (1986) has pointed out that interpretation is not a passive activity through which an audience tries to figure out what an author meant to convey. Rather, it is a way of making sense of a piece of communication by linking it to a context that is familiar or meaningful to the receiver.

The integration of corporate messages amongst consumers and other receivers is an active and creative process of interpretation.

Faced with numerous signs and symbols, consumers rarely read corporate messages in order to understand the intention of the sender. Rather, they make sense of them by linking them to their own world of relevance and experience. As marketing scholar Claus Buhl has demonstrated, consumers integrate corporate messages when, and only when, such messages allow them to confirm or extend their own personal interests: for example, as part of their own project of identity. When consumers find corporate messages relevant, they are co-creating this relevance themselves "through self-organizing activities in which the message is a resource of information rather than instruction" (1991: 120). Studying consumers reacting to an ad from American Express, Buhl found that readings are highly idiosyncratic processes in which receivers read meaning into a message by importing relevant information from their own world (Eco, 1979; Isar, 1974). While one reader, for instance, brought in the gendered role conflicts in his own family when focusing on a red handbag left on a chair in the ad, another reader related the left bag to her own economic situation, hoping to save money for a house with a restricted budget. While none of the readers had problems identifying the sender of the ad and the general advantages of owning an American Express card, they all interpreted the ad by importing personal meanings into its structure.

The discourse of corporate communications tends to assume that message consistency and message integration at the levels of campaign planning and exposure translate smoothly into consistency at the level of reception. As the following quote by professor of corporate communications Cees van Riel illustrates, corporate communicators seem to believe that consistency at the moment of reception can be actually planned and organized by the sender:

> Initially, 'integration' was taken to mean 'unification', or 'making uniform'. This interpretation was subsequently reduced to the requirement that the final picture created in the mind of the recipient must be consistent, and must not be marred by internal contradictions [...] This can only be achieved if the different elements of the communications mix are carefully coordinated during initial planning. (1995: 16)

If we leave this sender-oriented perspective and focus instead on reception, we find that the picture is more complex. At the receiver end of the communication process, corporate messages are confronted with receivers actively seeking to integrate and make sense of them in the context of their own lives. As scholars of consumer behaviour have demonstrated, contemporary consumers often interpret and use products and messages quite differently from their original purpose, reshape and adapt them to personal use, and modify and sometimes pervert their meanings in ways not imagined by their creators (Cova, 1996; Ogilvy, 1990). This has been demonstrated in so-called "brand communities", that is, virtual communities of brand devotees. Owners of Harley Davidson motorcycles, for example, are often described as a brand community in which members creatively re-construct the meanings and the uses of their favourite brand (McAlexander et al., 2002; Muniz and O'Guinn, 2001). Also the LEGO Group has experienced a re-construction of their brand by a strong brand community outside the corporate realm. Interestingly, this community of nerdish, adult fans playing, building and competing with the LEGO bricks was so far beyond the traditional LEGO target group (young boys), that they were discredited and not recognized by the LEGO Group as an energetic driver of brand and product development until much later (Antorini, in progress). But outside brand communities also, senders may often have difficulties shaping and controlling the meaning of corporate symbols and products. The manufacturer of BMW, for example, had probably not imagined how values associated with their car would change when the car became popular amongst Turkish immigrants and retirees. From being considered a luxurious and sporty car, the BMW is now loaded with new connotations, at least in some European countries. What does the notion of integrated communications mean under these circumstances? And to what extent are the efforts of the sender in this area at all relevant to the world of the consumer? The acquisition of products and symbols is always a creative process through which recipients create and confirm themselves. Contemporary communicators, therefore, must realize that reception is potentially a source of fragmentation, as seen from the perspective of the sender, and that they are no longer masters of meaning. Since intended receivers are never passive targets but partners in the production of experiences and identities, corporate communicators should think of integrated communications as a two-way process of co-orientation and co-construction. Acknowledging this condition, some advertisements for jeans or sports gear, for example, are designed as open structures that allow for multiple feelings and experiences among the end users (Firat and Christensen, 2005).

Creative and unplanned readings of corporate messages seriously challenge the sender-oriented notion of integrated communications.

The issue of communication impact is complicated even further by the lack of interest and involvement amongst consumers and other relevant target groups. In general, consumers are rarely interested and involved in what organizations say about themselves. So, one practical question to the corporate communicator is under what circumstances will consumers be especially interested? Popular management books on corporate communications and corporate branding frequently proclaim that consumers buy the company behind the product (see also Chapter 3, Fombrun (1996) and Kunde (1997)). Yet, practical evidence seems to suggest that many consumers do not care much about the *owners* of their brands (Davidson, 1998). Although brand loyalties and the emergence of critical stakeholders seem to indicate some deeper concern about organizational practices, organizations are also experiencing a growing indifference among their external audiences. In fact, when it comes to *corporate* messages, most consumers are, at best, indifferent. Adam Morgan, Joint European Planning Director of TBWA, argues that most people regard advertising as "a nuisance business", a type of communication we would prefer to do without. To talk about consumers as an audience presupposes that they are receptive to corporate messages, which is rarely the case: "Communication suggests active listening, but our target doesn't want to be communicated to, isn't waiting for a further message" (1999: 22). Morgan's description of what ordinary people typically are concerned about captures this indifference well:

> *Since we spend all our time thinking of our target's consumption and choices in, say, fish sticks, there is a natural tendency to be a little disappointed in listening to them tell us in focus groups that they don't really think about – or even want to think about – fish sticks at all. What they think about is how to get their son to soccer practice while their daughter makes ballet, or how they are going to find the money for college, or why their partner is in such a bad mood, or whether the cat needs putting down, or how to get the car cleaned before dinner with the Bukowskis on Thursday night. That's where their time and energy is devoted. In terms of "consumption" and brand decisions, they are on autopilot. (1999: 107)*

Most consumers are not deeply interested in what organizations have to say about themselves.

Given the bombardment with corporate messages, it is not surprising to find that consumers develop an indifferent or blasé attitude towards the enterprise of commercial communication (Baudrillard, 1983). Such a portrayal of consumers, of course, begs the question of how involved consumers and other publics were in the first place (Christensen and Cheney, 2000). Thus, we should be careful not to assume that the lack of interest that organizations observe in their surroundings today is fundamentally different from the communication situation that faced them earlier. As sociologist Michael Schudson argues, it is debateable whether external audiences have *ever* been *deeply* interested in what business corporations have to say about themselves. Obviously, there are exceptions. Shareholders are usually interested in communication indicating that the company is doing well. The same is true for employees, their families and the local community. And special interest groups such as environmentalists are often attentive to corporate messages – especially when they seem to differ from corporate practices. Yet, attention has always been a problem for mass communicators. The mere accumulation of corporate signifiers in contemporary markets suggests that one of the scarcest resources today is, and continues to be, attention and interest (Schudson, 1993). Still, the marketing and branding literature seems to presuppose such an interest. The literature on corporate branding, especially, is based on the notion of strong consumer involvement. Without dismissing the possibility that such involvement occasionally exists – that consumers sometimes display a surprising loyalty to specific brands, develop close relationship with certain symbols and slogans, or develop a special attachment to a particular company – it would be erroneous to assume that this is the usual picture. Communicators who acknowledge this limitation are no doubt more strongly positioned to craft persuasive messages than those who believe that interest and involvement are typical features.

Challenging the Differentiation Thesis

The differentiation thesis is equally flawed. When the description of the parity marketplace, filled by almost identical products, is combined with a call for greater communication involvement, the assumption seems to be that only *product* differences are being eroded in today's marketplace. Of course, the real issue here is not to establish whether contemporary products and brands are similar or not, but to understand what counts as "different" at any point in time. To think of planned communication as a separate and distinct sphere where differentiation and variation are more stable and unchangeable is to ignore the fact that images, positions and connotations also change over time. Looking, for example, at the growing number of almost identical corporate visions, missions and value statements, it is clear that an organization's standing in corporate communications is easily diminished by the activities of other players (see Box 5.4). While the pressure to stand out is relatively stable, the solutions may not be. Still, the organizations of today seem to be caught in a differentiation game that creates the very problems it sets out to solve. Communication is no less susceptible than products to the erosion of differences. Consequently, corporations need to stop deluding themselves that branding and other types of communication offer anything more than a temporary relief from the pressure to stand out.

Advocates of corporate communications seem to believe that communication endows companies with more stable points of differentiation than their tangible products are able to provide.

BOX 5.4   Advertising as a Game of Differentiation

In advertising, popular ideas and campaigns are constantly emulated by other players in the market to the effect that their originality and impact are diluted. The identity of Volvo, for example, as a very safe car – and, as it is put in an advertisement from the 1980s, a built-in "child's welfare organization" – was seriously challenged during the 1990s not because Volvo had difficulties living up to its promises but because other car producers began to emulate the *same* safety theme. Sometimes this emulation is very explicit. An advertisement from Subaru states: "Volvo has built a reputation for surviving accidents; Subaru has built a reputation for avoiding them". In a similar manner, the identity of IBM is constantly being challenged by competitors paraphrasing its slogan "Think". While ICL for a while suggested "Think ICL", other players used slogans like "Think Twice" or "Think Again". Today the "Think"-game continues. In a large, global campaign depicting a host of well-known people (for example, Gandhi, Picasso, Mohammed Ali), Apple suggests: "Think First. Think Fast. Think Different". The fact that its "difference" leans on an established slogan of the market leader does not seem to bother Apple. Most likely, people no longer associate "Think" with IBM. As a consequence, the Apple campaign may well come across as innovative, although strictly speaking this is not entirely the case. Although the imitators may not be in a position to threaten IBM's number-one position, their emulation of the "Think" slogan unavoidably reduces its value for IBM. Now, IBM can no longer say "Think" without evoking the clever twists of ICL or Apple (Christensen, 2001; Ries and Trout, 1986).

Competition has become a game of communication: a game in which differences and points of differentiation are constantly challenged.

In addition, the differentiation thesis claims that powerful retailers force organizations to adopt corporate communications programmes. This analysis also has its limitations in terms of the communication processes involved. While the analysis seems logical to the extent that manufacturers increasingly need to communicate with retailers in order to gain presence and visibility in the retail outlet, it tends to simplify the influence of power in this process. Having increased their power base, retail chains still depend on producers' brand communication in order to attract customers even when they try to use this communication primarily to strengthen their *own* corporate identity. If we realize that retailers prefer to carry the brands that are communicated most creatively, we see the contours of a far more complex and integrated communications process in which power is difficult to locate (Schudson, 1993). Marketers talk about "push strategies" when manufacturers stimulate sales by presenting their products to the consumers through the retail outlet. Conversely, a "pull strategy" is a strategy that stimulates sales by making the product desirable to the consumer in advance, for example through advertising. If retailers generally believe that consumers are influenced by advertising (that is, by pull strategies) they will choose to carry the advertised brands and thus, potentially, set a push strategy in motion. Although changes in the retail industry seem to call for an integrated approach to communication, it is not entirely clear who controls the integration process. This, of course, is not to suggest that manufacturers should avoid integrated communications; only to point out that integration, when pursued as a strategy by many players, may not be able to deliver the expected results.

The claim that integrated, corporate communications gives producers more influence vis-à-vis the retail industry is overly simplistic.

Challenging the Transparency Thesis

The growing exposure to critical voices and the sheer availability of corporate information make room for the claim that organizations have become increasingly open and exposed to their surroundings. The notion of transparency captures well the day-to-day experiences of many organizations. Yet, the assumption that such type of openness in fact makes organizations more transparent needs to be probed more carefully.

BOX 5.5   Two Sides of Transparency

Transparency suggests on the one hand that everything is clearly evident because we are able to see through all the obstacles and clutter in our way. On the other hand, transparency means that we are failing to appreciate something because we see right through it. In both cases, the visual metaphor is called to mind, but the two usages have very different implications. When we ask that legal or legislative processes be "transparent", we are really insisting nothing be hidden from view. In the second instance, however, we do not know what we are not seeing because we take it for granted in looking beyond. This is the case with any new communications technology that has been with us for a while: we do not "see" the telephone or the PC, once we're accustomed to using it, because we look beyond it to our communication goal or to the person at the "other end". But, watch a toddler play with toy telephone, and we are reminded of the object, the technology itself.

The notion of transparency at once suggests clarity or insight and blindness or ignorance.

The implications for the larger communication process are important as well. In fact, the goal of transparency, as we typically conceive of it, is somewhat illusory because it suggests a communication state in which all ambiguity, all uncertainty, are eliminated and a kind of pure "connection" or mutual understanding is achieved. We say "somewhat" illusory, though, because it is certainly true that some decision making, deliberative, or communication processes can be designed to obscure important goings on, often in the interests of power. The double-sided nature of transparency reminds us, however, that often we do not know what we are missing. So, it is difficult to know what to "ask for", or which part of a communication process to try to make clearer. Organizations, including their corporate communications managers, often fail to realize what assumptions they are making about their projects because they have ceased to ask questions of themselves and others.

A common assumption about transparency is that there is a wide-ranging desire for it, that *external* audiences in general want or even demand organizational transparency. To what extent is that the case? As consumers we like to express that we care that the companies behind the products or brands we purchase are "behaving" properly. However, when transparency is translated to a question of information this assumption is extended to include a general desire for more information. And here the issue becomes slightly more complicated. As we have argued, people (and organizations) are usually less interested in information than they claim to be (see also Box 4.3 in Chapter 4, Thompson and Wildavsky (1986) and Feldman and March (1981)). Except for a few professional audiences (for example, pressure groups) that clearly demand insight into organizational procedures and practices, most people are neither interested nor involved in such matters (Christensen and Cheney, 2000; Morgan, 1999).

The transparency thesis assumes a general demand for and interest in corporate information.

To equate transparency with information is to presume a *conduit* metaphor of communication by which messages are simply transferred from a sender to a receiver in accordance with the intentions of the former (Putnam et al., 1996). We have already challenged this perspective above by emphasizing reception as an active and creative process. Moreover, the transparency thesis takes for granted that people are able to *handle* the growing amount of information made available to them. This is rarely the case. As Nobel Prize winner Herbert Simon (1997) and others have taught us, our rationality is limited by our information processing capacity. Even if we imagine for a moment that the external audience had unlimited access to information about organizations, their images of the organizations in question would still be limited by their ability to *process* information – an ability shaped by their insight, time, and experience. Adding to this our propensity to reduce the complexity of new information to familiar schemes of interpretation, it would be a mistake to assume that information availability and corporate openness necessarily make organizations more transparent to their surroundings (Manning, 1986).

Information availability is a necessary but insufficient condition for corporate transparency.

In spite of its limitations, the transparency thesis dramatically shapes the practices of contemporary organizations. In order to cope with increased public exposure, organizations actively seek to define the standards for corporate openness and disclosure. Take, for instance, the case of social accountability where organizations in many countries now articulate charters to standardize corporate attitudes to, say, layoffs (see also Chapter 4). Without suggesting that individual firms control this process, transparency is continuously staged through inter-organizational enactments. Together with other central players in the market, organizations seek to produce a collective understanding of transparency, for example what types of information to disclose, how to present and summarize complex data and so forth. The advantages are obvious. By selecting, simplifying and summarizing data, organizations not only make themselves more accessible to external audiences but also allow themselves to (re)define their boundaries between "inside" and "outside", between openness and closure. Deciding what is available, when and how also means deciding what is not. By setting and complying with collective principles for corporate openness, organizations at once produce transparency as an environmental condition, create a joint understanding of what transparency means, and promote transparency as an important communication issue. Moreover, when standards for corporate disclosure are defined and institutionalized, they provide guidance to organizations and allow them to reduce uncertainty through the display of mimetic behavior.

Transparency is at once a condition shaping corporate communications and an assumption necessary for organizations to pursue and justify their corporate ambitions.

Today, transparency is not simply an external condition to which organizations seek to adapt but also an explicit strategy that *prescribes* transparency in corporate communications. Professor of strategy Violina Rindova (2000) even talks about "polished transparency" as a form of marketing aesthetics used to appeal to certain educated and inquisitive stakeholders. The use of beautiful photographs and sophisticated layouts in annual or environmental reports, for example, has a strong aesthetic appeal that stages "transparency" as a specific *form* of communication. The current trend of designing corporate headquarters in glass built on steel-skeletons is an obvious example of the desire to signal transparency. But there is also a more implicit trend to depict friendly, healthy and personally committed employees – rather than models – in magazines and annual reports that appeals to a sense of integrity and a "we have nothing to hide here" appearance or a "if you disagree, please contact me" invitation. Clearly, we need to ask ourselves what the limits are to this staging of corporate openness. If transparency is becoming part of the marketing or PR mix of contemporary organizations, how will this development shape our notions of corporate credibility and accountability in the future? Is the staging of transparency, then, simply a *simulation* of openness? If so, what does it mean to have access to or to "know" an organization behind its products? Should we expect audiences to become blasé or cynical about organizational attempts to create more transparency? And what kinds of measures will be needed for organizations that sincerely wish to communicate openness to their surroundings? No matter what the answers to these questions are, organizations need to realize that although transparency may be a necessary strategy to cope with inquisitive stakeholders, its meaning will change as corporate communicators seek to transform it from a market condition to an explicit business strategy.

When transparency is transformed from an environmental condition in to a business strategy, corporate disclosure is often reduced to simulated openness.

Do companies really embark on corporate communications programmes to become transparent to others? Hardly. Although the literature on corporate branding, as we have seen (in Chapter 3), takes its point of departure in the assumption that people increasingly buy the company behind the product, branding is not a practice developed to create consumer insight and knowledge. On the contrary, the aim of branding is to *reduce* transparency, to hide the fact, for example, that a pair of 100-dollar sneakers is produced in the same location as a pair of 20-dollar sneakers. In a situation of perfect transparency, such conditions are clear and visible to all players on the market. Corporations, however, try to avoid such situations because they reduce competition down to one parameter: the price. Although many products are essentially the same, branding is set in motion to deny this similarity and, of course, to institute a new set of differences as a bulwark against transparency.

The aim of branding is to conceal the process behind the product, to add intangible dimensions that obscure the fact that products and in fact organizations are increasingly similar.

Clearly, organizational transparency is difficult to achieve for cognitive and political as well as strategic reasons. Yet, it is increasingly taken for granted and prescribed by corporate consultants and decision makers. What is usually not debated, however, is the fact that external transparency presupposes a high level of *self-transparency*. How can organizations make themselves transparent to their surroundings if they are not transparent to themselves? Interestingly, many organizational practices and programmes are based on the belief that organizations are able to know themselves in detail. Think of managerial programmes such as Total Quality Management, Business Process Re-engineering, Knowledge Management and the notion of "the learning organization". Across their differences, these programmes try to improve organizational efficiency through meticulous self-description and self-correction. In line with these principles, the ultimate ambition of corporate communications is to map out in detail all communicative dimensions relevant to the projection of a coherent and legitimate image in the organization's surroundings. In the language of our body metaphor one could say that the discourse of corporate communications presumes that the body is capable of examining itself (Christensen and Cheney, 2005). When, for example, a corporate design programme sets out to integrate corporate symbols, messages and behaviours, it needs to find a position from where it can observe all these different dimensions of organizational communication, diagnose the problems or gaps and suggest proper treatments. Such a position, however, does not exist.

BOX 5.6   Self-Transparency

In his book *The Transparent Society*, the Italian philosopher Gianni Vattimo discusses the advent of postmodernity, a social condition he terms "the society of communication". In line with the works of the French sociologist Jean Baudrillard (1988), Vattimo claims that we live in a society of generalized communication, a society of the mass media in which virtually everything is expected to become an immediate object of communication. Whereas modernity was guided by the utopian ideal of absolute self-transparency, reflected in positive science and facilitated by open and "unrestricted discussion", it is the ubiquity of the mass media that finally makes this ideal technically possible. By offering information in "real time" about practically everything that happens on the globe, the mass media, according to Vattimo, seems to make it technically possible for us to realize what Hegel called Absolute Spirit: "the perfect self-consciousness of the whole of humanity, the coincidence between what happens, history and human knowledge" (1992: 6).

The ideal of *self*-transparency emerged with modern society and its notion of rational science and knowledge.

Still, such a potential in the mass media has not materialized. Late modern philosophy had already eroded the notion of a supreme or comprehensive viewpoint capable of unifying all others. At the same time, the mass media have facilitated what Vattimo calls "a general explosion and proliferation of *Weltanschauungen*, of world views" (1992: 5–7). With the increase in information about possible forms of reality, the notion of one single perspective or reality becomes impossible to sustain. This is clearly the case, for example, in the current debate about global climate changes where various individuals, institutions, political parties and media offer different, and often conflicting, perspectives on the issue, its development and its possible solutions. As a consequence, Vattimo says, disorientation and a general pluralism of voices and dialects are the order of the day (Bakhtin, 1981). The postmodern philosopher Jean-François Lyotard (1984) captured well this condition when he described the incredulity toward meta-narratives in contemporary society. Within this context, Vattimo claims, the realization of the ideal of self-transparency is beyond reach. In terms of our body metaphor, one could argue that the body no longer has only one, but several heads.

Rather than producing self-transparency, the intensification in communication leads to the exposure of pluralism, to a multiplicity of voices and perspectives.

While careful self-examinations and self-evaluations can be extremely valuable and generate important insight about internal processes, it would be erroneous to assume that such exercises make organizations transparent to themselves as whole entities. Self-transparency assumes that one part of the organization is able to step outside the whole, look inside and still describe it as a totality – including the observer who is "looking in". This, however, is not possible. Since our representation of the world never includes our point of observation, something always escapes the account or self-description referred to as the "whole" (Maturana and Varela, 1980). The notion of a whole or unity, thus, is merely one local representation among possible local representations (Andersen, 2003). Other "local" representations would be, for example, those of the assembly line workers, the marketing people or the engineers. 'Wholeness', in other words, is a definition: it is a point of reference in our struggle to grasp and hold on to that thing we call "identity". In the context of an organization, such a definition manifests itself as a privileged account or representation of the organization, typically embodied by a leader or a team of managers. Epistemologically speaking, thus, top management, is only a "part" that aspires to observe, capture and represent the entire organization. In contrast to other parts, however, this one has the power to claim that it represents the vision of the whole, no matter how limited or provincial its perspective might be.

The privileged perspective from where the organization can be observed in its entirety does not exist. The "body" does not have one, but many heads.

Although the diagnosis behind corporate communications has many flaws, shortcomings and ambiguities, it has become an important managerial agenda. Taking its point of departure in a seductive narrative about the communication arena on which contemporary companies operate, it promotes a communication ideal that calls for organizations to re-think their communications in corporate terms. Like many other discourses, the diagnosis behind corporate communications has produced its own universe of meaning: a universe in which the solution to the identified problems is inherently contained in its description of the environment. As an ongoing narrative about an increasingly complex and turbulent environment, this diagnosis is used as a powerful premise for decision making.

CASE: The Intricacies of Transparency

FAIR FORSIKRING[1]

Fair Forsikring (English: Fair Insurance) is a young non-life insurance company. The company was founded in 1998 by Storebrand, a Norwegian insurance company, and by Head & Company LLC, an American investment company. Since 2006, Fair Forsikring has been owned by Gjensidige, a mutual company and the largest insurance corporation in Norway. Fair Forsikring offers inexpensive insurances to private customers in Denmark through the telephone or the internet. The case illustrates the difficulties of pursuing both differentiation and transparency in a competitive and complex market.

The Industry

Seen from a customer's point of view, a general problem of the insurance market is lack of transparency. Many customers find it difficult to compare insurance products and to understand the, sometimes, subtle differences in the conditions of insurance policies. Although some websites have specialized in helping consumers compare and evaluate such products, the general perception is that the insurance market is extremely complex and difficult to get a clear vision of. In addition, consumers often feel that insurance companies are not interested in transparency but contribute themselves to ambiguity and uncertainty. In a market that could otherwise easily be standardized, special terminologies and "unique" products serve to sustain differentiation. Moreover, insurance is typically a low interest area. Although most people recognize the importance of having the right insurances, few people are willing to spend the time and the energy to investigate the market in detail. Finally, until recently all insurance companies in Denmark had the same conditions for policy termination: insurance policies could only be terminated once a year, 30 days before the annual expiration day. As a consequence, many insurance customers fell more or less chained to their insurance company.

The Vision

The vision of Fair Forsikring is to create an insurance company without these limitations. Through policies that are clear and understandable and practices that are open, transparent and fair, the vision of Fair Forsikring is to be the most trustworthy insurance company on the market. First, Fair Forsikring challenged conditions for policy termination, allowing its own customers to shift to other insurance companies with only two weeks notice. Second, Fair Forsikring established a so-called Customer Committee with the sole task of making decisions in cases where customers and Fair Forsikring disagree on the handling of specific cases. The Customer Committee is composed of seven individuals representing the customers of Fair Forsikring. The group, whose chairman is a lawyer, meets five times a year to deliberate on customer complaints. The judgments of the Customer Committee are binding to Fair Forsikring, but not to the complainer who can still challenge the decisions in other legal forums.

The Difficulties

While Fair Forsikring has been doing quite well, as judged by its annual growth, a number of difficulties are related to its specific vision and approach to the insurance market. By

(Continued)

(Continued)

building and promoting its identity and position on principles of openness and fairness, it unavoidably moves the whole insurance industry towards more transparency and flexibility. In part, Fair Forsikring has deliberately sought such a development. When the company was launched in 1998, it not only announced its unique policy termination practices in advertisements, but openly challenged existing practices in news programmes and other public media. While its position was initially disputed by leading representatives of the established insurance industry, it managed through clever PR practices to change the existing rules so that all insurance customers today can move to another company with a few weeks notice. Although Fair Forsikring may congratulate itself for influencing the insurance market so significantly, it no longer holds possession of that specific dimension of its "fair" identity, the short policy termination practices. The company needs to realize that most of its principles of fairness can easily be copied by other players. In spite of some inertia in the market, Fair Forsikring's practices on the arena of transparency may well become industry standards in the near future. The success of Fair Forsikring in promoting its principles and values is, in other words, challenging its specific points of differentiation and thus its raison d'être as an insurance company. The lesson for Fair Forsikring and other companies is that transparency is a weak differentiator. In fact, it may be an impediment in building sustainable identities and positions in a highly competitive market.

Points of reflection

1. What managerial ideal is embedded in Fair Forsikring's promise to customers, investors and employees?

2. What organizational and strategic implications are implied in Fair Forsikring's promise of transparency?

3. Having established its identity on a discourse of "fairness" and "transparency", what are the future competitive options for Fair Forsikring?

Chapter Summary

In Chapter 5, we argued that the environmental diagnosis behind the project of corporate communications is limited and flawed. Nonetheless, it significantly shapes the reality of contemporary organizations. The corporate communications literature advances a diagnosis of the market as cluttered and fragmented, shaped by me-too products and critical stakeholders. Moreover, it depicts conventional ways of managing communications as unfocused, disjointed and inefficient. While the diagnosis captures some important dimensions of today's communication environment, it tends to reduce communication to a simple sender-oriented exercise and ignores many of the complexities of human communication. In particular, the diagnosis disregards the possibilities that corporate communications may become a source of noise and clutter, that corporate messages themselves contribute to the erosion of differences and that "openness" in corporate communications may not produce the type of transparency hoped for by inquisitive stakeholders. Through a discussion of its most basic assumptions and premises, we attempted to deconstruct the diagnosis and this way help scholars and practitioners envision alternative futures for organizations and their communication. Before we can discuss such alternative futures, we shall elaborate on the organizational implications of corporate communications. This is the topic of Chapters 6 and 7.

Note

1   http://www.fair.dk/view.asp?ID=1

6

Corporate Communications as Control

The Body is Disciplined

> More than ever, domains of the self once considered private come under corporate scrutiny and regulation. What one does, thinks or feels – indeed, who one is – is not just a matter of private concern but the legitimate domain of bureaucratic control structures armed with increasingly sophisticated techniques of influence.
>
> Gideon Kunda (1992: 13ff.)

Introduction

As corporate communications involves the organization in its entirety, it requires more wide-ranging attempts to integrate organizational messages than we find in conventional marketing or public relations programmes. Integration is rarely something that occurs spontaneously and is therefore seldom left to local initiatives of self-organizing. Within the context of corporate communications, messages, symbols and behaviours are standardized, regulated and controlled. The body, in other words, is disciplined. In this chapter we argue that corporate communications has become an expansive project of organizational discipline and control. We explore how the project of corporate communications serves to discipline and regulate organizational behaviour at several different levels – from explicit efforts to organize and align messages to more indirect ways of managing the whole corporate body. In particular, the chapter will address the following issues and questions:

Chapter 6: Points of Challenge

- Organization is necessarily about discipline, regulation and control – even when these dimensions are subtle and hard to notice. In what ways can corporate communications be described as a project of bodily discipline?

- While the disciplining of corporate messages is phrased in terms of "contact points" and "contact plans", the structural regulation of integration is often translated as the need for a "communication czar". Why do such notions appeal to contemporary managers?

- Contemporary organizations discipline their members through normative or other forms of unobtrusive control, for example by shaping their values, feelings, aspirations and thoughts. What are the downsides of such types of control?

Organization as Discipline

We know that organizations have all sorts of goals. Many are designed to make a profit. Others are designed to govern and administer. Still others are devoted to social values and the public good. Across these differences, all organizations are in some ways about discipline and control. By this we do not mean that all organizations are obsessed with power. Rather, as business theorist and practitioner Chester Barnard (1968) observed, every organization has to engage in regulating individuals' attitudes and behaviours; otherwise it could not function. The individual, then, surrenders a degree of autonomy in order to participate in the organization and enjoy the benefits of collective action. This is true for organizations that use monetary incentives, those that use social incentives, and those that are grounded in values, according to sociologist Amitai Etzioni. Grameen Bank[1] for example, founded by Nobel Peace laureate Muhammad Yunus, provides micro-credits to the world's poorest people based on a belief that charity is not the answer to poverty. Rather than offering money for consumption, Grameen Bank provides loans on explicit conditions such as collectivity, creation of self-employment for income-generating activities and housing for the poor. Moreover, the bank rewards loaner groups that manage to have all their children complete primary school.[2] While the individual borrower surrenders a degree of autonomy to achieve a loan, the programme is set up for all to enjoy the benefits of collective action. Perhaps the only exception to *voluntary* "surrender" of some individual autonomy is "total institutions" such as prisons or slavery. In all other cases, there is an acceptance of a certain amount of organizational regulation and control.

All organization is essentially about discipline, regulation and control.

BOX 6.1   Discipline

Discipline is a commonly used term with two dominant meanings: it refers both to prescriptive control over others (or of one's self) and to bounded, organized bodies of knowledge. Thus, we will speak both of "disciplining a child" and of "the disciplines represented in a university". Both of these meanings are brought together in the French philosopher Michel Foucault's (1984) theory of modern society. Like many other social theorists, Foucault grants that modernity has tried to liberate people from certain presuppositions about centralized authority in the form of a chieftain, a dominant religion, or a monarchy – or even an oligarchy (such as in a feudal system). Of course, the trends away from these structures have been far from uniform, as recent history attests. In fact, new institutions of discipline have often replaced the old.

Modernity has liberated people from some types of discipline but has often replaced these with new forms.

(Continued)

(Continued)

At the same time, however, Foucault sees the rise of the individual as the presumed centre of the universe. That is, modern western individuality lays both possibility and responsibility at the doorstep of the individual person, celebrating what she or he can be. Where the individual is what Foucault would call "the episteme" or basic unit for conceptualizing the modern world, discipline acts to hold that individual – both physically and intersubjectively – in place. Thus, while we speak of freedom to choose, particularly in the domain of the marketplace or in fashion, we are bounded psychologically and emotionally by particular parameters. A great example is the celebrated notion of "professionalism" through which many jobs and careers are elevated and institutionalized. While power is accrued by individuals and groups within professions, however, certain behavioural styles are preferred. This can have important moral as well as practical implications in a meeting, for example, where neither euphoria nor moral outrage are in line with the group's way of being (Schmidt, 2000). Discipline thus operates in the domains of control and knowledge simultaneously. What we "know" about ourselves, say, as professionals in any field, also can become a means by which we govern values, attitudes, dress, gesture and speech. Also, the prevailing discipline for a group may exhibit support for certain categories or identities: along the lines of gender, race, class, religion, or politics. This is clear when we see the link between discipline and ways of being at work (Cheney and Ashcraft, in progress). Discipline, thus, is inescapable to the extent that an organization, including both small work teams and large professional associations, asks members to surrender some autonomy in the interest of collective power and prestige.

While discipline and control vary across organizational arrangements and organizing practices, we find numerous attempts to restore a disciplined body in contemporary organizations. In Chapter 5, we discussed how management programmes such as business process re-engineering, total quality management, and knowledge management represent attempts to generate meticulous self-descriptions in the interest of organizational efficiency. And while the goal of complete self-transparency is not attainable, these programmes share the ambition of disciplining organizational processes by having one part of the organization, the "head", step outside the whole and oversee it in its totality. In all these situations organizations try to conceive of themselves as bodily totalities with organs that are not only identifiable but also interdependent and possible to oversee and control.

Disciplining Corporate Messages

In the context of corporate communications, discipline is manifested at many different levels. First of all, we find elements of discipline in the ways organizations tell themselves and each other to manage their messages. Most conspicuous is the insistence on turning all organizational activities into strategic communications. Having argued for years that the range of corporate communications has expanded to the corporate "body" *in toto*, scholars and practitioners of corporate communications now insist that everything *must* communicate. This imperative is expressed explicitly in the field of corporate identity management. Co-founder and chairman of Wolff Olins Ltd, Wally Olins, for example, says:

> Everything an organisation does must be an affirmation of its identity. The products that the company makes or sells must project its standards or values. The buildings in which it makes things and trades, its offices, factories and showpieces – their location, how they are furnished and maintained – are all manifestations of identity. The corporation's communication material, from its advertising to its instruction manuals, must have a consistent quality and character that accurately and honestly reflect the whole organization and its aims ... A further component, which is just as significant although it is not visible, is how the organization behaves: to its own staff and to everybody with whom it comes into contact, including customers, suppliers and its host communities. (1989: 7)

Far from being limited to the arena of organizational design – Olins' primary domain – this all-embracing aspiration to manage all corporate messages is today reproduced across the integrated communications literature. Professor of marketing Tom Duncan, for example, calls for "controlling or influencing all messages which customers and other stakeholders use in forming an image of, and maintaining a relationship with, an organisation" (1993: 22). And professor of marketing Tony Yeshin chimes in: "... it [IMC] aims to ensure cohesion and the delivery of a single-minded message to the target audience" (1998: 68). And, professor of marketing Paul Smith says "Integrated marketing communications is a simple concept. It brings together all forms of communication into a seamless solution. At its most basic level, IMC integrates all promotional tools so that they work together in harmony" (1996: 19–22). Often this aspiration is reproduced by the communication practitioner. Marketing scholars Helen Stuart and Gayle Kerr, for example, cite a manager for saying: "Every piece of external communication ... has to scream the same core message of whatever it is that your brand represents ... It's got to be everything that your company does" (1999: 177). Jerry Richardson, Chairman of Flagstar, the company behind brands like El Pollo Loco, Quincy's and Denny's, shares this vision: "Showing our employees that our future success depends on unity and a single vision for our entire company is a high priority" (cited in Fombrun, 1996: 269). In line with professor Åberg's notion of "total communication" (see Chapter 2), this perspective calls for organizations to supervise and regulate everything the organization says and does, both internally and externally.

With its ambition of turning all organizational activities into premeditated messages, corporate communications paves the way for new types of communication surveillance and control.

In the literature on integrated communications, message regulation and control is defined more specifically by the notion of "contact points". Contact points are points at which customers meet or are exposed to an organization, for example through experiences with its products, its sales people, its advertisements, its call centres, or its reputations. The critical issue for the manager of integrated communications, according to marketing professor Don Schultz and his associates, is "how to control the input of information that consumers use to build, adjust, and maintain the product/service/brand concepts in the marketer's category" (1994: 47). Recognizing that marketers can only control a limited amount of the total information customers gather about products and services, Schultz et al. limit their integrative efforts to *strategic* points of contact between the organization and its critical audiences. These points of contact, however, need to be managed and controlled carefully. Schultz et al. suggest that organizations identify the "contact inventories" and "contact paths" of all customers so that the organization can develop a "contact plan" that helps the organization launch its messages at the right time and at the right place. In line with this perspective, Tom Duncan and his colleague Clarke Caywood have suggested using quantitative and qualitative research to uncover all the consumer's contact points with the brand or the company, including the contacts initiated by the consumer as well as those initiated by the company:

> For example, all customer contact points with an airline – from the travel agent to the baggage handler and counter service representative, as well as experience with airport signage, airline cleanliness, on-time flight, safety, and so on – are considered part of the contact points with the airline. (1996: 29)

Likewise, GM created the subsidiary Saturn as a "spunky little brand" in 1990 with innovative ideas for selling cars.[3] In particular, marketing consultant Anders Gronstedt (2000) explains how Saturn identified 40 customer contact points that together make up the experience of buying a car. Ranging from the moment a customer is exposed to an ad for a Saturn car to the service received while owning the car and, eventually, trading in the car for a new one, these contact points were identified in order to help Saturn manage a consistent image of the Saturn brand. While Saturn has now somewhat adjusted and downplayed its innovative organizational ideas, the brand still adheres to its customer-oriented flexibility. Using new media, Dell provides another example of strategic contact points between companies and their critical audiences. Recently Dell launched the Direct2Dell blog to serve as a strategic contact point for Dell's millions of global customers in over 100 countries. Dell labels its blog "one2one" to signal that its ambition is to give customers an "accessible alternative to more formal, one-way channels of communication".[4] The ambition behind such strategic contact points is to take what are many perhaps disparate messages, meld them into one, and give a voice and perhaps also a persona to the organization speaking. The label of "contact points," is therefore suggestive of technical competence, confidence and control. At a broader strategic level, message control is also expected to encompass long-term brand communications as well as relationships with customers, all in order to ensure consistency in the ways the brand and its values are presented (Duncan, 2005).

Message regulation and control are defined as a question of identifying and managing all contact points.

In the context of corporate communications, where the customer is only one among several important audience groups, the number of potential contact points increases dramatically. In addition to easily identifiable communication parameters, like product related messages, image and profiling activities, sponsorship programmes, human resources programmes, work instructions, technical communication, internal marketing, training programmes, and so on, the ambition of integrating and regulating corporate messages is expanded to include informal, unexpected and thus less controllable messages about the organization. And while some of these messages may be captured by programmes of customer relations, crisis communication, issues management, labour relations, financial relations, business-to-business communication, lobbying and government relations, it is highly unrealistic to assume that organizations are able to manage more than a limited number of messages within one contact plan (Dolphin, 1999; Goodman, 1994; Harrison, 1995). Organizations may succeed in integrating a limited set of corporate messages. Yet, this integration "package" may not include the most important points of communication, for example, word-of-mouth, anti-corp blogging, social trends, and so forth. Only a limited part of what organizations say or do operates in the service of their formal communication. Dell's one2one blog has met with some appreciation, but it has also faced even more critique by bloggers complaining about all the critical issues that Dell did *not* mention. While the wish is strong to unilaterally control all messages globally, new technologies like blogging particularly disclose the difficulty and complexity of this ambition. Although the expansion of the corporate communications project and the ideology behind is understandable, we need to acknowledge the fact that an organization, as a living organism, cannot be reduced to its formal communication. The contact plan, although firmly integrated and regulated, may have a tendency to become auton-omized from the real communication issues surrounding the organization.

With the increase in messages, audiences and media, organizations can only hope to manage a limited number of customer contact points.

A Disciplining Structure

In the context of corporate communications, discipline is not limited to the ambi-tion of embracing everything the organization says or does – all possible "contact points" – within one unified identity. In addition, we find a desire to concentrate the responsibility for the expanded notion of strategic communications in the hands of top management. With its notion of integration, thus, the project of corporate communications has provided management with a powerful argument for central-ized surveillance.

BOX 6.2   Surveillance as Bodily Discipline

In the works of Michel Foucault we find the notion of the body linked to processes of power, regulation and control. From his *The Order of Things* (1970), through *The Birth of The Clinic* (1973), to *The History of Sexuality* (1978) Foucault demonstrates an ongoing concern with bodily discipline organized through processes of surveillance or normalisation. Foucault talks about a new regime of "governmentality" which subjects the human body to various forms of social control.

The metaphor of the body symbolizes processes of surveillance, discipline and control.

In *Discipline and Punish* (1977) these processes are studied in the context of the modern penal institution where Foucault locates a new type of power and control based on the ability (of the prison inspector) to observe all pris-oners at once. The control happens without the use of sprinklers, chains or heavy locks, but is organized through a chain of buildings with one central watchtower in the centre. Knowing that all their actions are visible, even in moments when they are not being observed, prisoners adapt their behaviour and act *as if* they constantly under supervision. The very possibility of being observed, thus, implies a disciplining of the prisoners' behaviour. According to Foucault however, this type of control is not limited to prisons but shapes the entire social body. Drawing on Bentham's notion of the *panopticon* (pan: all; optic: see), Foucault demonstrates how the modern body (and soul) is disciplined through numerous means of observation: in the private sphere, in public places, and in the workplace setting. Foucault refers to this type of discipline as "panopticism". Much like prisons, modern organizations, according to Foucault, are total institutions organized on panoptical principles where the few are capable of keeping the many under surveillance. In the modern organization, many situations are subjected to meticulous planning and registration from one central location, for example, the flow of work processes, the institutionalization of participation and the managing of consent (cf. Barker, 1999; Burawoy, 1979; Kunda, 1992).

Modern organizations, according to Foucault, are organized on panoptical principles where the possibility of being observed has a disciplining effect on the behaviour of the individual.

As several writers have emphasized, integrated communications requires leadership able to cut through partisan interests and establish the authority of a coherent corporate voice (Duncan and Caywood, 1996). Professor Don Schultz and his associates have argued that despite decentralization's desirability in pushing decision making closer to customers, "[i]ntegration cannot be accomplished by middle managers or from those in the lower levels of the organization. It must come from the top, and it can't be just a memo or a directive ... There must be a commitment from top management to integrate and to remove the barriers which prevent integration" (1994: 5). Emphasizing the need for consistency across all media forms as well as across customer groups, Schultz et al. suggest that a communications "czar" endowed with the power to regulate and control communications across the organizational setting should be appointed. Following this suggestion, Schultz and Kitchen (2000) point out that the need to control the entire marketing communication process from one central location is even more pronounced in a global context. They write:

> Often called the communication czar or corporate communication director, [the marcom] manager is designated to consolidate control and responsibility for all forms and types of corporate and product brand communication in one place, increasingly in the office

of the CEO or chairman of the organization. For many groups attempting to build their brand value or simply to gain control over the communication being distributed about the brand or the organization, this approach makes good sense. In this structure all activities related to the brand or brand communication and therefore market or marketing communication are brought together in one office or one central location. (2000: 169ff.)

Schultz and Kitchen not only suggest that the *overall* responsibility of brand and marketing communications is concentrated in one central location, but also that the actual *content* of each communications program is organized centrally in an effort to ensure conformity in messages and avoid the dispersion of communication resources. Interestingly, Schultz and Kitchen suggest that such centralization helps the organization become customer focused. Recently, the American College of Radiology has appointed a communications czar, or head of a commission on communications. It is stated that: "In appointing a communications czar, the American College of Radiology seeks to both broaden its audience and streamline its efforts" (Van Houten, 2006). Barry D. Pressman, newly appointed communications czar, states that the ambition is:

... to develop a cohesive and effective program of communicating the college's message to our many audiences. ... the college is communicating in many ways, but not necessarily with any central organizational control. So that is what the commission is trying to do: centralize and improve all communication by looking for duplication, maximizing advantages that exist in the size of the organization, and developing a plan for improving our overall communication ability, both internally and externally. (Van Houten, 2006)

The project of corporate communications advocates a structural disciplining of an organization's communication.

Although the idea of centralizing the responsibility for the organization's communication activities is expressed most explicitly by Schultz and his associates, this call for structural concentration is a general feature of both the IMC literature (Duncan and Moriarty, 1998; Miller and Rose, 1994) and the literature on corporate communications (Dolphin, 1999; Goodman, 1994; Kunde, 2000). Emphasizing the importance of delivering a "harmonious message to all constituents", professor of corporate communications Paul Argenti and his colleagues point out that "... while communication is something that everyone does, the communication function must ensure that communications emanating from the business units are aligned with and support the company's overall strategy" (2005: 88). Here, Argenti and his colleagues capture the dual nature of integrated communications: its expansion to still more areas of the organization's life *and* its concentration in the hands of top management. With its ambition of bringing together all communications that involve an organization as a corporate entity, corporate communications is a managerial project concerned with authority, regulation, and control. Corporate communications consultant Richard Dolphin puts it this way:

> Communications have become a resource and as such they must be controlled in the same way that any other resource is managed. Communication is now a major and sophisticated specialty and its directors are men and women of signal influence, if not power. (1999: 15ff.)

Corporate communications, thus, is regarded as a managerial vision that promises to establish and maintain unified organizational identities through clear lines of communication regulation and control. As the project of corporate communications has expanded from a more bounded and specialized activity to an organization-wide issue and concern, the implied control has expanded too. Interestingly, the call for structural concentration of the communication function may be the primary reason why corporate communication appeals to managers. Like integration, corporate communications employs a rhetoric that advocates a higher degree of centralization and regulation of the company's communication (Cornelissen, 2001). Moreover, this is often supported by the communication field as such because it entails granting a more central position, closer to the management, of those in the organization who represent the communication discipline. Indeed, the practice of communication (including corporate communications, marketing and PR) is gradually assuming a more powerful and strategic role in many organizations, even when these activities are not being financially underwritten or their architects well rewarded in a particular company.

The project of corporate communications has a strong rhetorical appeal to managers because it promises to provide a structural foundation for message control and regulation.

Few writings have challenged the assumption, promoted by corporate communications and related fields, that organizations need to centralize their communications into one functional department. One notable exception is the work by Professor Joep Cornelissen (2001, 2003). Cornelissen takes his point of departure in the literature on integrated marketing communications and its most central propositions regarding the best management practice. As Cornelissen points out, writings on IMC suggest that contemporary marketing communications management is by characterized (1) "zero-based" media planning, (2) high levels of coordination between separate communication disciplines and (3) a consolidation of communication disciplines into a single department. "Zero-based" media planning refers to the practice of choosing the most cost-effective communication solution in each situation, irrespective of where in the organization communication assignments have traditionally been located. Reviewing a range of empirical studies on communication management, Cornelissen concludes that tradition still plays a significant role in determining how communication activities are organized. The studies indicate a relatively high level of interdepartmental interaction and coordination between the different subdisciplines. Yet, historical inertia, a lack of adequate planning tools and subjective preconceptions about "what works" seem to prevent "zero-based" media planning from becoming a widespread practice. Simultaneously, the empirical studies provide little evidence to the proposition that various communication disciplines are gradually merging into one communication department. Most organizations studied were characterized by a functional organization of communication in separate sub-departments. The organizational prescriptions of IMC theory, thus, are not descriptive of the *practice* of contemporary communication management. Rather, they are rhetorical in the sense that they help (communication) managers edify and legitimize changes in the way they organize and regulate market-related communications. Interestingly, Cornelissen points out, the specific organizational arrangement may not make a major difference in terms of how effectively communication is managed. Yet, it is timely to discuss, as we will do in more detail in Chapter 7, whether organizational arrangements designed to support the regulation and control of all communications are consistent with contemporary notions of organizational flexibility (Leitch, 1999).

Communication activities are rarely organized into a single communications department.

Disciplining the Corporate Mind

Organizational attempts to control communications are not always as explicit and direct as we find it in the discourse of "contact points", "contact plans" and "communication czars". The modern organization is an important locus of discipline and control and while its manifestations are increasingly implicit or unobtrusive its impact may still, as we shall argue below, be rather significant.

BOX 6.3   Unobtrusive Control

The German sociologist Max Weber understood the principles of control deeply. Weber showed how control worked in his three famous types of authority systems (involving the legitimate uses of power): charismatic, traditional and legal-rational. The charismatic leader or organization achieves control through compelling personal qualities, such as dynamism and inspirational talk. The traditional system, such as a monarchy, relies on a "line" of authority that is either embodied in a family or simply carried forward with the idea: "This is the way things have always been done". Legal-rational authority, as exemplified by bureaucracy, is quite different: it uses common adherence to rules, regulations and norms to govern collective behaviour.

Control works through systems of authority: charismatic, traditional and legal-rational.

Control, as a more "active" way of describing power, can be overt or subtle, acknowledged or unacknowledged, physical or symbolic. When a "boss" is literally standing over you at work, you know who is in charge and then count on that person's benevolence. Assembly-line technologies and cubicle-style offices rely heavily on the architecture of the workplace to govern behaviour. That is, a great deal of "supervision" is done without the direct intervention of people, as when employees at Amazon.com receive automated computer feedback about where they stand with respect to a certain number of transactions to be handled per hour. In addition to vertical and direct forms of control, organizational communication scholars have phrased the notion of "concertive control" to describe systems of control that rely more on horizontal means, such as the enforcement of group norms (Tompkins and Cheney, 1985; see also Barker, 1993; Bullis, 1999). This is the type of control found most often in value-based organizations, such as non-profits, social movement organizations and many religious congregations. But, concertive control can be seen as well in many "flat" high-tech firms in Silicon Valley, California, and elsewhere around the world. Of course, none of these systems of control exist in a pure form. So, it is important to look at any organization with an eye toward the "mix" of different types of control exercised. This is where things get really interesting because we may be surprised to find combinations such as technical control combined with charismatic leadership. Or, an organization that calls itself "entrepreneurial" but may in fact be very bureaucratic.

Unobtrusive or concertive forms of control often co-exist with traditional control systems.

Organizations exercise unobtrusive control whenever they set out to manage their employees through the implementation of corporate values, corporate identities and other projects of staged sharedness. Through the regulation of collective values and identities, organizations seek to tap into the emotional dimension of their members: that is, their personal desires, identity projects and aspirations. According to organizational scholars Mats Alvesson and Hugh Willmott (2002), the discourses of quality management, service management, innovation and knowledge work are manifestations of a growing managerial interest in regulating the "insides" of employees, that is, managing their self-perceptions and points of identification (see also Deetz, 1995).

For example, FedEx's values about outstanding service and reliability are reconfirmed on their website where "employee volunteer stories" report how members on the job and even in private voluntarily have enacted the FedEx values, often in dangerous or difficult situations. In an unobtrusive way, proud stories about parcels being saved in stormy weather, a wedding ring being brought to the groom just in time, and FedEx couriers assisting the New York Police Department during the blackout in August 2003, contribute to an implicit regulation of identity. Currently, programmes that tap even further into the private sphere are gaining terrain. While norms for physical appearance in dress codes, hairstyles and make-up have been around for a number of years, the new value programmes include norms for personal dietary habits, health and fitness programmes, non-smoking policies, work–life balance analyses, and sometimes even choice of psychologist. While these new services emerge to motivate members, they also serve as powerful standards for the development of a preferred identity that is not to be questioned. This aspiration corresponds to what professor of sociology Gideon Kunda has called "normative control":

> Normative control is the attempt to elicit and direct the required efforts of members by controlling the underlying experiences, thoughts, and feelings that guide their actions. Under normative control members act in the best interest of the company not because they are physically coerced, nor purely from an instrumental concern with economic rewards and sanctions. It is not just their behaviors and activities that are specified, evaluated, and rewarded or punished. Rather, they are driven by internal commitment, strong identification with company goals, intrinsic satisfaction from work. [...] In short, under normative control it is the employee's self – that ineffable source of subjective experience – that is claimed in the name of the corporate interest. (1992: 11)

In his book about organizational culture, Gideon Kunda describes the demand for integrity and authenticity in an US high-tech company. The company subscribes to every possible management trend, enjoys a good reputation, says all the politically correct things and is known and admired across the country. However, its employees suffer from nausea and stress. Their experience of the company's culture is that of a public prison in which they are constantly on display and have to simulate values and attitudes that they neither believe in nor experience in practice. The company's demand for consistency between "on stage" and "off stage" gives cause for internal tension, rage and ridicule. At the same time, it is impossible for employees to break out because the company's public identity is so prominent. An employee who discredits the company and its values has by definition deemed himself useless in the eyes of the public – and hence also in his own eyes.

Commitment to and identification with corporate values are enthused through processes of normative control.

The desire to manage the behaviours, thoughts and feelings of employees is not new. Yet, the project of corporate communications has radicalized the notion of employee dedication by making commitment and ownership explicit preconditions of professional communication. Prescribing employee commitment and loyalty to the voice of the company, contemporary organizations seem to assume that their members can be turned into disciples of "the word". In a speech, transmitted via television satellite to more than one hundred thousand Wal-Mart associates, Sam Walton said: "Now, I want you to raise your hand – and remember what we say at Wal-Mart, that a promise we make is a promise we keep – and I want you to repeat after me: From this day onward, I solemnly declare that every time a customer comes within ten feet of me, I will smile, look him in the eye, and greet him. So help me Sam" (Walton and Huey, 1992: 223). And Ole Madsen, franchise manager at McDonald's, says: "If you can't think the 'McDonald's' way, you have no business being in the organisation – let alone being responsible for one of its restaurants" (cited in Kunde, 2000: 173). Even though such ideals and expressions may seem harmless, they contain strong elements of discipline and normative control. As demonstrated by the auto-communication perspective, the very declaration vis-à-vis an audience calls for commitment. Management consultant and author of *Corporate Religion* Jesper Kunde puts it this way:

> The company which has complete control of – and keeps in step with – its international organization can control both the organisation and the market with the aid of a strong Corporate Religion. A company's success depends simply on direction ... A Corporate Religion ensures that all employees in a company share the same qualitative values ... It might sound totalitarian, but with a clearly defined Corporate Religion, there is nobody who will have problems on the course because everybody's job is connected to the company's Corporate Religion. (2000: 48, 103)

While identity regulation, as Alvesson and Willmott point out, is "a pervasive and increasingly intentional modality of organizational control" (2002: 622), they urge us to be cautious not to assume that management are omnipotent in its ability to shape employee identification and commitment. In the process of aligning their messages and regulating their many different voices, organizations may well produce resistance amongst employees. Any attempt to regulate the organization's identity from above is precarious and likely to be contested by competing discourses and interpretations. As we shall discuss in more detail in Chapter 8, the difficulties of maintaining a monological and hegemonic identity narrative in an organizational context, where centrifugal forces unavoidably challenge the community declared by management, are a serious challenge to the project of corporate communications, at least in its present articulation. As a particular way of organizing, however, the *attempt* to apply consistency and assert community in and around contemporary organizations is an interesting (albeit troublesome) managerial dream in itself. Realizing that organizations emerge in their communication, we need to be sensitive to the new types of organizations that come out of these communication ideals and practices.

With its ambition of integrating all communications, corporate communications has become an explicit arena for corporate control that extends far beyond corporate messages per se.

Discipline through Participation

Not all attempts to control communications come across as regulative. As employees conform to the managerial desire of commitment, they will develop an orientation to work captured in statements like the following: "I feel like putting a lot of time. There is a real kind of loyalty here. We are all working on this together – working a process together. I'm not a workaholic it's just the place. I love the place" (Deal and Kennedy, 1982: 9). Or "IBM is really good at motivating its people; I see that through Anne. [She] might be brainwashed by some people's standards, but it's good brainwashing. They really do instil a loyalty and drive to work" (spouse of IBM employee, quoted in Collins and Porras, 2000: 115). The distinctive feature of corporate communications, as opposed to other types of managerial communication, is precisely its ambition to implicate the heart or soul of the employee, to prompt the employee to live the corporate brand and to participate in its continual celebration. Contemporary organizations employ a host of methods to engage employees and to stimulate ownership and commitment. Whereas some of these methods are explicitly managerial, others are more participatory in nature. As management theorists H. Peter Dachler and Bernard Wilpert pointed out in 1979, it is important to sort and evaluate the many programmes of participation according to their actual goals and practices. For example, in their survey they found that European systems of employee participation were much more likely than North American systems to feature workplace democracy as an end in itself (Dachler and Wilpert, 1979).

BOX 6.4   Participation as Control

Since the Second World War, "participation" has been one of the most talked about aspects of businesses and other organizations. And, there is a host of terms associated with this idea of ways that employees are engaged in enhancing productivity, setting goals and perhaps even shaping the policies of organizations. Participatory management, socio-technical systems, quality circles, reengineering and teamwork have all been programmes under the banner of employee participation. Experiments as well as routine applications of worker participation have been tried in countries including Japan, Tanzania, Sweden, Israel and Canada. One of the most important distinctions to be made with systems of participation, as communication scholar Cynthia Stohl (1995) has noted, is whether they involve something *added* to or beside the work of the organization or whether they refer to an actual restructuring of work. For example, quality circles are like committees, often constructed with cross-sections of the workforce, but making for extra meetings by employees. Conversely, many models of teamwork (such as semi-autonomous work teams or self-directed work teams) require the reordering of work processes in the direction of greater coordination, but sometimes also increased worker responsibility.

The term "participation" includes a host of activities from extra team or departmental meetings to company restructuring plans.

When we probe systems of employee participation, just as when we penetrate political systems that call themselves "democratic", contradictions become apparent. For example, many systems of employee participation are imposed by top management, with little or no employee input into their design. Communication and management analyst James Barker (1999) has found that even in highly team-oriented work structures, there may be persistent elements of bureaucratic control over employees. Likewise, sociologist Graham Sewell (1998) has discovered that electronic surveillance of employees at work often is used alongside so-called entrepreneurial models of shop floor governance. Communication scholar Dana Cloud goes further to suggest that in today's workplace terms like "teamwork" and individual "entrepreneurship" are used as smokescreens for getting employees to work harder and for maintaining even tighter

(Continued)

(Continued)

control by management (Cloud, 2005; Cheney and Cloud, 2006). This is why we must study participation together with forms of leadership and forms of control. Some systems of employee participation may be quite "disciplined" even while touting freedom for the employee. In some cases, such contradictions may not be readily seen, even by the policy makers or top managers.

Some participatory systems are just as disciplinary as traditional organizational hierarchies.

In an influential article on the practice of participation from 1969, director of a non-profit research institute, Sherry R. Arnstein noted, that while virtually everyone applauds the idea of participation, the applause comes to a halt when participation is advocated by those not in power. Her examples are Mexican-Americans, Puerto Ricans, Indians, Eskimos and whites, for whom participation signals citizen power, but in practice they experience that participation without redistribution of power is an empty and frustrating process for the powerless. Participation, according to Arnstein, "... allows the power holders to claim that all sides were considered, but makes it possible for only some of those sides to benefit" (1969: 216). Her often-cited "Ladder of Citizen Participation" spans a continuum of participation from "citizen control" to "manipulation". In her studies of federal social programmes such as urban renewal and antipoverty programmes Arnstein noted that participation tends to reflect the latter end of the continuum.

Obviously, there is a tension between management regimes that requires and desires a level of unanimity of action with the age of "participation" and employee "entrepreneurship" (Sewell, 1998). As the box above illustrates, these trends are not in complete opposition to one another, but they are not always easily reconciled in a company that celebrates "teamwork" and "employee involvement" while insisting on speaking consistently on all important policy matters. In the famous Mondragón worker cooperatives of the Basque country in Spain, for example, this tension has been resolved in a tentative way through the reinterpretation of a long-held value of participation in favour of its non-political meaning of having "employees give 110% to their jobs" (Cheney, 1999).

The notion of communicating consistently across different audiences and different media is potentially at odds with the values of participation and employee entrepreneurship.

Some programmes of participation expand the process of discipline and control to selectively include strategic players in the organization's surroundings. When organizations organize strategic dialogues with select stakeholders, for example, they unavoidably define an arena of participation that includes some actors and excludes others. In such an approach, there is a tendency for participation programmes to become closed communication domains shaped by the interests and goals of a narrow group of actors. Some corporate dialogues, for example, take place in executive networks or clubs where corporations and NGOs discuss pertinent issues and possible solutions behind closed doors. This happens when Amnesty International launches the "Amnesty Business Club" or when "Nordic Partnership" invites an exclusive corporate elite to debate CSR initiatives. While the dialogues held in London and Copenhagen between Royal Dutch Shell and Greenpeace in the aftermath of the Brent Spar crisis of 1995, for example, expressed an openness on the part of Shell to include the opinions of its surroundings, they simultaneously allowed Shell to regulate and, to some extent, control the direction and the content of the dialogues. So-called "symmetrical" communication systems, initiated and organized by organizations in presumed attempts to adapt to the demands of strategic publics, may turn out to be relatively closed domains disciplined by the interests, expectations and enactments of the participating organizations. The more proactively such communication systems are managed, the more the direct role of the general public is circumscribed. Potential criticism from non-invited parties can be rejected with reference to the fact that a dialogue between concerned parties *has* taken place, that risks *have* been discussed and, above all, that agreement *has* been reached. Thus the dialogue becomes closed around itself (Cheney and Christensen, 2001a). When decisions and compromises established in such domains define the political agenda for the issues discussed, we have a case of corporatism.

When organizations integrate the voice of critical stakeholders, they introduce new and more sophisticated forms of corporate discipline that implicate the environment.

BOX 6.5   Corporatism and Political Discipline

Just like "corporation", the word "corporatism" is derived from the Latin word *corpus* (= body). Originally, however, corporatism was not related to the notion of a business corporation. Corporatism is an old phenomenon in

(Continued)

(Continued)

Western politics dating back to a medieval notion of society as a body in which the components (or organs) serve specific functions of the whole (see also the Prologue). Corporatism can be regarded as an attempt to recreate a society in which the interests of the components merge with those of the state. A modern version of corporatism was found in Mussolini's Italy, where political influence was organized with the obligatory representation of business organizations and trade unions from each of the industries. Together with government officials from the fascist party, these groups (corpora) regulated working conditions. Moreover, they influenced the composition of the Deputy Chamber (and later of the Fascist and Corporative Chamber). Today, corporatism refers to a political way of governing in which a number of groups (professionals, experts, religions, and so on) are granted representative monopoly of the state within a limited area. By indirectly regulating such officially-incorporated groups, the corporatist state is able to circumscribe their ability to challenge its authority. In contrast to pluralism, in which different groups (parties) are able to compete to gain political influence and control of the state, corporatism alows *un*elected bodies to play a critical role in the decision-making process (Cawson, 1986).

Under systems of corporatism, *un*elected institutions play a critical role in political decisions.

In practice, corporatism typically implies that political issues are "cleared" between political decision makers and powerful strategic stakeholders before they are presented to the general public. Under corporatism, for example, corporations resolve potentially burning issues with other organizations, politicians and institutions outside the parliamentary system. Neo-corporatism is often used in a more neutral sense to describe bargaining arrangements where, for example, unions, private corporations and the government together resolve issues of wages and working conditions.

A few years back, a Scandinavian minister of energy and environmental issues was interviewed on public television about a report his office had recently issued on the use of energy resources in the twenty–first century. The journalist asked him how he, as a minister of these two domains, was able to balance his interests in the area of energy resources with his concerns for the environment. The minister's reply was simply this: "Greenpeace has read the report and given it an 'A'". The answer is interesting for both political and rhetorical reasons. By referring to Greenpeace in his brief reply, the minister obviously sought to lend legitimacy to his policies. More importantly, he made it clear that the issue raised by the journalist had *already* been debated in a different forum with representatives from a powerful and highly visible interest group. The fact that this group is an *un*elected organization and the debate was closed to other voices did not weaken the power of the minister's implicit argument: if Greenpeace is happy with the report, there is no reason why the rest of us should complain. The problem with the minister's reply was not the fact that the opinion of a special interest group was heard in the process. When an important public discussion is closed off by reference to another discussion, which has already taken place and to which there was neither general access nor insight, we have a case of corporatism. Although corporatism is not a new phenomenon, it is once again becoming an important issue as organizations increasingly influence and shape the political agenda. To the extent that such answers are accepted as legitimate it becomes difficult to maintain an open debate about issues of social, political or ethical relevance.

Under corporatism, public debate and discussion are regulated and disciplined within closed domains of communication – domains that often appear open and participatory.

Social Discipline and Control

Organizational discipline does not take place in a social vacuum. While the organization is a central locus of control, it is often society that defines what counts as appropriate behaviour amongst individuals and organizations. According to the French sociologist Émile Durkheim (1893/2000), a social body without norms to regulate its individual bodies is characterized by "anomie", a social condition characterized by dissatisfaction, frustration and deviant behaviour. Although the world of today is different in many ways from the newly industrialized environment in which Durkheim wrote his theses, contemporary society also seeks to counter anomie by assuming a common belief system, a collective identity or a shared set of values. This way, society constitutes a regulative force that imposes limits on the ambitions, propensities and actions of its members (Coser, 1977). The processes of regulation and control that we find in the organizational context are unavoidably informed and shaped by social values and expectations. Thus, when organizations aspire to develop and present themselves as corporate brands, this ambition is unavoidably shaped by a society that celebrates explicit communication as a source of existence.

The values and norms that discipline and control organizations and their members are most often imposed from society.

Through the regulative force of social norms, individuals and organizations have a tendency to subscribe to the same ideas, aspire the same things and imagine the same solutions as everybody else. As a consequence, organizations are often more similar than their leaders like to believe. US sociologists Paul Dimaggio and Walter W. Powell have analyzed the propensity of organizations to develop similar structures or patterns of behaviour. They refer to this propensity as "isomorphism" (*iso* = same; *morp* = form or shape). Organizations take on similar forms primarily because they want to be recognized as legitimate institutions in society. Organizations compete not only for resources and customers but also for power and social recognition. In this process, they often end up imitating other organizations, even when their greatest desire is to differentiate themselves from each other. Think, for example, of corporate value statements. While corporate values are assumed to represent something fundamental and unique to the organization and its members, a study of the expression of corporate values shows that organizations have a tendency to express their uniqueness in similar ways (Martin et al., 1983). A glance at corporate websites reveals the isomorphic nature of corporate values. While Heineken subscribes to corporate values like respect, enjoyment and quality,[5] Boeing says: leadership, integrity, quality, people working together, customer satisfaction, diversity, citizenship and shareholder value.[6]

Social discipline is evident in corporate values that are frequently surprisingly similar.

Organizational sociologists John Meyer and Brian Rowan (1977) have coined the notion of "ceremonial conformity" to describe the fact that organizations adapt their structures to signal conformity with external norms and expectations. While certain sponsor organizations, such as the state, condition their support on particular hierarchical structures (*coercive isomorphism*), similarity can also develop for other, less obvious, reasons. Organizations also develop similar structures when they model themselves on organizations they perceive as more legitimate or successful (*mimetic isomorphism*). Such behaviour may be a result of uncertainty, a lack of inventiveness or other reasons. Finally, we find examples of organizational isomorphism when individuals with similar educational backgrounds share competencies, position, status and orientation across different positions and organizational membership, thus contributing to the creation of uniformity in organizational behaviour (*normative isomorphism*). According to Dimaggio and Powell, isomorphism makes it easier for organizations to negotiate with other organizations, to attract competent employees, to be recognized as legitimate actors and to fit the administrative categories that are seen as appropriate in order to obtain public and private contracts. Such conformity, however, does not necessarily improve organizational efficiency. While Heineken and Boeing may argue that their corporate values create direction and motivation as well as express unique identities, Gideon Kunda's (1992) studies, mentioned above, demonstrate how conformity to corporate values may lead to anxiety, demotivation, and cynicism.

The notion of isomorphism expresses the propensity for organizations to imitate each other, for example by developing similar structures or adopting similar programmes of change.

The diffusion of corporate communications and its associated notions of integration, consistency and alignment may well be explained in terms of organizational isomorphism. Along with marketing professor Andrew Lock, Joep Cornelissen has suggested that IMC is a management fashion that appeals to executives not because it provides a well-defined theory or a set of practices but because its jargon holds a promise of progress and rationality (Cornelissen and Lock, 2000). The term management fashion usually refers to the way organizations and the people who work for them are eager to adopt and participate in the hype of every new organizational improvement programme in a lemming-like manner, and then drop it for yet another one without any real sense of follow-through. "Rewind ten years and the dominant management mantra was re-engineering. Fast forward to the present day and a new acronym has become the height of fashion: corporate social responsibility" (Dearlove, 2004: 8). Referring to a management activity as a "fashion," thus, seems to imply that it is not serious, that it does not work, and that anyone who subscribes to it is not focused on bottom-line results. However, in his influential research on management fashions, Professor Eric Abrahamson has argued that management fashions are *precisely* about rationality, efficiency, and progress. Abrahamson defines a management fashion as "… *a relatively transitory collective belief, disseminated by management fashion setters, that a management technique leads to rational management progress*" (1996: 257). As Abrahamson points out, management fashions differ in significant ways from aesthetic fashions in clothing or hairstyles. While aesthetic fashions only have to appear modern and appealing to the eye, management fashions must come across as both rational and progressive. Management fashions, in other words, must present themselves as efficient ways of realizing important objectives while appearing new and improved, that is, better than the older ways of doing things. Based on the work of Abrahamson, Cornelissen and Lock point out that while IMC as a theory lacks academic content and rigor and is often characterized by prescription and oversimplification, its rhetoric of "synergy", "holism" and "integration" provides managers with an appearance of rationality. The norm of rationality, in other words, promotes organizational conformity.

Through appeals to social values such as rationality and progress, management fashions discipline the actions of corporate decision makers by justifying organizational conformity.

Management fashions identify what are legitimate actions and hence the proper tools and goals for organizations and their employees. Presenting IMC as a natural step in the evolution of marketing communications, writings on IMC, according to Cornelissen and Lock, do exactly that: define and justify the proper goals and practices of contemporary communication management. At the same time, the fashion may still have real consequences in terms of the action it produces. By using the language of integration, managers are able to initiate and justify numerous changes in the ways communication is organized within the organizational setting. The notions of "contact points" and "communication czars" illustrate well such changes. Management fashions, thus, serve to ensure organizational renewal without deviating from an acclaimed pursuit of rationality and efficiency. Under conditions of uncertainty, managers will be inclined to adopt or imitate management techniques and programmes used by other and more influential organizations. Because stakeholders increasingly draw public attention to organizational practices, managers will feel a growing need to present their decisions and actions as rational and legitimate.

Social norms, values, trends and fashions regulate and discipline corporate behavior.

BOX 6.6   Mediated Visibility as Discipline

According to professor of sociology John B. Thompson, the communication media have reversed the direction of discipline in contemporary society. The media's power to make the invisible visible for us all to see has a disciplining effect that Foucault's perspective on surveillance neglected. Acknowledging the work of Foucault, Thompson argues that while the panopticon makes the many visible to the few, the media make the few visible to the many. In this respect, contemporary society bears a resemblance to the societies of the *ancient régime.* Traditional societies, as Foucault pointed out, were societies of spectacles – societies where the power to rule was linked to the ability to demonstrate strength and superiority to the general population, for example through public executions. Likewise, the communication media allow the rulers of today's world, political or corporate leaders, to display and celebrate their strength and importance to the masses. In contrast to the spectacles of the ancient world, however, the new type of visibility, facilitated by the media, does not necessarily serve those in power.

> ... *mediated visibility is a doubled-edged sword. The development of the media has created new opportunities for political leaders, but it has also created new risks and political leaders find themselves exposed to new kinds of dangers that stem from the uncontrollable nature of mediated visibility. (Thompson, 2005: 41)*

Today, according to Thompson, it is primarily those who exercise power who are subjected to the discipline produced by mediated visibility. No matter how much political and corporate leaders seek to manage their media visibility – often with the help of advertising or PR consultants – their ability to control it is limited. The use of webloggs, for example, has demonstrated how spatially isolated individuals may assert a collective influence on corporations by turning mass media into the mass' media. In 2004, a US bicycle owner experienced by coincidence that his bicycle lock could be opened with a simple pen. He communicated his experience via a weblogg and this exercise was commented on, repeated and even illustrated by a video by so many other "bloggers" that it ended up as an article in the *New York Times*.[7] The name and reputation of the bicycle lock manufacturer, Kryptonites, was severely damaged by the "bloggstorm" and the company had to promise to replace all its old locks to regain its credibility.

The mediated visibility has a disciplining effect on those in power, including corporations.

Mediated visibility, however, should not be confused with the type of transparency postulated by the literature on corporate communications. Corporate decisions, scandals and misconduct have for a many years been exposed in the media without producing a marked increase in the ability of the public to see through the complexities of corporate behaviour. Although we live in an era where everything, according to the French sociologist Jean Baudrillard (1988), is "exposed in the raw and inexorable light of information and communication", we cannot take for granted that such exposition uncovers any "secrets" hidden from the general populace. Rather than creating transparency, mediated visibility becomes a source of uncertainty or fragility where the very possibility of being observed by the public implies a disciplining of corporate behaviour.

CASE: The Discipline of Integration

The SAS INSTITUTE[8]

Founded in 1976, the SAS Institute is the world's largest privately held software company. Being a leader in business intelligence software and services, SAS produces data warehousing and data mining software used to gather, manage and analyze enormous amounts of corporate information. Clients such as Air France and the US Department of Defense use SAS software to find patterns in customer data, manage resources and target new business. SAS also offers industry-specific integrated software and support packages. Over its 30 years, SAS Institute has grown from seven employees to nearly 10,000 worldwide and from a few to more than 40,000 customer sites. James Goodnight, who is chairman, president and CEO of SAS, owns about two-thirds of the company and is on the Forbes list of the world's richest people. Co-founder and EVP John Sall owns the remainder. The case illustrates the disciplining power of an integrative culture in which private life issues often blend with the organization of a work life.

The Work/Life Programme

"If you treat employees as if they make a difference to the company, they *will* make a difference to the company" is the philosophy behind the SAS Institute's corporate culture. At the core of SAS's business model is the idea that satisfied employees create satisfied customers. The SAS Institute is particularly known for its comprehensive programme to promote employee welfare. SAS employees, thus, work in an environment that explicitly claims to foster and encourage the integration of the company's business objectives with their personal needs. This integration of private life in the work sphere is referred to as the SAS Institute's work–life programme. The company has a very low employee turnover, is well known for its employee loyalty and for having attracted some of the most talented minds in the software business. While the SAS has always prioritized the well-being of its employees, recent programmes and facilities at its headquarters in North Carolina outperform prior initiatives. These include two on-site childcare centres, an eldercare information and referral programme, an employee healthcare centre, wellness programmes, a 58,000 square foot recreation and fitness centre, robust benefit packages, convenient benefits and flexible work schedules, and many other initiatives to facilitate a better work/life balance for employees. Moreover, SAS Institute employees have a tradition for giving generously of their time and talents, volunteering for community work in order to make their communities better places to live and work. SAS employees donate their time through the Employee Volunteer Fund (EVF), which offers a $500 contribution to schools or non-profit groups with the requirement that an SAS employee spends an average of eight hours a month over a year volunteering with that organization. By combining money and time, this programme is designed to provide a double benefit to the community: hundreds of employees participate, which translates to valuable volunteer support for SAS communities and thousands of dollars in financial contributions.

Royal Treatment or Brain-Washing?

The SAS Institute has received many awards for its work–life programmes and its unique corporate culture. For eight consecutive years, the company has been rated in the top 20 of *FORTUNE*'s "100 Best Companies to Work for in America" and was inducted into the list's "Hall of Fame" in 2005. In addition, the SAS has been listed numerous times by *Working Mother* as one of the 100 Best Companies for working mothers. Moreover, SAS's corporate culture has been featured in a segment titled "The Royal Treatment" on CBS's *60 Minutes*. More recently the SAS was featured as the Best Place to Work on the *Oprah* show. According to Suzanne Gordon, Vice President and CIO of SAS, its corporate culture is the main reason for SAS's sixth-place ranking in Computerworld's Best Places to Work in IT 2006 survey. "Our continued presence on the list and high ranking this year reinforce what I believe about working at SAS", said Gordon. "It's not just benefits and amenities that fulfill our IT staff. It's the culture of trust and respect, and the ability to contribute strategically to the company's success. Their hard work and innovation make it an honor to lead them". While the notions of culture, values and respect are often associated with the SAS Institute, this does not mean that people work less. CEO Goodnight sets the standard for working at the SAS Institute and he plays a direct role in many aspects of the company's operations, remaining deeply involved in the development of SAS's products:

Some have called it management by walking around; I call it management by loitering. I'm personally involved in what goes on at SAS and for that you must have movement. I try to avoid set meetings. A lot of people feel they are working very hard if they are in meetings for every hour of the day. I don't adhere to that belief at all. I think people who spend a lot of their time in meetings are just wasting time. They think they are busy, but they're not really accomplishing any work.[9]

In spite of wide-spread recognition and accolades, visitors to the SAS Institute's headquarters often ask themselves if this *really* is a good place to work or if the celebration of shared values and the integration of work and life are sophisticated forms of corporate discipline. All the employees at SAS seem to be able to reproduce almost verbatim the history and philosophy of the company. And most employees use the services provided by the company on childcare, eldercare, health care and fitness. "Is there a life outside or beyond SAS?" is a frequent question asked by visitors. And what happens to one's

(Continued)

(Continued)

social life if you leave the company? Is it healthy for people to have one's personal life so deeply integrated into one's work life? And is such an organization better prepared for change than a classically bureaucratic organization?

Points of reflection

1. In what ways are the values at the SAS Institute a source of autonomy for the employees? And can these values also be regarded as a system of discipline? Is the work/life programme at the SAS Institute, in other words, a sophisticated version of the panopticon?

2. Will the work/life programme help the SAS Institute survive in the future?

3. What are the ethical limits to corporate discipline of employees?

Chapter Summary

Chapter 6 takes its point of departure in the observation that organization is essentially about discipline, regulation and control. With its ambition of managing all communications consistently, however, the project of corporate communications has intensified the preoccupation of contemporary organizations with these dimensions. At its most basic level, organizations seek to regulate corporate messages through the management of all customer contact points. Simultaneously, the organizational responsibility for corporate communications is increasingly concentrated in the hands of "communication czars" or other members of top-management. We argue that the project of corporate communications, in large part, appeals to managers because it justifies such movement towards message regulation and control. Corporate discipline and control, however, are not limited to direct surveillance. Through normative and other forms of unobtrusive control, organizations seek to manage the minds of their employees, for example through the articulation of shared values or the implementation of employee participation programmes. And, hoping to be recognized as legitimate players in the social world, organizations increasingly allow their communications to be disciplined by the values, norms and fashions of the wider society. In the next chapter, we argue that the desire for discipline and control is necessarily counteracted by the call for differentiation, flexibility and responsiveness.

Notes

1 http://www.grameen-info.org/. See also: http://www.grameen-info.org/bank/Whatis Micro-credit.
   htm
2 http://www.grameen-info.org/bank/ExpandingMicrocredit.html
3 http://www.usatoday.com/money/autos/2003-12-04-saturn-cover_x.htm
4 http://www.direct2dell.com/about.aspx
5 http://www.heinekeninternational.com/pages/article/s2/12230000000050-13660000000065/
   values.aspx
6 http://www.boeing.com/companyoffices/aboutus/ethics/integst.htm
7 http://www.nytimes.com/2004/09/17/nyregion/17lock.html?ei=5090&en=52de64f51b99 1525
   &ex=1253160000&adxnnl=1&partner=rssuserland&adxnnlx=1162897131-7gkiz6v   MnCn
   W3ctrryqdXA
8 http://www.sas.com/corporate/worklife/index.html. See also: http://www.sas.com/news/
   feature/12jan06/fortune.html
9 http://www.itworldcanada.com/Pages/Docbase/ViewArticle.aspx?ID=idgml-83ce33da
   64a6-4ffe-9a99-e2a941aa6698

7

Corporate Communications and Flexibility

Towards an Agile Body?

Coordinating different people's actions ... means reducing the range of actions available to each one of them. And while the reduction in variety may increase efficiency, it also tends to undermine the ability to promote new values, to perform new tasks or to handle new situations. For this reason many people are now asking how organizations can be made more flexible and adaptive.

Nils Brunsson (1985: 4f)

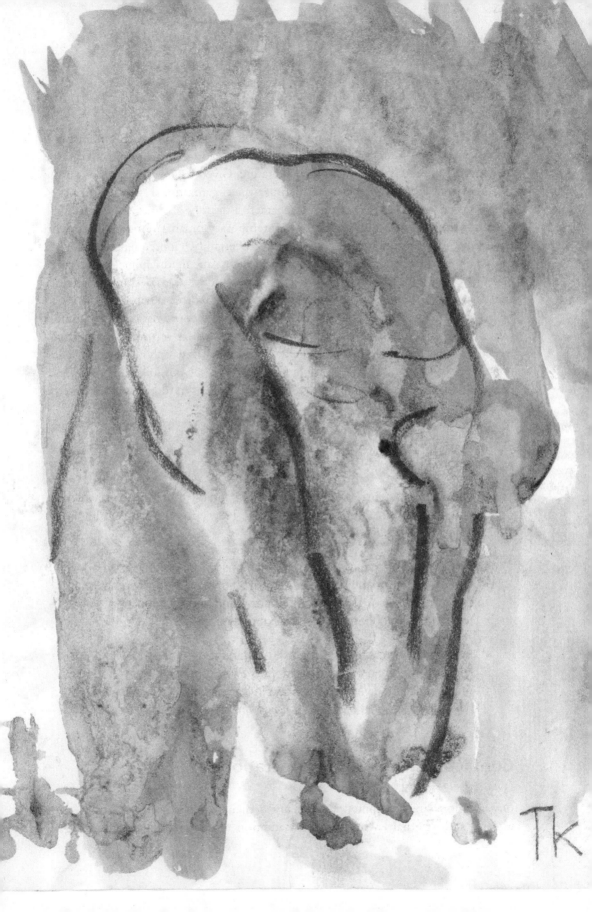

Introduction

Corporate communications is not a distinct and separate type of communication but a management ideal with wide-ranging organizational implications. Yet, those implications are rarely discussed in the literature. Given its potential impact on the organizational domain, we need to scrutinize the organizational "anatomy" of corporate communications. What are the characteristics of an organization that subscribes to corporate communications? Contemporary organizations are faced with challenges of globalization, turbulence and uncertainty. Consequently there is a growing need for organizational forms capable of balancing discipline with change and regulation with flexibility. In this chapter we address the question of whether the corporate communications project is able to support a flexible organization. Specifically, we discuss how the practice of aligning and coordinating all communications may co-exist with other managerial ideals, such as organizational responsiveness and adaptability. Because integration is not the only challenge facing contemporary organizations, we should be sensitive to the possibility that corporate communications may clash with other corporate agendas of today. In particular, the chapter will address the following issues and questions:

Chapter 7: Points-of-Challenge

- Organizations are shaped by multiple logics that do not always complement and support each other. How is integration counteracted by processes of differentiation?

- The project of corporate communications and its notion of integration presume a tightly coupled organization. Yet, that presumption is challenged by organizational buffers and loose couplings. What roles do such buffers and loose couplings serve?

- In a world of increasing complexity, organizations respond with ambitions of integration and consistency. Simultaneously, they hope to retain sufficient diversity to operate in complex markets. Is that possible under the aegis of a corporate communications programme?

Conflicting Ideals and Expectations

Organizations are confronted with many demands and expectations from their internal and external environments. In addition to aligning and coordinating all messages and means of communication, there is a persistent demand on contemporary organizations to be flexible (Zorn et al., 1999). A number of trend-setting books from the 1990s – e.g. *The Learning Organization* (Senge, 1990) or *Reengineering the Corporation* (Hammer and Champy, 1993) – stressed that today's winning organizations are characterized by sensitivity, empathy, learning, willingness to change and improvization. Thus, organizations are expected to be adaptable to changes in their surroundings, to be sensitive and receptive to new trends, to be able to learn fast and rapidly transform new input into changed procedures; in other words to be able to demonstrate responsiveness at all organizational levels. These characteristics, however, do not necessarily match the qualities endorsed by corporate communications.

An organization is a complex entity shaped by the co-existence of several different logics that do not necessarily complement and support each other.

BOX 7.1   The Dialogical Principle

The French sociologist Edgar Morin describes complex systems, like for example organizations, as "unitas multiplex": entities characterized by order *and* disorder, coherence *and* incoherence, unity *and* disunity. To grasp the complexity of living systems, Morin points out, we need to acknowledge the co-existence of multiple logics or principles and to realize that these logics are not only complementary but also antagonistic with respect to one another. Morin's term for the co-existence of different logics is "dialogics". The dialogical principle signifies "the symbiotic unity of two [or more] logics, which simultaneously nourish each other, compete against each other, live off each other, oppose and combat each other to death" (1992: 77; see also 1984, 1987). An obvious example is the tension between individualism and community that we find in modernity – a tension which is intensified considerably in contemporary, late-modern society.

Along with unity and complementarity, organizations are shaped by competition and antagonism between different ideas, practices and principles.

The dialogical principle points out that unity in complex systems, such as organizations and societies, is not the same as one-dimensionality or uniformity.

(Continued)

(Continued)

Behind the façade of unity there are fractures created by the encounter between different organizing principles. One example is the tension between integration and differentiation. In their classical work on organizations and environments, organizational theorists Paul R. Lawrence and Jay W. Lorsch (1967a, 1967b) found that integration and differentiation are opposing organizational forces that need to be balanced when environmental complexity increases. According to Lawrence and Lorsch, differentiation is "the state of segmentation of the organizational system into subsystems, each of which tends to develop particular attributes in relation to the requirements posed by its relevant external environments" (1967b: 3). Complex systems such as organizations inevitably differentiate into specialized units (or subsystems), with their own objectives, timeframes, forms of interaction and degrees of formalization. The coordination of these subsystems is essential for the system to be operational. Unfortunately, most writers on organizations have been so preoccupied with problems of achieving integration and collaboration that they have ignored the equally vital need for differentiation. To be effective, Lawrence and Lorsch claimed, organizations must approach the levels of differentiation and integration required by their specific environments. Such a balance is no less important in the turbulent world of today.

While "integration" is essentially another word for organization, it needs to be balanced by differentiation to stimulate organizational flexibility.

Contemporary organizations, thus, need to be able to do several things at once. While they are urged to institute and maintain a platform of shared symbols, messages and values in order to ensure stability and consistency in all communications, they are simultaneously expected to question and be willing to replace established ideas with new practices and activities. In line with our body metaphor, such organizations can be described as "ambidextrous organizations" (Achrol, 1991). Ambidexterity is normally used to describe people who use both hands with the same level of proficiency. Marketing professor Ravi Achrol, however, employs the term in the context of new organizational forms to characterize organizations that are capable of balancing the need for regulation and control with the growing demand for innovation and flexibility.

In complex environments, organizations must be able to handle multiple and sometimes conflicting ideas and principles simultaneously, that is, within the same organizational unit.

The question is if corporate communications as a mindset and disciplinary practice is capable of meeting this challenge. Marketing commentator Matthew Syrett remarks:

> *Integration is a marketing catchphrase of the moment. Its value proposition seems unquestionably strong – the whole of a marketing initiative can be greater than the sum of its multidisciplinary parts if those parts work tightly together to assist one another. While certainly capable of delivering on this promise, integrated marketing is not without its inherent vulnerabilities. One area of definite risk with integration lies in its rigidity – its inability to handle change and dynamic competitive forces … Success for integration requires much planning and management to orchestrate the varied mix of marketing disciplines. This need for strong coordination forms an Achilles heel for integration, since it often prevents rapid responses to unexpected situations and emergent opportunities. (2004: 1ff.)*

A One-Dimensional Organization

The field of corporate communications is limited primarily by a one-dimensional notion of what an organization is. Assuming that the integration of communications is the most important mission of contemporary organizations, writings within the field seem to suggest that all other organizational practices need to defer to the corporate communications programmes. The ITO (input-through-put-output) model of communication planning by professor Cees van Riel (1995), for example, seems to place communication at the centre of all organizational processes. Even though the literature on corporate communications often talks about organizational flexibility, the discipline seems to take for granted that flexibility serves – or rather *should* serve – the interests of communication. This point and its implications will be elaborated on below.

The discourse of corporate communications expects the organization to operate in the service of the communication *plan*.

When the literature on corporate communications pays attention to organizational issues, these issues are typically phrased as "barriers" to integration (Pettegrew, 2000–01; Schultz and Schultz, 2004; Wightman, 1999). The lack of horizontal communication, for example, is often mentioned as a significant barrier. Since many organizations lack adequate communication between departments, they have difficulties, we are told, exchanging and sharing crucial information about developments amongst consumers and other target audiences. As a result, their ability to detect and learn about changes in environments, perspectives and practices is limited (Pickton and Broderick, 2001). The lack of horizontal communication is usually a structural problem: most organizations simply do not have any formal forum for horizontal communication. Moreover, job descriptions, professional affiliations and departmental structures have a tendency to pigeonhole employees into narrow roles with little overlap and little insight into the functions and concerns of their colleagues. When employees are assigned to separate functions in different and sometimes competing organizational departments, they are rarely motivated to communicate and to learn from each other (Gayeski and Woodward, 1996; Schultz and Schultz, 2004).

Inadequate horizontal communication makes it difficult for organizations to integrate their communications in practice.

In addition to inadequate horizontal communication, the literature talks about turf battles, ego problems and managerial parochialism as significant barriers to integration (De Pelsmacker et al., 2001). For example, it is often claimed that marketing people have difficulties communicating with production people, in part because the marketers feel closer to the customer and the production people see themselves at the centre of the organization. Similar problems, of course, exist amongst other professions. Moreover, companies that organize their departments in independent units with independent objectives will typically find it difficult if not impossible to get the different departments to work together on a shared profile. The same thing applies in particular to companies that have been through a merger.

Even *within* the field of marketing, one finds considerable barriers to integrated communications. A lack of commitment to integrated communications, for example, is often rooted in a structural isolation of communications tools and communication managers from each other plus a general absence of interdisciplinary communication expertise (Smith, 1996). Because advertising, point-of-purchase, sales promotions, public relations and so on attend to different audiences, these activities often develop different operational practices, including media strategies, timing and the use of creative appeals. As a consequence, the organization's communication is fragmented, organized in "functional silos" (Gronstedt, 1996; see also Prensky et al., 1996). Also, because the integration of communications potentially restricts the creative freedom for each communication parameter, communication professionals, such as art directors, may oppose integration in practice – even when they subscribe to the general idea behind it. Adding to these barriers the tendency for established practices and perspectives to resist change, managers who initiate corporate communications programmes are facing a difficult task of compelling specialists in different communication subfields to give up their acquired autonomy for the benefit of the organizational voice as a whole.

Communications professionals may resist corporate communications in practice even when they endorse the general idea of integration.

Corporate communications, we are told, requires strong leaders, that is, leaders who have the necessary authority to make decisions when special interests and resistance to change block the process. Although communication, as we have seen, has received increased managerial attention in many companies, the involvement of management is still the crux of the matter in projects of corporate communications. But even with strong leaders behind it, it may be hard to implement integration in practice. As we saw in Chapter 5, integrated communication has come to represent so many different activities and perspectives that concrete models for action are difficult to identify. This may paralyze action. In her study of Total Quality Management, communication scholar Helene Giroux has illustrated, for instance, that an organizational ideal is more easily implemented when the ideal is narrowly defined and the group of implementers is clearly identified. As soon as the ideal is expanded to a wider range of professions, it looses the precision that is needed to manage it in practice (Giroux and Taylor, 2002; see also Giroux and Landry, 1998). A similar point can be made about integrated communications. While the ambiguity of the concept has been significant in allowing its expansion to still more aspects of an organization's life (Cornelissen et al., 2006), the same ambiguity makes it difficult to delimit the integration process and thus to manage it in a clear and simple way. This problem paves they way for unsubstantiated organizational ideals and instructions.

The problem of implementing integrated communications is frequently acknowledged by writers within the field. Yet, most seem to articulate this problem in prescriptive terms as either an issue of organizational (re)design or as a question of overcoming structural "barriers". Without dismissing these managerial problems, we wish in this chapter to approach the organizational dimension of corporate communications at a deeper theoretical level that does not determine *a priori* how an organization is supportive or what corporate communications should look like.

In the discourse of corporate communications, organizational flexibility is reduced to a question of overcoming organizational barriers to integration.

As marketing and communication scholars Lars Thøger Christensen, Fuat Firat and Simon Torp point out, the language of "barriers" implies a limited view of the organization. Similar to the way managers use the language of "change" (Zorn et al., 1999) the notion of "barriers" suggests that the organization is the primary problem:

> *It suggests that integrated communications is a fixed and predetermined product – for example a corporate branding programme developed by management together with a*

consultancy firm – that only needs to be "transported" smoothly through the organisational "container" and unpacked correctly by its members. Anything that blocks or limits the smooth passage of the product is considered a "barrier" to integration. Objections, for example, by sales personnel that the integration project ignores the needs and wishes of specific customers are considered a barrier rather than a significant source of information. Such understanding of the organisational dimension is problematic for several reasons. Firstly, because it implies that management is uniquely qualified to define the best integration projects and practices without the continuous input from rank-and-file members of the organisation. Secondly, because it regards the rest of the organisation as an obstacle or a source of noise in a communication process that would otherwise run smoothly and seamlessly. Instead of regarding the organisation as a resource for the accomplishment of integration, the literature on integrated communications tends to approach the organisation as a refractory entity that needs to be disciplined and controlled. (Christensen et al., in press)

The organization in other words, is considered a simple, functional mechanism entirely at the disposal of the corporeal project. This is hardly the case. Also, the notion of barriers suggests, epistemologically speaking, a privileged perspective or position from where the organization (or parts thereof) can oversee its communication in its totality. As we argued in Chapter 5, such a privileged perspective does not actually exist.

The notion of "barriers" suggests that the organization is a refractory entity that needs to be disciplined by the communication plan.

The "organization" we find represented in the integrated communications literature is an organization that operates in the full service of the corporate communications programme, in other words, an organization defined, shaped and controlled by its overall corporate message. In the language of organizational theory, such an organization may be described as *a tightly coupled system*.

BOX 7.2   Tightly Coupled Systems – and their Limitations

In a tightly coupled system, input and output are closely connected. Slack is limited and all inputs affect the system as a whole. Think, for example, of a mechanical system like the classic time clock: all its cogwheels are tightly coupled and interdependent. As a consequence, mechanical errors or problems in one part are immediately felt in other parts. In a tightly coupled system, thus, changes involve the system in its entirety (Glassman, 1973; see also Orton and Weick, 1990; Weick, 1976). Applied to the organization, a tightly coupled system would imply that every attempt to reorganize is felt instantaneously in all corners of the organization (Weick and Sutcliffe, 2001). That is why a tightly coupled system, from a decision maker's point of view, may seem rather appealing. Changes or perturbations in one part of the system are instantly registered and transformed into proper actions in other parts. The tightly coupled organization, in other words, is compliant and efficient in securing an immediate and appropriate response to all internal and external inputs. As such, it appears to be a perfectly integrated mechanism.

Tightly coupled systems respond immediately – and as a whole – to new inputs.

Such a type of integration, however, is vulnerable – especially in environments that are susceptible to change. Tight couplings seem to support control and predictability. Yet, its flexibility is limited exactly because changes and responses involve all dimensions of the system at once. To ensure such total compliance, the tightly coupled system needs to limit autonomous interaction and responsiveness at the level of its subunits. Local ideas and solutions to local problems, in other words, cannot be enacted freely. As a consequence, the system is left without sufficient flexibility to deal swiftly with changes in its surroundings. The limitation of tight couplings is exemplified by the potential corporate repercussions of a failure in one component within an integrated corporate communications programme. If the failed component – for example, a delivery date or the tactical execution of a campaign – is tightly synchronized with other components in the programme (a public announcement or a marketing event), the failure will immediately spread to the rest of the organization affecting the quality of several other tasks and processes (Syrett, 2004).

Sociologist Charles Perrow (1984) has pointed out that crises and failures resulting from unexpected events are more likely to occur in tightly coupled systems. When Exxon's supertanker Valdez hit the Bligh Reef in Prince William Sound in 1989, thereby causing the largest spill in US waters of almost 11 million gallons of oil, the company did not send a cleanup emergency team until 14 hours after the disaster. Moreover, within 48 hours of the spill, very little headway had been made in retrieving the oil due to disagreements between the company and the government about methods and impacts. Although Exxon was known for its highly efficient production methods, a steep hierarchy, its "mean and lean" philosophy, and for having the strongest balance sheet in the industry (Goodpaster and Holloran, 2006), the company proved to have a rigid organizational system unable to handle unexpected events in efficient ways. Internationally Exxon was criticized for being "unprepared, moving slowly, communicating poorly, displaying arrogance rather than contrition, and failing to show leadership" (Goodpaster and Holloran, 2006: 400). The lead attorney for the following class action plaintiffs argued that Exxon must pay punitive damage since "the culture of the [Exxon] company has gone so sour we need to … shock them into some kind of corporate personality change" (Schneider, 1994: 34). Although the literature on corporate communications does not articulate its ideal organization in terms of tight couplings, its notion of communication control seems to suggest a tightly coupled organizing practice informed and shaped by a discourse of consistency, alignment and regulation. As we shall see below, such practice conflicts with important findings in organizational theory.

Acknowledging Difference and Variety

Whereas corporate communications presupposes a number of integrative practices (alignment, regulation, discipline and so forth), the demand for flexibility pulls the organization in the opposite direction, that is, in the direction of variety and decentralization. The importance of organizational variety had been demonstrated already by system theorist W. Ross Ashby (1956, 1958) in the 1950s. Ashby explained that living systems need to develop and maintain sufficient systemic diversity in order to accurately sense diversity in their surroundings. His "law of requisite variety" states that the internal diversity of a controlling system must match the complexity of the environment it seeks to control (Conant and Ashby, 1970). The law of requisite variety implies that organizations need to maintain a sufficient level of internal diversity in order to recognize variety in their external environments. Put differently, organizational processes (for example, scanning processes and ways of handling and exchanging information between departments) must be *as* equivocal as the inputs organizations seek to manage and adapt to (Weick, 1979). Although the project of corporate communications presupposes a streamlining of the organization's communication and hence a certain degree of standardization, the organization simultaneously has to cultivate its internal differences in order to maintain the ability to observe differences in its external environment. Analogous to the law of requisite variety, sophisticated climate prediction systems are designed to continually improve our ability to assess and forecast climate change, and to develop models according to the changing complexity of the environment.[1] Such systems rely on targeted research efforts continuously informed by and adapted to regional demands as well as significant external collaborations with networks of climate scientists worldwide.

Organizations need sufficient systemic diversity – what has been called "requisite variety" – to sense and recognize important differences in their surroundings.

The desire for control and predictability, however, means that requisite variety is frequently absent in organizations. Some organizations, for example, are obsessively concerned with their corporate design wanting to appear exactly the same way across all situations and all markets (Christensen and Cheney, 2000). Others exhibit their desire for control in attempts to align the values and attitudes of their employees with the philosophy of management. Yet others reduce variety by employing only those people who are willing to uncritically support the organization's visions and values (Kunde, 2000). With the renewed emphasis on total or "bodily" images of organization, corporations are increasingly dependent on the involvement and loyalty of their staff. This dependency may lead some organizations to believe that their members should behave as loyal devotees to the corporation and its creed.

Buffers and Loose Couplings

The project of corporate communications, and its notion of integration, are challenged by findings that demonstrate buffers in organizational communication. If communication across the organization, or among organizations, cannot be as "seamless" as the literature prescribes, the project of corporate communications needs to be reformulated accordingly.

BOX 7.3   Organizational Buffers

In 1967, organizational theorist James D. Thompson pointed out that organizations need to maintain buffers between flexibility and stability. Organizations, according to Thompson, are at once open systems that seek, and to some extent create, uncertainty and closed systems that aim for stability. In a sense, thus, an organization consists of several organizations – some "core" processes that carry out routine tasks (for example, production, logistics and accounting) and some boundary processes that create change (for example, research, product development and marketing). Often the latter operate as buffers, absorbing new trends and input without disturbing the routines of the former. A pharmaceutical company like Johnson & Johnson, for example, needs to continuously question

(Continued)

(Continued)

existing practices, services and products in order to innovate and improve quality. At the same time Johnson & Johnson needs to insist on the impeccability of existing products and production processes to appear legitimate and trustworthy to its internal and external audiences. The separation of flexibility and stability, Thompson continued, is essential for the organization to function efficiently. Thompson therefore prescribed a structural de-coupling of the organizational functions that deal with uncertainty and flexibility (for example, R&D or marketing) from the core of the organization concerned with rationality, predictability and control (production, logistics, and so on).

Organizations maintain buffers between certainty and uncertainty, stability and flexibility.

Thompson's perspective may well be criticized for being too mechanistic and simplistic for contemporary organizations where the "core" of the organization is no longer defined by its technology and production. Indeed, his observation needs to be reformulated in a world where the speedy development and dissemination of technology mean that the product is often transient while the communication is responsible for providing stability. In addition we may note that it is often expected of today's employees that everyone in every department is able to handle the dual demand for flexibility and stability. What is the buffer under such circumstances? Yet, Thompson's notion of buffers between flexibility and stability captures a significant feature of organizing in all living systems and indicates that integration is necessarily partial and incomplete.

Echoing the findings of Thompson, biologist Robert B. Glassman (1973) argued that complex living systems like organizations are loosely coupled internally. The different organs of the body, for example, are able to carry out multiple activities without involving other organs. Eye movements, thus, are not tightly coupled to the movements of hands and feet. The notion of loose coupling refers to the ability to handle flexibility and stability simultaneously but in different parts of the system. Because changes and perturbations do not affect all parts of the system equally and at the same time, such a division of labour is more efficient than the tightly coupled system described above. Whereas stability in the tightly coupled system is rigid and fragile because it only allows for adaptations that include the system *as a whole,* the loosely coupled system insures its existence by limiting the flexibility to local and relatively independent variables. Because the procedures for adaptation are not standardized and specific, as in the tightly coupled systems, they are able to develop a greater degree of sensitivity to the external environment. This increases the adaptability of the system without weakening or undermining its organizational structure.

To ensure flexibility and adaptability, complex living systems such as organizations are loosely coupled internally.

The loosely coupled system is stable because its flexibility is handled locally and by relatively independent subsystems. When subsystems have few variables in common with each other, they are able to be sensitive and responsive to external changes without affecting or disturbing the system as a whole (Weick, 1976; see also Orton and Weick, 1990). Through the function of a perceptive marketing department, for example, an organization is able to be open and flexible vis-à-vis *certain* kinds of external changes: for example, variations in some consumer preferences. Simultaneously, and because of the buffer provided by the marketing department, other departments such as production and finance can operate as more closed and stable domains.

As the German sociologist Niklas Luhmann (1990) has argued, systemic openness and closure are each other's preconditions: closure on some dimensions makes it possible for the system to be open on others (Morin, 1986). In a similar manner, loose and tight couplings necessarily *co-exist* in complex organizations. Think, for example, of the chameleon, which has a unique ability to change its outer colour and blend in with its environment. While the colour of the chameleon is tightly coupled to its immediate surroundings to which it adapts, it is at the same time loosely coupled to internal functions like various biochemical processes. Without such a division of labour between loose and tight couplings, the chameleon would explode if it were placed on a piece of multi-coloured fabric (Christensen et al., in press)! The changes the chameleon undergoes on its surface can be thought of as first-order changes or, in the words of British anthropologist Gregory Bateson, "changes in order not to change" (Bateson, 1972). Without suggesting that organizations are themselves chameleons, the loosely coupled features that allow the chameleon to retain stability while adapting to external changes are essential for all living systems operating in complex and changing environments. While the principles of buffering and loose couplings cannot be translated directly from the physical world to the universe of communication, the analogy is still important in the field of corporate communications. Due to the essential ambiguity of communication, there will always be fractures of interpretation between what is said and what is understood. Consequently, there will always be buffers or loose couplings at play – even when full integration is the goal.

In living systems, loose and tight couplings presuppose and facilitate each other.

The interdependence of loose and tight couplings is well-known in many managerial situations. If a subdivision is "tightly" coupled to external variables that change quickly, and at the same time loosely coupled to other internal departments, it allows the organization as a whole the possibility of maintaining good relations with its external environment without subjecting itself to their dynamics as a whole. For example, while Novo Nordisk's People, Relations and Reputation (PRR) department is doing a meticulous job of engaging with stakeholders in understanding and responding to their concerns on behalf of the organization, its IT and logistics department need not preoccupy themselves with the same task. They can rely on engaging with the PRR department to obtain important information about changes in stakeholder expectations while pursuing the detailed implications for their specific work tasks. As we shall argue later in this chapter (as well as in Chapter 8), a healthy interplay between loose and tight couplings may be reached by combining horizontal communication structures with intensive upward communication processes. Such a combination allows the organization to discover new ideas and solutions while at the same time operating under the auspices of a shared set of norms and values.

A healthy combination of tight and loose couplings allows the organization to develop close relations with its environment while insulating certain processes from external uncertainty.

Generally, close relations with customers and responsiveness with regard to the market will reduce the organization's possibilities for internal regulation and control (Chase and Tansik, 1983; see also Chase, 1978). Conversely, if one insists on a complete integration of all of an organization's communications, one must simultaneously allow for looser couplings elsewhere, for example vis-à-vis the market. The internal regulation and integration presupposed by corporate communications are, in other words, reciprocally related to the organization's sensitivity to its environment. This becomes most apparent when companies standardize their communication across national and cultural differences. Bang & Olufsen's aspiration to project a uniform and global image of itself onto every market, exemplified for example through their campaign "A life less ordinary", implies a potential blindness to input, such as market analyses that contradict or question this image.[2] But Bang & Olufsen is not alone with this problem. In line with Theodore Levitt's convergence thesis (Chapter 2), a growing number of organizations have streamlined their communication in ways that do indeed create tightness and consistency in the messages sent but at the same time leave no room for variation and local adaptation. Some of the most globally streamlined corporate communication examples are Coca-Cola, Disney and McDonald's.

When an organization integrates its communications in accordance with the corporate communications perspective, it runs the risk of reducing its sensitivity to its surroundings.

BOX 7.4   Buffers, Variety and Organizational Learning

Organizational theorist Monty L. Lynn (2005) has revisited and revised the classical writings on variety, buffers and loose couplings. Lynn defines buffering as the regulation and/or insulation of organizational processes from the effects of environmental uncertainty or scarcity. While it may look as if buffers have been minimized in new organizational arrangements such as lean manufacturing, cross-functional teams, just-in-time inventory systems and so on, they are in fact just as important in contemporary organizations as they have ever been. Instead of eliminating buffers, such arrangements have only decentralized or relocated the buffering process into smaller or different elements. Buffering, according to Lynn, makes it possible for organizations to handle *unexpected* changes in their surroundings by absorbing discontinuous input that cannot be matched by their current level of requisite variety. As the organization learns from the new situation and increases its requisite variety accordingly, the regulation or insulation provided by the buffers can be reduced.

Requisite variety and buffering are complementary dimensions in the process of organizational adaptation and learning.

In line with the classical writers on this issue, Lynn suggests that environmental complexity at some point becomes too complex to deal with by a centralized control system. The need for message and image control, predicated by writings on integrated communications, thus must be tempered by a persistent concern with issues of variety, differentiation and flexibility. Today many organizations seek to formalize their engagement with variety, differentiation and flexibility, for example through principles of diversity recruitment or multi-stakeholder dialogues. But variety and differentiation may also emerge as vital dimensions in organizational cultures that nurture diversity and flexibility for different reasons. In his study of the Diablo Canyon nuclear power plant's safety principles, professor of organizational behavior and psychology Karl Weick (and Sutcliffe, 2001) illustrates how buffering processes re-emerge in smaller processes in an otherwise tightly

(Continued)

(*Continued*)

coupled system. In such high-risk organizations, Weick stresses the importance of developing what he calls organizational "mindfulness", a mentality
that encourages employees to develop a preoccupation with failure, a
reluctance to simplify interpretations and an ongoing sensitivity to operations. He argues that such constant self-analysis of seemingly minor and
unproblematic slips in the nuclear power plant develops an openness for
learning and a habit of alertness (Weick and Sutcliffe, 2001).

Balancing Control with Flexibility

We need not subscribe to excessively dramatic depictions of organizational environments as "turbulent" or "chaotic" to acknowledge that organizations need to
develop their potential for flexibility. Unless the field of corporate communications
recognizes the organizational significance of variety, buffers and loose couplings, its
notions of alignment, coordination and control may well become sources of rigid-
ity in the organizational practice. System theorists have argued that the application
of simple control systems on complex events implies that certain information
escapes attention. Moreover, complexity is often dramatically increased (Morin,
1992). The attempt, for example, to regulate communication networks through the
control of a single parameter leads to distortion of other parameters (Mulgan, 1991).
The French sociologist Jean Baudrillard (1990b) gives examples of how social systems in trying to predict and prevent catastrophes may end up producing side-
effects that are more destructive than the events they were trying to evade.

**To acknowledge and adapt to environmental complexity, the project of
corporate communications needs to balance central control with flexibility and decentralization.**

Complex systems have the capacity to maintain themselves through the constant
adaptation of internal states to changes in the environment. Such a capacity moves
the system towards greater diversity and complexity (Mulgan, 1991). Rather than
centralized control, which is always difficult and costly to impose when complexity is high, it may be argued (see box below) that such a capacity is best fostered in
a decentralized structure where information flows more freely and rank defers to
expertise (Weick and Sutcliffe, 2001; see also Sproull and Kiesler, 1992).

BOX 7.5   High Reliability Organizations

According to professors of organization Karl E. Weick and Kathleen Sutcliffe, organizations can stimulate their own complexity by becoming sophisticated controllers. Sophisticated controllers, according to Weick and Sutcliffe, are skilled at perceiving and utilizing subtle variations and nuances missed by other observers. To people without a prior knowledge of opera, for example, all arias may sound the same. And without insight into the art of painting, it may be difficult to appreciate the differences in style and genre in the fine arts. However, just as an individual can learn to observe distinctions in a piece of music or in a piece of painting, organizations can sensitize themselves to observe and attend to variations that they could not previously recognize. Weick and Sutcliffe's term for such sophisticated controllers is "high reliability organizations" (HROs):

> *HROs take deliberate steps to create more complete and nuanced pictures. They simplify less and see more. Knowing that the world they face is complex, unstable, unknowable, and unpredictable, they position themselves to see as much as possible. They encourage boundary spanners who have diverse experience, scepticism toward received wisdom, and negotiating tactics that reconcile differences of opinion without destroying the nuances that diverse people detect.* (2001: 11ff.)

Unlike the role of horizontal communication in the detailed planning and control system suggested by proponents of integrated communications programmes (Schultz and Schultz, 2004), these boundary spanners are not expected simply to coordinate a *preset* integration project. In the context of high reliability organizations, boundary spanning serves to confront established practices and programmes with alternative ideas and understandings. This ambition implies that organizations must nourish diversity, quantitatively as well as qualitatively, employ and give voice to a wide variety of professions and perspectives, and perhaps even be willing to hire a professional "jester" (Peters, 1988). The jester challenges unexamined assumptions and helps the organization stay out of the ruts. It is the willingness and ability to organize themselves in such a complex manner that help organizations perceive diversity and thus to handle unexpected situations.

The advantage of internal differentiation and variety is a richer and more varied picture of the environment, which in turn cultivates a more elaborate set of organizational precautions.

In a complex organizational setting, control changes too. To enable complex information exchanges – that is, exchanges that are richer and contain more variety than the simple coordination processes of the corporate communications literature – organizations need to replace exogenous (or imposed) control by endogenous and more organic forms of control. Geoff Mulgan (1991), director of the Young Foundation and founder and director of the UK think-tank Demos, refers to such control as "efficient weak power controls", that is, control which is not a delimited resource held by some and exercised over others but a capacity embedded within the structure, a capacity that helps the organization adapt to different situations and thus to meet its goals. Such capacity is sometimes found in self-managing work teams, but may also appear in networks.

In line with Mulgan, marketing professors Ravi Achrol and Philip Kotler (1999) point out that networks and other flexible organizational arrangements necessarily challenge traditional instruments of authority and control such as hierarchy, power and contracts. Compared to these instruments, networks, according to Achrol and Kotler, are superior when it comes to flexibility and learning. Hierarchy may facilitate strong ties within and among functional units and thus foster a sense of integration. Strong ties, however, also cause members, as we have argued, to think and act alike, which reduce requisite variety. By contrast, networks create what sociologist Mark Granovetter (1973) referred to as dense but weak ties among people with different functions, interests, and knowledge. "The strength of weak ties" refers to their ability to stimulate new links and facilitate the transmission of information that challenges the taken-for-granted routines and assumptions. Such an ability is unlikely to appear in a corporate communications programme concerned primarily with a notion of consistency defined *a priori* and managed in a top-down manner. 'The strength of weak ties' shows up in contexts as diverse as individual job hunting, organizational innovation, and grief work. In all these cases, new inputs into the "system" that come from unexpected sources may take on far greater importance that they would seem to have on the surface.

When control is endogenous and decentralized it allows organizational members to develop new links and networks that stimulate information exchange and, thus, the formation of new ideas.

Rather than supporting integration across the organizational setting, the control system suggested here supports the formation of small organizational units, which are integrated internally through intense communication, but at the same time able to operate autonomously vis-à-vis the environment (Piercy and Cravens, 1995; Quinn, 1992). In line with Glassman's conception of a complex and adaptable system discussed above, tight couplings in some organizational processes are, in this vision, balanced by loose couplings in others. One approach to such a balance between tight and loose couplings is professor of corporate communications Cees van Riel's notion of "Common Starting Points" (CSP). Van Riel describes CSPs as "central values which function as the basis for undertaking any kinds of communication envisaged by an organization. Establishing CSPs is particularly useful in creating clear priorities, e.g. to facilitate an eventual control and evaluation of the total communication policy" (1995: 19ff.). An early example of Common Starting Points is the Dow Corning Corporation's response to market growth and expansions as well as national debates about corporate ethical stances to bribes and gifts. The Dow Corning Corporation decided in the early 1970s to articulate a corporate code of conduct and to develop guidelines for communicating ethical standards of business conduct around the world. The organization was a few years before reorganized into a global matrix with a high degree of decentralization, and top management identified a need to ensure a code sufficiently general enough to encompass the corporate variety of cultures and business practices, and at the same time specific enough to be a useful guide for local action (Harvard Business School, 1989). While such Common Starting Points may serve to clarify global priorities while allowing for local flexibility, they are no guarantee for maintaining horizontal communication and organizational adaptability. Ten years after the implementation of Dow Corning's global business conduct, the company was driven into the well known serious controversy over the safety of its silicone breast implants (Sellers et al., 1995).

Corporate communications based on "Common Starting Points" potentially allows the organization to cultivate a more agile corporate body.

It is uncertain, however, if the call for flexibility facing contemporary organizations can be sufficiently complied with through the implementation of Common Starting Points alone. To remain flexible, organizations need to balance their concern for consistency with sufficient local autonomy to allow the organization to retain its sensitivity and responsiveness vis-à-vis its customers and other significant stakeholders. The CSP perspective may (as we argue further in the Chapter 8) be just as controlling and disciplining as other approaches to corporate communications. Rather than being only *starting* points, CSPs are values to which the organization returns again and again when orchestrating its communications. Although van Riel emphasizes that the parameters or "wavelengths" defined by the CSPs "by no means imply absolute uniformity" (1995: 19), the flexibility and deviations permitted resemble what organizational sociologists Paul du Gay and Graeme Salaman (1992) refer to as "controlled de-control," that is, attempts to dictate and dominate autonomous processes. Karl Weick puts it this way:

> ... whenever you have what appears to be successful decentralization, if you look more closely, you will discover that it was always preceded by a period of intense centralization where a set of core values were hammered out and socialized into people before the people were turned loose to go their own "independent," "autonomous" ways. (1987: 124)

What appears to be local autonomy within a corporate communications programme may well be restricted by regulations and surveillance.

To embrace and match the complexities of the environment on an *ongoing* basis, organizations need to establish structures that allow them to be efficient and flexible at the same time. Christensen, Firat and Torp have proposed a model of flexible integration that combines sophisticated horizontal structures, based on semi-autonomous workgroups, with intensified vertical (especially upward) communication. Whereas the horizontal structures allow the organization to experiment locally with new ideas and solutions, the vertical communication ensures that such new ideas and solutions are conveyed promptly to management. This way, the organization can draw far more actively on the experiences, ideas and enactments of its frontline members. Because of their boundary spanning functions, such members often have a more detailed insight into the needs, wants and wishes of customers and other external audiences. By formalizing the voice of such members, the organization is better equipped to stay in tune with changes in the market (Christensen et al., in press). In the following chapter, the significance of this voice within the corporate communication project will be elaborated further.

CASE: The Organization of Innovation

OTICON[3]

Since 1904, Oticon A/S (hereafter Oticon) has been a designer and manufacturer of hearing aids. Located in Scandinavia, Oticon employs approximately 1000 people around the world. The case illustrates how a company can nourish flexibility in order to stimulate and sustain innovation. In a wide-ranging change process, Oticon managed to transform a bureaucratic, hierarchical company into a networked, multi-tasking and innovative organization. Furthermore, the case suggests that flexibility and loose couplings need to be nurtured in order to last. The desire for control and predictability is powerful, even in organizations that encourage decentralization, loose couplings and flexibility.

The Spaghetti Organization

For more than 15 years, Oticon has been an icon of innovation and flexibility. The company has attracted international recognition for its daring organizational experiments to encourage innovation and improve competitiveness. Oticon became known as "the spaghetti organization" in 1991, when Lars Kolind introduced his vision of the future organization to all employees. While the spaghetti metaphor was first mentioned casually in an interview with CEO Lars Kolind, its appeal proved so strong, that it even sticks to

---

the organization today, 15 years later. The notion of the "spaghetti organization" symbolically describes a unit composed of numerous and interwoven strings of interaction, a unit that always moves, never stays the same, yet somehow remains a coherent "portion".

The call for innovation became urgent in the 1980s when Oticon's international leading position as the world's largest hearing aid manufacturer was challenged by American competitors. While Oticon had managed for many years to build successfully on its strength as a mass producer of high quality hearing aids, American competitors threatened Oticon's leading position with customized hearing aids based on new and, for Oticon unfamiliar, digital technologies. Oticon's former international recognition dwindled remarkably and by the late 1980s Oticon had fallen back to third position on the world market. The company experienced severe economic problems and the family feeling of unity, coherence and belonging, that had characterized the Oticon spirit in the period of international expansion, disappeared. According to employees, Oticon suddenly came across as "fragmented and disillusioned". The top management, who had led the company for 25 years, decided collectively to resign, and a new CEO, Lars Kolind, was appointed in September 1989.

The New Vision

In the media, Lars Kolind's vision was presented as an "organizational revolution". To managers and employees the revolution was presented in a rather informal tone under the heading "Think the Unthinkable", capturing the essence of the project – to learn to think beyond conventional boundaries and to imagine the unusual. More specifically, Lars Kolind encouraged managers and employees to imitate the spectacle industry. Here the standard of spectacle had successfully been replaced by contact lenses because spectacles were viewed as a handicap that had to be hidden until later as the spectacle was re-launched as a fashion phenomenon. "Today, spectacles are a way of demonstrating identity", said Lars Kolind. Why should we at Oticon not be able to turn hearing aids into a life style product? How can we master the leap from big behind-the-ear devices to the more invisible in-the-ear devices and turn hearing aids into fashion? Or perhaps something else? Moreover, Kolind told managers and employees to stop perceiving themselves as staff in a manufacturing company. Rather, they were encouraged to regard themselves as members working in the healthcare industry. Oticon was on the move "From the industry of hearing aids to the industry of hearing care", as Kolind phrased it.

CEO Lars Kolind himself embodied the idea of breaking with Oticon's well-established traditions: his informal way of communicating by addressing people by their first names and by hand-written memos, his direct management style of confronting people with reflexive questions about their practices and ideas, his academic university degree in mathematics, and his professional track record outside the hearing aid industry.

(Continued)

(Continued)

Kolind was compassionately engaged in the international boy-scout movementm and had four young children that he insisted on picking up after school as often as possible. At his first reception, he was serving water and milk to the audience while the former CEO served champagne. Employees found it difficult to categorize Kolind. On the one hand, he was found to be a puritan, extremely competitive and focused on economics. On the other hand, he was seen as caring, sensitive and concerned about employees' well-being.

The Strength of Multiple Voices

At the core of the spaghetti vision was a set of corporate values: dialogue, creativity, voluntariness, egalitarianism, flexibility, decentralization and trust in the individual. These values contrasted remarkably with prior experiences in Oticon. A radical reorganization of daily routines and norms was enacted to make these values live. The focus was neither directed towards business strategies, product programmes nor market expansion but rather on how Oticon's managers and employees could improve their creativity and innovation.

A central idea was to expose everyone to multiple voices, critiques and alternative solutions. To implement that idea, "professional strangers" were introduced to the organization. While apprenticeship and internal recruitment characterized the traditional career path at Oticon, a number of people were now hired with untraditional backgrounds, including a librarian, a designer, several economists and a few political scientists. Also, a number of journalists and managers from other organizations visited Oticon. From different perspectives, they reflected and asked questions about organizational routines and actions. Moreover, Kolind strategically opened the doors to the public, inviting the media to interrogate managers and employees on their experiences and opinions about working in a "spaghetti organization". Being confronted with curious "external strangers" even critical employees experienced how they transformed scepticism to support. One "spaghetti-sceptic" project manager reported how he was taken by surprise at his own transformation when talking to an audience of business managers, and someone interrupted him asking "Is everyone at Oticon as excited about this as you are?"

A careful redesign of the office space reminded managers and employees of the spaghetti vision by urging them to reflect on the benefits of existing practices, by engaging in discussions with colleagues to increase horizontal communication, and by seeking new ideas to do things differently. More specifically, the spaghetti organization included a new office building with open-spaced offices, in which the CEO, managers, and employees were able to relocate themselves from desk to desk according to what teams and project they were working with at the time. For example, development engineers were found dispersed in the office landscape, moving around with their trolleys, small cases on wheels, in which they kept all their personal and professional belongings making it easy to move from area to area. All department and middle manager-titles were abolished and everyone was working in ad hoc teams supervized by project managers. Project teams were only temporary and so was the title of project manager. Once a project was completed, a project manager had to convince management that s/he was the best person to conduct another project.

The organizational structure and the flexible office were central features, and a number of symbolic arrangements were introduced in support: the locking of elevators urging people to take the stairways and meet new colleagues, the banning of thermoses and the setting-up of "coffee-islands" to encourage everyone to drink coffee with colleagues rather than in isolation, and the transparent meeting rooms making dialogue and work visible to everyone. Also, labs for development engineers were located in the middle of the office landscape and equipped with windows. The large transparent tube for the paper shredder upstairs running down through the canteen reminded everyone that dialogue is better than writing memos to each other. Most remarkably, perhaps, was the fact that managers, including the CEO, were found in the open office space moving around with their trolleys like everyone else. Former managerial privileges, such as large private offices fenced by a secretary, belonged to the past. Managers were "on the floor", available for anyone with a question or a suggestion in accordance with the organizational value of egalitarianism.

Within a few years Oticon was able to turn its economy from a loss to high profits. Time from product idea to release was reduced significantly and the number of new commercially successful products increased. Today, fifteen years later, Oticon's economy is even better.

The Routinization of Flexibility?

Although strongly emphasized, the spaghetti organization did not require that all managers and employees subscribe fully to a decentralized structure. But the accentuation of flexibility and innovation was pivotal for motivating new perspectives on existing perceptions and routines. Yet, despite the persistent accentuation of almost anarchistic structures, Oticon never turned into anarchy. While contemporary organizations recognize the necessity to emphasize diversity and develop sensitivity to differences in environments, in practice the need for predictability and stability often overshadows the quest for flexibility. Thus, while the emphasis was given to flexibility and innovation, quite a number of managers and employees reported that their work routines did not change much with the introduction of the spaghetti organization. Some employees soon started to regret that "the spaghetti had turned into ravioli". Soon after the organizational turnaround, a new middle manager level surfaced. First informally but then gradually more formal departments re-emerged, and structures for decision making and

(Continued)

fixed principles for action developed. Although the media still refer to Oticon as the spaghetti organization, some years after managers and employees do not recognize the spaghetti in practice. Despite the many features installed to sustain flexibility, multiple voices are silenced and organizational flexibility is crystallized into a more traditional, compartmentalized, fixed structure for product development.

Points of reflection

1. How does Oticon's spaghetti vision balance the need for integration, in the sense of speaking consistently, while promoting organizational differentiation to enhance innovation?

2. How did the notion of "buffers" change in Oticon, as the company moved from a traditional hierarchy to a spaghetti organization?

3. What are the main challenges for Oticon in trying to maintain its vision of a flexible and innovative organization? Or, put differently, why has Oticon returned to a more traditional compartmentalized structure?

Chapter Summary

Chapter 7 takes as its point of departure the fact that organizations operating in complex environments must be able to handle multiple and sometimes conflicting ideas and principles simultaneously within the same organizational unit. Integration and differentiation, for example, are opposing organizational forces that need to be balanced as environmental complexity increases. Expecting the organization to operate in the full service of its communication *plan*, corporate communications, however, tends to ignore the complexities of organizational practice. In addition to differentiation, complex organizations are characterized by buffers, loose couplings and systemic diversity. Together these traits challenge the conventional understandings of integration that we usually find in the field of corporate communications. When an organization integrates its communication in accordance with the corporate communication perspective, it runs the risk of installing a tightly coupled organizing practice that reduces sensitivity to its surroundings. To acknowledge and adapt to environmental complexity, the project of corporate communications needs to balance central control with flexibility and decentralization and to allow for more sophisticated forms of communication across the organizational setting. In the next chapter, the practical implications of these points will be fleshed out in more detail.

Notes

1   See for example: http://iri.columbia.edu/pred/
2   See for example: http://www.elliottsoflymington.com/links/index.html, and: http://images. google. dk/images?svnum=10&hl=da&lr=&q=B%26O+a+life+less+ordinary&btnG=S% C3%B8g
3   http://www.oticon.com/eprise/main/Oticon/com/_index. See also: Morsing and Eiberg, 1998; Morsing and Kristensen, 2001; Kjaergaard, 2004; Foss, 2003.

8

Corporate Communications as Polyphony

A Body with Multiple Voices

> If we conceive of organization as many dialogues occurring simultaneously and sequentially, as polyphony, we begin to hear differences and possibilities. We discover that each voice, each person, is his or her centre of any organization. And it is from each of the dynamic centres that change occurs.
>
> Mary Ann Hazen (1993: 16)

Introduction

In the complex business environment of today in which identity and legitimacy are constantly at issue, it is difficult to imagine a world in which corporate communications does not play a significant role. Without some alignment of symbols and messages in a cluttered marketplace, some clarity and continuity in communications, organizations will have difficulties being recognized as distinctive corporate brands. And without a minimal level of consistency between messages, procedures and behaviours, words and deeds, organizations cannot expect to be recognized as legitimate players in a globalized world. Some bodily unity, in other words, is essential in today's communication. Yet, the ambition to demarcate, enclose and manage everything the organization says and does within a unifying corporate expression remains the essential weakness of the perspective. The aim of this chapter is to point out alternative ways of approaching corporate communications that acknowledge the value of diversity and the wisdom of many different voices. In particular, the chapter will address the following issues and questions:

Chapter 8: Points of Challenge

- The ambition of corporate communications is to convey clear and explicit attitudes and values across different organizational audiences. To what extent, however, are clarity and explicitness essential dimensions of organizational integration?

- In order to build legitimacy and prevent hypocrisy, corporate messages are expected to be consistent with corporate behaviours. How can hypocrisy help organizations develop and adapt to new situations?

- Contemporary organizations are told to orchestrate all communications from a central perspective. How can the insights and experiences of the organization's many voices be brought into play under the aegis of such a perspective?

Management as Polyphony

The advantage of the corporate communications perspective is that it operates from a broader and far more sophisticated conception of the communication task than we typically find in organizations that manage their communication from a marketing or a public relations perspective. As we have seen, communication is no longer the exclusive domain of communication specialists, but an expanding dimension that potentially involves all members of an organization. Although contemporary management is concerned with consistency, corporate communications may still be approached as a case of polyphony.

BOX 8.1   Polyphony

The notion of polyphony refers primarily to music in which two or more independent melodic parts (or voices) are combined into a coherent musicial entity. Polyphony is contrasted to music with a single voice (monophony), music where many voices sing the same melody (unity) or music where multiple parts are dependent on or subservient to a single dominant voice, as when an instrument accompanies a singer (homophony). Most complex and interesting music involves multiple overlapping or interactive parts. But to have full polyphony each part must retain its independent musical identity. Polyphony, thus, requires autonomous parts whose integrity is sustained even when they blend into a coherent entity. Often polyphony is realized by having the parts contrast with or stand in relief to each other. Whereas polyphony in some extreme cases involves the simultaneous performance of totally different scores or texts, most often it is dialogical in the sense that the parts play up against each other in a continuous discourse.[1] The distinctive quality of polyphonic music is its utilization of diversity and complexity within a coherent unit (compare with our definition of *integration* in Chapter 2).

Polyphony presupposes the combination of diversity and unity within in a coherent entity.

The technique or art of combining two or more melodic parts to achieve a coherent or harmonic relationship, while retaining the individual integrity of each part, is called *counterpoint*. Obviously, this technique or art is extremely difficult to master and will usually involve the active participation of all parts to bring about musical coherence (for example, the recurrence of a shared melodic theme). Consider what this principle means when applied to team brainstorming about a problem, or negotiations between two departments, the revaluation of an organization's goals, or to the way an organization presents itself in the world.

In the context of polyphony, corporate communications becomes a highly sophisticated managerial practice.

To approach management as polyphony means to challenge conventional prescriptions for corporate communications practice. The most prominent prescriptions in the field are explicitness, clarity, consistency and orchestration. As we have seen, corporations increasingly tell themselves to be explicit and clear in their communications and to orchestrate their symbols and messages consistently across different situations and different audiences. Although these principles make good sense at first glance, they present a number of significant limitations when it comes to recognizing and taking advantage of different insights and voices in the organization. Challenging each of these principles below will help us move towards the articulation of an alternative agenda for corporate communications.

Explicitness or Tacitness?

When the basic premises of a group, including values, attitudes, and understood history, are stated explicitly, the result is not necessarily a feeling of community. People enter organizations and use them for many different reasons and purposes. Some people use the organization as a temporary springboard in their career; others plan to hang around till they retire. Some people use the organization to build their identity; others to gain a living. Since management mostly takes place under the assumption of sharedness and commonality, these differences are often ignored or repressed (Weick, 1979). In this context, explicitness not only increases attention, as management might hope, to the shared dimensions of the group but also to the disagreements and discrepancies that inevitably shape social life. The marketing people and the engineers, for example, may find out that they have more in common with colleagues in *other* organizations than with each other. And, they may come to realize that the understanding of integration advanced by management does not match their own. Studies of strong organizational cultures have indicated that these are not necessarily based on an *explicit* articulation of community (Weick, 1995). Competent managers, therefore, know when to be explicit and when to let the situation speak for itself. Professors of management Richard Tanner Pascale and Anthony G. Athos express it this way:

> *Explicit communication is a cultural assumption; it is not a linguistic imperative. Skilled executives develop the ability to vary their language along the spectrum from explicitness to indirection depending upon their reading of the other person and the situation.* (1981: 102)

Contrary to common belief, people do not have to agree on goals in order to act collectively, that is to act rationally and predictably as a group. People participating in a political demonstration or a labour strike, for example, often account so differently for their motives and behaviour that the notion of shared meaning becomes difficult to uphold (Donnellon et al., 1986). In fact, many organizations work well as integrated communities as long as the precise definition of the community is left out or toned down. On the contrary, the demand to spell out the sharedness of the organization's members may impede approval and agreement. As professors of management Richard Dunford and Ian Palmer point out, while talk may help organizations identify a common issue of concern, it simultaneously defines "a territory upon which grounds for disagreement can be articulated ... once talk constitutes a community of interest, a forum exists within which divergent opinions can be circulated in a way that is not possible amongst fragmented players" (1998: 215). While efforts to articulate a shared point of departure *can* be a very fruitful process for an organization because it nurtures an awareness of strengths and limitations, it is through the same process that organizational members are reminded of the limitations of their community. Thus, the very same ritualistic weekly or monthly meeting of a committee that reaffirms members' sense of connection to one another may in fact give testimony to the difficulties of achieving consensus. This is why it is important to understand how meetings function on multiple practical and symbolic levels, depending in part on how much is invested in the goal of deep mutual understanding in addition to the arrival at a decision on how to "speak" as a group, say, through a report, or resolution, or some other kind of outcome. Very few small groups, let alone large organizations, take the time or use the types of processes necessary for deep intersubjective understanding between differing values, opinions and areas of knowledge. However, for an organization's policy makers to march to a tune that is completely out of step with the majority of members risks discord or worse, cynicism and alienation. None of this means, of course, that laying bare our claims and assumptions will necessarily yield agreement; often the contrary is true.

Explicitness does not necessarily promote agreement, commitment and an *esprit de corps*.

Clarity or Ambiguity?

Like explicitness, clarity is a double-edged sword. On the one hand, marketing professor Nicholas Ind has an important point when he says: "Visions that tend towards a middle of the road view are unlikely to engender the sort of devotion needed to coalesce the organisation ... It is the power of the shared values and the organizational commitment to a few simple ideas that drives the organisations forward in a cohesive way, so that the actions of employees endorse the quality of the products and services to create a relationship of trust with their consumers" (1997: 11, 50). When distinctive positions, on the other hand, are spelt out too precisely, some audiences may feel that their freedom and creativity in enacting their own interpretations are curtailed. This may reduce motivation and loyalty. While writings in corporate communications and corporate branding call for organizations to eliminate ambiguity (Hatch and Schultz, 2001), such a practice does not necessarily serve the interests of the organization as a unified and coherent community. This may explain why many organizations use rather vague and general language when articulating their *raison d'être*. Vision and mission statements, thus, are often characterized by clichés and platitudes that do not explain much about the company behind the products. This is true for nations as well as organizations. The Volvo Group presents its mission statement in the following words: "By creating value for our customers, we create value for our shareholders. We use our expertise to create transport-related products and services of superior quality, safety and environmental care for demanding customers in selected segments. We work with energy, passion, and respect for the individual."[2] Likewise, the Sara Lee Corporation's vision is: "To be the first choice of consumers around the world by bringing together innovative ideas, continuous improvement and people who make things happen."[3] And, in its "Vision 2020" Caterpillar aspires to be "An admired global leader making progress possible."[4] The same tendency is found when organizations select their values. Values are typically formulated in vague and imprecise phrases that rarely provide the organization with the points of differentiation it may hope for. Yet, the lack of precision might allow the organization to talk about itself without pushing anyone away. A Danish study of corporate values in private and public sector organizations showed some of the most frequently used values were "innovation", "quality", "openness" and "customer orientation" (Morsing, 2005).

Clarity does not necessarily promote loyalty and consent. In the usual sense of the term, clarity may actually prevent managers from establishing accord with some corporate audiences.

BOX 8.2   Strategic Ambiguity

Professor of organizational communication Eric Eisenberg has phrased the term "strategic ambiguity" to account for the practice of managers to generate support for their ideas by employing an ambiguous and imprecise rhetoric. While most communication researchers and practitioners, according to Eisenberg, encourage clarity, such advice ignores the fact that communicators often have multiple and conflicting goals when communicating inside and outside the organizational setting. Communicators, for example, constantly need to strike a balance between being understood, maintaining a specific self-image and not offending others. The strategic use of ambiguity promotes what Eisenberg calls "unified diversity", the ability of differences to co-exist within the unity of the organization:

> Strategic ambiguity is essential to organizing because it allows for multiple interpretations to exist among people who contend that they are attending to the same message – i.e., perceive the message to be clear. It is a political necessity to engage in strategic ambiguity so that different constituent groups may apply different interpretations to the symbol. (1984: 231)

Eisenberg emphasizes that strategic ambiguity does not move people towards having the same views. Rather, it makes it possible for them to maintain their individual differences and interpretations while believing that they are in agreement. Recognizing that a tension between the individual and the system, the parts and the whole, exists in every social system, Eisenberg finds it necessary for communicators to cultivate ambiguity because it allows them at once to express and protect, reveal and conceal – in other words, to be both open and closed.

Strategic ambiguity allows for multiple interpretations and in this way creates space for different identities and different audiences to co-exist within the confines of the organizational unit.

This does not have to signal a slide into manipulation. What it does mean is that we should recognize the ways language and other symbols operate on different levels. Sometimes unity requires more abstract affirmations of values that all can share. Even apparently univocal messages may have multiple meanings. Language is essentially polysemic, giving rise to a proliferation of uncontrollable meanings. The Russian linguist Mikhail Bakhtin has introduced the notion of *heteroglossia* to describe the centrifugal powers of language and the coexistence of distinct varieties within a single linguistic code. Heteroglossia challenges the assumption that communicators must conform to the same linguistic code in order for communication to take place (Bakhtin, 1981). Following Bakhtin, professors of management Michael Humphreys and Andrew Brown point out that "… organizations are not discursively monolithic, but pluralistic and polyphonic, involving multiple dialogical practices that occur simultaneously and sequentially" (2002: 422).

Even without precision and clarity, the articulation of an organization's values provides employees with a voice against management. When the company tells itself and its surroundings what it stands for, for example "innovation", "quality", "openness" or "customer orientation", it simultaneously defines an arena of potential criticism – and most likely, criticism will arise! Since employees know that corporate messages involve and obligate them in a deeper sense than conventional advertising (see Chapter 3), they are often the first to notice if organizational practices do not correspond to words. As several studies have shown, employees may use the company's official rhetoric as arguments against management in times of disagreement and conflict. During a strike caused by layoffs, employees at Disneyland accused management for abandoning the organization's family values (Smith and Eisenberg, 1987). Similarly, cabin crews at the Scandinavian Airlines System accused management during a labour conflict for not living up to its own ideals – service, anti-hierarchy and mutual dependency – which the company had advertised and promoted widely (Dahler-Larsen, 1997). Of course, such a critique presents an obvious chance for an organization, if it is open enough, to question its own practices and to reestablish consistency between words and actions. The question of consistency, however, is more complex than what this logic suggests.

Consistency or Hypocrisy?

While consistency is generally considered a virtue, the demand for consistency will often be difficult to honour for organizations operating in complex environments. If all stakeholders (including shareholders and customers) were expecting and demanding the same things, it would be easy for organizations to act consistently. This, however, is rarely the case. In complex environments, organizations face many different stakeholders and typically these stakeholders confront the organization with conflicting goals and demands. While the neighbouring community, for example, expects an organization to preserve jobs locally, environmentalists insist that corporations first of all respect the surrounding nature. Complex environments, in other words, are inconsistent. To operate in such environments requires a willingness and an ability on the part of the organization to make continual adjustments in its preferences and behaviours. Under such conditions, the repeated insistence on consistency may become an obstacle to organizational adaptation (March, 1988).

The desire for consistency between words and actions may be a liability in complex and changeable environments.

Nonetheless, because a lack of consistency appears hypocritical and false, the demand for consistency will be voiced regularly by both internal and external audiences. Challenging the call for consistency, however, professor of organization James G. March argues that hypocrisy – defined as inconsistency between words and action – is a necessary transitional practice in an environment that changes rapidly. While it is obvious that organizations often have difficulties living up to their own ideals or publicized intentions, we should not, says March, restrict them from claiming these ideals and intentions as their own. In line with the perspective taken in this book, March regards language as a highly creative force able to shape reality significantly. For that reason, he favours a relatively unrestricted articulation of ideals. As he points out, a bad person with good intentions *can* be a person who experiments with the possibilities of becoming a good person. Consequently, it would be more sensible to encourage experiments than reject them, for example by allowing organizations to talk about their ideals and good intentions instead of insisting that their behaviour leaves much to be desired (March, 1994). Since corporate messages have the potential to prompt an organization to change its behaviours to become, for example, more socially or environmentally responsible (see Chapter 4), it makes sense to allow organizations some latitude in experimenting with the ways they talk about these and related issues (Livesey and Graham, 2007).

Hypocrisy may be a necessary transitional practice that helps organizations experiment and adjust to new situations.

The impossibility of satisfying all goals and demands from stakeholders simultaneously implies that organizations cannot escape some level of hypocrisy. In line with March, professor of organization Nils Brunsson (2003b) argues that organizations, in order to manoeuver in a world of conflicting demands, need to compensate action in one direction with talk and decisions in the opposite direction. In 1980, the government of Sweden had to react to a referendum that showed a clear interest in the Swedish public to close down all nuclear power plants. Simultaneously, the Swedish industry insisted on greater and cheaper electricity. The government managed to adapt to both parties by splitting decision and action: it decided to close down all power plants by 2005, that is, 25 years later (Brunsson, 2003a). While most people consider the practice of separating words and action unethical, especially if the practice is applied as a conscious strategy, Brunsson demonstrates that organizational hypocrisy is often unintentional. In the process of "muddling through" a world of conflicting demands (Lindblom, 1959), organizations inevitably end up producing differences between their words and their actions. Following this line of thought, Brunsson suggests provokingly that hypocrisy may be regarded as an organizational *solution* rather than as a problem. Some stakeholders are fully satisfied with symbolic actions such as an apology or openness to a critical inquiry. As professor of organization, Jeffrey Pfeffer has pointed out:

> *Assessing organizational actions is an activity that takes resources and attention. It is unlikely to be undertaken except by those who stand to be significantly affected by what the organization really does. Since most people are not so profoundly impacted, for most*

people, symbolic responses are sufficient given their limited involvement in knowing the organization. Symbolic responses may also be sufficient because in the absence of the ability to specify precisely what is desired or to assess the multiple dimensions of organizational outputs, parties in contact with the organization may desire only some reassurance that their interests are being seriously considered within the organization. In this case, a symbolic response conveys information that the organization is responsive to the demands being made, and this symbolic gesture may be sufficiently reassuring. (1981: 33)

Organizations often produce hypocrisy when they seek to be responsive to differing and incompatible demands.

BOX 8.3   Walk the Talk – or Vice Versa?

The expression "walk the talk" is generally used as a prescription for managers to practise what they preach. As such, it represents a protection against hypocrisy and a sensible recipe for integration. However, although the recipe seems politically correct, it limits the manouverability of managers and thus their potential for learning. Based on his notion that discovery resides in action, Karl E. Weick argues that "walk the talk" impedes innovation and reduces the likelihood of change: "When told to walk their talk, the vehicle for discovery, the walking, is redirected. It has been pressed into service as a testimonial that a handful of earlier words are the right words" (1995: 183). Being oriented primarily towards previous talk, managers trying to practise what they preach miss the chance of discovering something new. "Walk the talk", thus creates organizational inertia because managerial action primarily serves as a confirmation of (or "salute" to) previous statements.

"Walk the talk" impedes organizational experimentation, innovation and the ability to learn.

Good managers, according to Weick, practise "talk the walk". They are adept at putting into words the decisions and actions already made or the activities (the "walking") they spend most time doing. "Talk the walk" increases flexibility because it allows the manager to experiment, test assumptions and discover new ways of doing things without being rigidly confined by earlier statements. Moreover, by allowing the manager to retrospectively construct a narrative that explains why the organization's reality looks the way it does, "talk the walk" helps cultivate meaning and coherence in the organization. The opportunism inherent in "talk the walk" is necessary, argues Weick, because organizations need to stimulate curiosity and innovation when operating in complex environments.

"Talk the walk" cultivates new meanings while allowing the organization to explore, experiment and change.

As managers, employees or consumers we are used to the fact that very few organizations live up to their declared ideals. And, we often condone the hypocrisy. Still, for the organization itself it is imperative to signal consistency in order to … well, sustain consistency. If the organization abandons the ideal of consistency it runs the risk of disintegrating. The renaissance political writer Niccoló Machiavelli[5] was aware that although it is not necessary to possess *all* virtues, it may sometimes be necessary to *pretend* to possess them. For good reasons, Machiavelli's work is often described as cynical because it describes the achievement and maintenance of power by a determined ruler indifferent to moral considerations. At the same time, his recommendations for the emperor to use illusions in order to achieve and uphold supremacy can be regarded as a first attempt to uncover or deconstruct the secrets of power (Ehnmark, 1986; see also Skinner, 1981). As (post)modern consumers, employees, investors and journalists, we are familiar with many of the illusions employed by contemporary organizations to present themselves as legitimate players in the market; we know that there are many truths about an organization and we are fully aware that most of them are neither acceptable nor consistent. We also realize that an organization has to choose and highlight one description amongst other possible descriptions and that this choice inevitably involves a certain amount of idealization. This is not an apology for deceit, but a reminder that organizations – like human beings – sustain themselves to some extent through idealizations.

Corporate communications entail idealized narratives on organizational clarity, consistency and unity.

BOX 8.4   The Tyranny of Intimacy

Professor of sociology Richard Sennett is concerned that social interaction in contemporary society is being impoverished by an overwhelming quest for intimacy. In *The Fall of Public Man,* (1964) Sennett unfolds his thesis

(Continued)

(Continued)

about how the display of emotions turns the public into passive spectators rather than an active force – a public. Sennett calls this "the Tyranny of Intimacy". For a manager, he argues, the loss of impersonality in public is a distortion of the distance between the manager's own sentiments and impulses and those of his audience. And, in this process the audience will focus on his motivations rather than assessing him in terms of his acts. Rather than engaging in a critical debate about the issues of concern, a critique of the issue will be perceived as a critique of the person. Consequently, the critical debate suffers and the case loses ground.

Impersonality and masks are necessary to avoid emotions and intimacy that will cause impoverishment on the corporate dialogue, to the detriment of both individual and company.

Drawing on the theatre metaphor, Sennett points to the necessity for people, including managers, to play a role as they appear on stage. He argues that wearing a mask is the essence of civility, which he defines as "the activity which protects people from each other and yet allows them to enjoy each other's company" (1964: 264). Incivility, according to Sennett, is to impose oneself on others. To criticize a mask and a role is not to criticize the manager himself. Without the ability to play an act on stage, a person loses the ability of self-distance. He blends the self with the person on stage, and burdens himself and others with a self-conscious doubt: is what I'm showing really me? The manager's expressions are made contingent on authentic feelings, but he and his audience are left with the narcissistic problem of never being able to dissect what is authentic in one's feelings.

The strength of idealization is simplification: it suspends the need to consider a wealth of superfluous information. More importantly, idealization can be used to develop the organization, provided that its managers are willing to accept some difference between words and action. Such a difference, which is the driving force in an auto-communication process (see Chapters 1 and 3), can be used as a lever for organizational development, as a starting point for soul-searching and as a "mirror" in which the organization can continually observe and evaluate itself. When an organization communicates with itself, it not only confirms its identity but simultaneously seeks to announce its ideal self-image in its surroundings. For such an announcement to do more than simply salute the triumphs of the past it needs to have an element of aspiration, belief and hope: in other words, a *difference* between what the organization is now and what it aspires to be.

To develop itself, an organization must be capable of accepting and handling differences.

Such an approach is no less trustworthy than one which claims to ensure consistency in everything the organization says and does. After all, who is judging whether corporate messages are consistent or not? While consistency is justified with reference to the consumer and his or her need for clarity and order, the orchestration of organizational messages is usually regarded as a managerial prerogative (Schultz et al., 1994).

Orchestration or Local Articulation?

Consistency in meaning as prescribed by the corporate communications literature is largely concerned about orchestration at the levels of message construction and delivery. Contemporary organizations, thus, seem utterly concerned about delivering uniform and unambiguous descriptions of themselves. The more resources organizations have invested in integrated communications, it seems, the more important it becomes to management that everybody understands the message the "right" way (Christensen and Cheney, 2000).

BOX 8.5   Corporate Consistency: Orchestration or Narcissism?

As professors of organization Per Olof Berg and Kristian Kreiner have illustrated so well, corporate symbols are rarely left to speak for themselves, especially when organizations invest in corporate architecture and corporate design. Analysing the symbolic meaning of corporate architecture, Berg and Kreiner show how CEOs, communication managers and other architects of organizational identity are keen to deliver official descriptions and interpretations of their own buildings. Expounding on the meaning of Volvo's pentagon-shaped Kalmar plant, the vice president of corporate planning told Berg and Kreiner that "it was a signal to the whole company that we were fully backing up what we were saying about work democracy, technological innovations, etc" (1990: 57). In the process of making sure that corporate symbols are interpreted "correctly", corporate managers tend to communicate mainly with themselves.

(Continued)

(Continued)

Attempts to integrate organizational symbols and messages seem to breed corporate vanity.

While management has the authority to expound the "correct" meaning of corporate symbols, this right should be used with care. As we have argued earlier, auto-communication borders on self-seduction (Christensen and Cheney, 2000). Design management, for example, is often a very inward-looking exercise where the organization orchestrates and adjusts its own communication in accordance with ... well, its own communication. In the process of aligning design parameters organizations run the risk of over-estimating the significance of their own communication. This point is illustrated by another interesting example from Berg and Kreiner in which a marketing manager of a leading Swedish office furniture manufacturer explains the round shapes used in the organization's headquarters:

> *The domed roof, in its form and design, consequently symbolizes the rounded details in our assortment. In the interior we have rounded doors and some corners are similarly rounded instead of being right-angled in order to accentuate the identity of the product ... In the exterior, logo, architecture, and product program we are everywhere confronted with the same round basic form. From the moment we enter the reception we are also confronted with the positive sense of well-being associated with success. No communication problems here.* (1990: 49)

Considering the amount of resources that organizations spend building their identities, the desire to orchestrate corporate symbols and messages is understandable. However, while some level of orchestration is necessary, such sender-oriented exercise tends to disregard the creative readings of the receiver. Acknowledging the creativity of reception does not imply that consumers and other audiences *necessarily* see corporate messages as inconsistent or fragmented – only that the organization loses its ability to orchestrate its own messages once they enter the universe of the receiver (see Chapter 5). Still, organizations often hope to influence or control this universe too. As a consequence, consistency becomes more a question of being in a position to deliver an authoritative interpretation of corporate symbols than a question of discovering a necessary and logical connection between and among those symbols.

Consistency in corporate communications is a question of the power to deliver the authoritative interpretation of corporate symbols and messages.

When orchestration is reduced to the practice of regulating symbols and messages from the top of the organizational pyramid, the organization deprives itself of the possibility of securing member support behind its communications. Support and ownership require a *real* involvement of the members who are expected to demonstrate involvement (see Chapter 3). The expectation that people will loyally support projects on which they have no direct influence is naïve and outdated. For more than half a century, progressive organizations have experimented with alternative forms of involvement. In his classic study of the US Forestry Service Herbert Kaufman (1960) illustrated how organizational identification is associated with the ability of members to articulate their own interpretation of the organization's identity. Kaufman described how the US Forestry Service used its rangers not only to maintain and preserve its forests and parks but also as public relations representatives. Giving public talks to the local community, the rangers found themselves regularly explaining the corporate missions, plans and principles of the US Forestry Service. Although this was not an entirely flexible assignment, each ranger was able to personalize the presentation and thus articulated the identity of the organization in a way that included him or herself as an individual. In addition to creating understanding and goodwill in the public, the US Forestry Service managed to use its external communication in the service of internal management issues like motivation, loyalty, commitment and belongingness. Following our discussion of auto-communication we can say that the ability to speak on behalf of one's workplace is a powerful way to stimulate involvement and workplace identification.

Involvement presupposes involvement: a willingness on the part of the organization to grant participation and voice to its employees.

Many organizations in the Western world subscribe to such a philosophy. Yet, few seem to be able to implement it in practice. On the one hand, organizations talk about delegating responsibility and giving voice to everybody. One the other hand, they are concerned that such delegation erodes the clear and consistent story. Under the impact of corporate communications and its notions of consistency and integration, this concern has come to prevail. As a consequence, contemporary organizations frequently enforce an official story about the company's values on their employees. This is a serious mistake primarily because enforced stories have a tendency to provoke anti-stories, that is, stories that contradict, parody or counteract the official story of management and its implied values.

BOX 8.6   Storytelling

Storytelling can be defined as "the art of portraying real or fictitious events in words, images, and sounds".[6] Storytelling is essential to humanity. Human beings tell stories for many different purposes – often to entertain,

(Continued)

(Continued)

but also to teach or convey social values. The stories about who we are and where we come from define our communities and societies. Similarly, the stories that an organization tell about its mission, its values and its daily practices are central manifestations of its identity.

Storytelling is a consitutional dimension of social life in human societies and organizations.

As contemporary managers have come to realize, stories inform, influence, confirm and guide organizational members and in this way help reduce uncertainty, create meaning and facilitate identification with the workplace (Brown, 1990). Stories, thus, can become important to management in efforts to develop specific organizational cultures. Constructing stories about the organization allows management to highlight specific themes, adopt certain perspectives and assign acceptable motives and action. A good corporate story can convey complex messages in a way that sticks in the minds of the audience. In 1997, for instance, the CEO of BP John Browne initiated a story about BP's intentions to fulfil its promise of working towards global environmental improvements (see also Chapter 4). Under lots of media attention, he announced BP's decision to leave the Global Climate Coalition, a lobby-group group of 50 corporations and trade associations, claiming that global warming was unproven and action to prevent it unwarranted. John Browne argued it was time to act to prevent greenhouse warming rather than continue to debate whether it would occur. With this new and unexpected stance, BP sought to earn a reputation as an environmentally progressive corporation in an industry that largely refused to accept the likelihood of global warming. While BP's intentions and actions were criticized by some of the media, Browne's attempt to stage BP as environmentally friendly led to praise from environmental groups including Greenpeace and provided a story that is widely retold and remembered. Obviously, stories initiated by management are sometimes challenged or contradicted by anti-stories developed among rank-and-file members of the organization as well as among involved non-members. The people who have the most powerful corporate story define the organizational reality.

Stories define our reality by shaping our understanding of the past and the future.

Through stories, the past is brought into the present in ways that allow us to re-interpret our history. Through the articulation of new stories, thus, organizations can change not only who they want to be, but also who they *were*. While organizational identity, for example, is often described as something authentic – as "the quintessence of an organization" (Balmer and Greyser, 2003) – organizations re-interpret their authenticity and, thus, their history quite frequently. And while identity is seen as an expression of the organization's "character", it still needs to be sold to its members through convincing and orchestrated stories.

In a publication featuring stories from its employees, American Airlines has tried to balance the dual need for orchestration and voice. The book, called *A Spirit of Greatness,* recounts stories about day-to-day interactions between staff and customers. Lurain Murray, for example, who works at American Airlines' First Class check-in desk, relates how she often, when there are no First Class passengers, calls over Economy Class passengers to her desk. The typical reaction is: "Ma'am, I'm not traveling First Class." Her reply, which the company must be very happy with, is: "All American Airlines passengers are First Class; we just don't have that many seats in front." While the management at American Airlines clearly recognizes the difference that committed employees make in providing exceptional customer service, they also understand the power of voice. By allowing rank-and-file members of the organization to articulate their individual interpretations of corporate values in an external medium, American Airlines is able to set a process of auto-communication in motion – a process that potentially cultivates commitment, identification and customer satisfaction.

Rather than orchestrating the many stories about the organization from one central location, ownership and involvement are created by giving space and possibilities for *local* articulation.

In a similar manner, the Danish-based producer of hearing aids and sound systems, Danavox, has issued an elegant booklet that presents a number of the company's employees by combining aesthetically appealing close-up pictures with interviews and personal information. Nikolai Bisgaard, for example, who is Vice President of Research & Development and responsible for the development of new hearing instruments is presented this way: "When Bisgaard is not at Danavox, there's a good chance of finding him in one of four places: out in his kitchen among the pots and pans, on a tennis court, skiing or on vacation in France". Likewise we are told that Carsten Trads, who is the Vice President of Sales & Marketing and at Madsen Electronics, is very interested in sound – both professionally and in his private life: "He's been playing the trumpet for many years and likes to relax to the sound of music, especially classical music and jazz". By letting their employees relay information that traverses the boundary between the public and private sphere, Danavox demonstrates – internally as well as and externally – that it values its members as "real people" and has the weight to express its appreciation in a fancy, external medium.

As these cases illustrate, it is not necessary to orchestrate all communications from one position in the organization in order to facilitate integration. The opportunity for an employee to express him or herself in an external medium holds a strong integrative potential. The success of such a strategy, of course, hinges on the willingness of employees to embody a collective message as long as it allows them to articulate their own identity and their own values in the process.

By giving employees voice in external media, organizations can instil pride, stimulate identification and potentially enhance commitment and ownership for corporate symbols and values.

According to professor of communication Stanley Deetz, commitment is more important to organizations than sharedness and agreement. Good communication, Deetz argues, is not a matter of defining a common ground or securing consensus between different interests, but of allowing and cultivating a variety of perspectives in order to make sure that established positions are challenged on a continual basis. To facilitate commitment, organizations need to allow for the contestation of established positions and practices through decisional involvement. Deetz's perspective implies a tolerance for organizational subcultures and the diversity of the multiple voices of different professions and backgrounds. In line with our discussion of organizational flexibility (see Chapter 7), Deetz points out that a requisite diversity and contestation are necessary to stimulate creative solutions and assure a mutual commitment among the involved parties, even when opinions, ideals and goals differ. Deetz's (2006) perspective, thus, is a *processual* perspective – a perspective focused on participation rather than sacrosanct solutions.

CASE: Licence to Critique

The Copenhagen Municipality[7]

The municipality of Copenhagen is an organization with 40,000 employees to serve 500,000 citizens. It provides services to the citizens of Copenhagen, the capital city of

Denmark, within a diverse range of activities including housing, traffic, education, integration, culture, leisure, health care, the environment and urban development. During the last couple of years, the municipality has been in the process of unfolding a corporate values programme designed to foster consistency in the municipality's messages and behaviours while simultaneously developing the quality of its services and interactions vis-à-vis the citizenry. This case illustrates the advantages of pursuing a flexible type of integration in which integration is seen as a process of development rather than a product in itself.

The Ambition

In many organizations, values are regarded as a beacon or a set of instructions that defines, sometimes in minute detail, how employees are supposed to think and act in specific situations. That way, the values constitute an answer to questions of proper conduct within the organization and vis-à-vis its various constituencies. In order to stimulate employee involvement and organizational flexibility, the Copenhagen Municipality is approaching the issue of values-based management differently. The municipality is defining its values as "a living value base", that is, a set of corporate values that continuously evolves through input from employees and citizens. Their ambition is to pave the way for an open and self-reflective culture in which the values themselves are only stepping stones in the process of developing a better city. Typically traditional values programmes are concerned about *congruence* (do the values reflect organizational reality?), *sharing* (are the values recognized and accepted by everybody?) and *discipline* (are the values able to manage the behaviour of employees?). This programme by contrast, emphasizes the potential of the values to make a *difference* or, put differently, to become a "horizon" towards which the initiatives and the decisions of the municipality are continuously evaluated. Rather than disciplining employees, the values are meant to inspire inquiry and reflection. And rather than announcing a field of agreement and communality, the values are meant to challenge and activate the diversity of the municipality in order to stimulate its capacity for change.

The Practice

The values of the Copenhagen municipality are respect, equality, dialogue and trust. In contrast to most corporate values, however, these values are not seen as important in themselves. Together they constitute an "authorized speech position" from which employees and citizens can challenge the attitudes, decisions and practices of the municipality. Instead of providing final answers, the values are meant to authorize employees and citizens to ask penetrating questions about the type of respect, trust or equality that the municipality demonstrates vis-à-vis its constituencies: Do our actions convey respect for the elderly? Do our letters indicate a relationship of equality between the citizens and

(Continued)

(Continued)

us? Do we approach our students with trust? And so on. In fact, management explicitly invites employees and citizens to reflect on the values and confront them with the practices of the municipality. This programme – called "licence to critique" – is fundamentally different from other approaches to value-based management and most conceptions of corporate communications. The managers of the programme are fully aware that such an approach to integration presupposes a high degree of openness, reciprocity and trust that allows information to flow freely in the organization.

The Advantages

Drawing much more actively on the experiences, ideas and enactments of the organization's rank-and-file members, the municipality has designed its integration process to be sufficiently complex to match the complexities of the environment (Christensen et al., in press). The licence to critique approach encourages the formation of intensive and information-rich ties between the organization and its clients as well as between different professions and work groups inside the organization. The municipality, in other words, allows its employees to become sophisticated observers skilled at detecting diversity in the environment, capable of spanning disciplinary and hierarchical boundaries and adept at creating and utilizing horizontal and vertical communication channels to convey new ideas (see Chapter 7). Such capabilities are unlikely to appear in an integrated communication programme concerned primarily with a notion of consistency defined *a priori* and managed in a top-down manner. The licence to critique slogan underscores the possibility for employees and citizens to legitimately and safely challenge the attitudes, decisions, and practices of the municipality. Interestingly, the slogan not only authorizes employees to pose critical questions, but also to suggest or initiate *alternative solutions* in specific situations. By allowing its employees to enact a high degree of autonomy and local responsiveness (endogenous control), the municipality simultaneously cultivates its requisite variety and thus its ability to change. The disadvantage is that the licence to critique is abstract and difficult to implement on all levels because it requires equality between all parties. Hence it disregards issues such as power, prejudice, limited resources and differences in interests and linguistic competences. Despite these limitations, the licence to critique programme holds a promise of more dynamism and involvement than that provided by other approaches to values and integrated communications.

Points of reflection

1. How does the Copenhagen Municipality's approach to value-based management differ from conventional approaches?

2. What are the main challenges of the Copenhagen Municipality, given its processual perspective on integration?

3. Will its project be successful? Or will it be terminated?

Central or Local?

The alternative to centralized control in corporate communications is not to relinquish attempts to create integration and consistency in organizational messages, symbols and behaviours. Following the arguments above, one way for organizations to pursue integration is to create room for the individual employee or workgroup to contribute with alternative interpretations, ideas and practices. In order for corporate communications, as a principle of organizing, to be sufficiently complex to match the complexities of the environment, it needs to draw much more actively on the experiences, ideas and enactments of the organization's rank-and-file members as we saw, for example, in the case of the Copenhagen Municipality. Obviously, some common principles and ideas are indispensable before the members can be turned loose to enact their autonomy.

Sophisticated corporate communications implies a fine balance between centralized, global and dencentralized, local articulations.

The notion of "Common Starting Points" (CSPs), coined by professor of corporate communications Cees Van Riel (see Chapter 7), is often cited as a feasible approach to the problem of pursuing integration and consistency while allowing for local interpretations and enactments. According to professors of communication management Judy Motion and Shirley Leitch, the advantage of the CSP type of value integration is that it does not presuppose consistency between and among all symbols and messages from the organization. Rather, it assumes that organizational symbols and messages reflect and support, in a broader sense, the values which the organization espouses and adheres to. While the CSP approach, in other words, calls for organizations to ensure consistency in value expressions, it allows for a variety of "tunes" to be sung under its general tutelage (Leitch and Motion, 2002). This solution, Motion and Leitch claim, allows the organization to be "lighter on its feet", to be more open towards new ideas and to move faster when such a need arises.

Common Starting Points is often cited as a solution to the challenge of balancing control and autonomy in corporate communications.

Motion and Leitch have proposed an extension of van Riel's CSP approach – a so-called "semiotic model of corporate identity" – that combines the Common Starting Points with notions of "multiple identity enactments" (MIE) and "Common End Points" (CEP). Motion and Leitch use the notion of "multiple identity enactments" (MIEs) to describe the fact that all interactions between an organization and its stakeholders are expressions of organizational identity. Rather than suppressing differences, which most programmes of identity management tend to do in the name of consistency, Motion and Leitch argue that organizations should strike a balance between consistency and multiplicity. Such an approach, they claim, brings the identity to life and helps the company adjust to new conditions. CEPs are the goals the organization has set for itself – goals, which according to Motion and Leitch, should guide all identity enactments. Motion and Leitch also suggest that their approach leads to a reduction of centralized identity control. Unfortunately, however, it seems to reinforce a vertical and, thus, hierarchical communication structure and ignores or downplays the importance of horizontal communication exchanges. Although the semiotic identity model may allow for multiple interpretations, it still assumes the existence of a privileged (managerial) perspective from where corporate communications and corporate identities can be properly overseen and managed.

CSP and CEP approaches to corporate communications reinforce a vertical and, thus, hierarchical communication structure.

We fully recognize the necessity of pursuing consistency and the crucial role of management in this process. Yet, we would challenge the implied notion that integration is a fixed and well-defined product that only needs to be unpacked correctly by the organization's members. To move beyond this conventional understanding, organizations must allow their rank-and-file members to contribute more actively to the ongoing definition of what integration is and should be. This calls for intensified communication along both vertical and horizontal dimensions. Along the vertical dimension, the spirit of the Common Starting Points (CSP) and Common End Points (CEP) informs and shapes what the organization does. Along the horizontal dimension, we find more experimentation and occasional departures from the centralized and largely vertical structure. Such departures, facilitated by local responsiveness amongst boundary spanners such as frontline personnel, are necessary to ensure that the organization's values, goals and practices stay vibrant and in tune with changes in the market. While the departures need to be explained and justified to management, they are essential for the organization in its efforts to explore new ideas and thus cultivate its requisite variety (Christensen et al., in press).

Vertical approaches to integration must be supplemented by common process rules that stimulate horizontal communication and allow the organization to explore new ideas and solutions.

With its ambition of integrating all symbols, messages and behaviours, the project of corporate communications is clearly dependent on the existence and maintenance of some shared corporate values, for example in the form of CSPs and CEPs. In addition, however, complex organizations need a set of common *process* rules that is able to guide members in the process of discovering and applying new ideas and solutions (Christensen et al., in press). In today's world where the pressure to innovate and change is so pronounced, such common process rules may well be more important than CSPs and CEPs. In the case of the Copenhagen Municipality common process rules were given by the slogan "Licence to critique". This slogan underscores the possibility for employees and citizens to legitimately and safely challenge the attitudes, decisions and practices of the municipality. Such inquiry into different belief systems and behaviour stimulates the development of new attitudes and practices.

CASE: Exploring the Consistency of Corporate Competencies

Silvan[8]

Silvan is a Scandinavian home repair store chain, with more than 250 outlets in Denmark, Sweden, Norway and Finland. Silvan is also represented in Lithuania and China. In Scandinavia, Silvan is an established brand within the home-repair store industry and a leading provider and distributor of building materials. In 2000, Silvan launched a corporate communications campaign designed to establish consistency between the nature of its products and the competencies of its employees. The case illustrates how internal and external consistency can be developed as on ongoing process rather than as a centralized and top-down product. By exploring the many dimensions of its own identity and its own competencies, an organization can learn to handle diversity in its internal and external environments.

The External Campaign

Silvan's campaign took its point of departure in the general perception that the success of home repair shops is based on a combination of low cost products and poor service. While home repair shops sell handyman products at very competitive prices, their employees are rarely able to provide qualified assistance to customers who are asking for more skilled guidance. Inspired by Wal-Mart and Home Depot – companies that seek to combine service and guidance with competitive prices – Silvan wanted to change its image and position vis-à-vis other Scandinavian hardware chains. The external side of Silvan's campaign – called "We *also* do it ourselves" (meaning *We* are handymen ourselves) – was designed to demonstrate in humorous ways that Silvan employees are all home repairers, capable of making significant home improvements themselves.

The Internal Process

Prior to the launch of the external campaign, Silvan had been through an extensive revitalization process focusing on the development of employee competencies. Realizing that its external campaign would only be trustworthy if all its employees could live up to the slogan, Silvan set out to educate its 1500 employees in a broad range of home repair skills. In addition to seminars, training camps, competitions and joint

(Continued)

(Continued)

projects – all focusing on developing handyman skills and experiences – Silvan offered all employees one extra week of holiday per year provided the week was spent on a home repair project. The project was to be documented before, during and after and finally reported to management: how did the project work out, what materials and skills were used, what was learned, etc.? Employees embarking on such a project had the right to ask for help and support from the organization, for example demonstration videos. Moreover, employees were offered a discount on all materials used. The best home repair project of the year was awarded a prize.

The Benefits

By developing individual competencies amongst employees, Silvan managed to heighten the collective self-esteem in the organization. As its managers are aware, such self-esteem is essential for commitment and involvement and indispensable when recruiting new employees. One indication that the project has been a success is that employee turnover has been reduced considerably. More importantly, by stimulating employees to explore and develop their personal competencies, Silvan was able to map out its own skills and competencies as an organization. Urging members to ask for help and support, the organization simultaneously learned from its members and uncovered the nature of its own limitations as a home repair organization. All limitations were subsequentially reduced through the development of new competencies, demonstration videos, etc. As such, the project managed to combine the integration of internal and external communication with a wide-ranging knowledge management process in which the organization simultaneously improved its ability to learn how to learn. Obviously, such a strategy is not without imperfections. When corporate messages commit an organization beyond the communication or marketing department, they potentially exhibit the organization's weaknesses. Thus, Silvan depends on competent employees to continuously – and regardless of working hours – be able to enact the promise of the company slogan. This can be difficult in a line of business that often depends on part-time employees to cover "irregular" hours. In spite of this limitation, such projects allow organizations to combine managerial projects of integration with an ongoing sensitivity to the ideas, skills and visions of their members.

Points of reflection

1. How does Silvan's corporate communications project achieve a balance of control and autonomy amongst employees?

2. To what extent is the Silvan case a reflection of mainstream corporate communications? And how is it different?

3. Can Silvan extend its integration project even further to include, for example, customers and other stakeholders?

Chapter Summary

In this chapter, we have discussed the possibility for corporate communications to become a managerial practice focused on polyphony rather than unity. Proceeding from a critique of conventional principles in the field – explicitness, clarity, consistency and orchestration – we argued that the usual understanding of integration limits flexibility and employee involvement in the corporate communications project. While explicitness and clarity in communications may become a hindrance in establishing consent amongst different audiences, strategic ambiguity allows for different ideas and identities to co-exist within the confines of the organizational unit. Simultaneously, the desire for consistency between words and actions may be a liability in complex and changeable environments. In fact, and in contrast to most writings in the field, we may need to realize that organizations inevitably produce hypocrisy when they seek to be responsive to differing and incompatible demands. For some organizations, hypocrisy is a necessary transitional practice that helps them experiment and adjust to new situations. Without justifying or promoting corporate deceit, we emphasized that contemporary organizations must learn to accept and handle differences at many levels. Accepting differences is also a precondition for employee involvement in the corporate communications project. Involvement necessitates involvement: a willingness on the part of the organization to accept and engage the different voices of its employees. The strength of such a practice is its flexibility. When corporate values and other dimensions of corporate communication become objects of reflection and negotiation, they allow for multiple interpretations and for a realistic understanding of the fact that situations change over time. Moreover, they increase ownership and motivation.

Notes

1   http://en.wikipedia.org/wiki/Polyphonic
2   http://www.volvo.com/group/global/en-gb/Volvo+Group/ourmission/
3   http://www.saralee.com/ourcompany/mission.aspx
4   http://www.cat.com/cda/layout?m=38035&x=7
5   Machiavelli was an Italian political theorist who lived in Florence during the Renaissance. His book *The Prince* (1513) is regarded as a cynical manual for rulers who want to hold on to power by all possible means.
6   http://en.wikipedia.org/wiki/Storytelling
7   http://www.ipc.um.dk/en/servicemenu/Links/PublicAdministration/Municipality Of Copenhagen/ See also Knudsen (2003, 2004)
8   http://www.silvan.dk/templates/DT_InfoPage_Narrow.aspx?id=14822

Epilogue

Challenging the "Bodily" Pursuit

> Thus, rather than thinking about the body as a regulated topic, we should conceptualize the body in a more fluid manner to allow for ... important social changes in the wider social context.
>
> Bryan Turner (1996: 21)

Modernity and Decorporation

The French historian and philosopher Olivier Mongin (1982) uses the image of traditional society as a body to describe modernity as an ongoing process of "decorporation". According to Mongin, modern society dissolves the corporeality of ancient community by disintegrating its tightly knit systems of authority, hierarchy and solidarity. In contrast to the unity of traditional society built on strong interpersonal bonds, intimacy, emotional depth, moral commitment, social cohesion and continuity in time (Nisbet, 1966), modern society bases its legitimacy on the rights and wills of the individual. The transition from traditional society to modernity found perhaps its most dramatic expression with the beheading of Louis XVI during the French revolution, a symbolic (as well as a physical) process whereby the divine head was separated from the social body. In modernity, thus, the body is not whole or complete: a condition that poses new challenges to projects of identity.

The process of modernity involves a continuous "de-corporation" of society.

In modernity, identity is always at issue both for individuals and organizations (Cheney and Christensen, 2001a). Being decorporated, the modern individual no longer owes status to the larger social Body but finds its identity *in itself* and in the continuous pursuit of self-interests and individual rights vis-à-vis other social actors and institutions. Individuals are thus continually in search of themselves. Obviously, this leaves modern society and its institutions with an inherent weakness. Without a clear, shared symbolism to unite and integrate its members, modern society regularly needs to reinvent and rearticulate collective visions and collective representations. In fact, organizations as well as individuals experience periodic and sometimes ongoing identity crises. By intensifying modernity's propensity to question total "bodily" visions, postmodernity can be regarded as an intensification of these conditions.

While the dream of "bodily" coherence persists in modern societies, the efforts to articulate collective visions often lack persuasive power.

Re-Corporation and the Deformed Body

What interests Mongin in particular are the attempts of the present age to reestablish and reassert unified social bodies. He finds such attempts in various versions of totalitarianism or absolutist government. As he points out, totalitarianism can be seen as an endeavour to recreate a unity that at once evades the hierarchy of traditional society and the divisions between groupings and individuals that we find in modern democratic societies. The body of the totalitarian society, however, is not harmonious like the body of traditional society where the power of the sovereign was granted by, and subjected to, the transcendent power of God. By denying hierarchy and divisions, the totalitarian body, Mongin argues, is founded on the illusion that the head not only coincides with the rest of the body but simultaneously and at once controls all bodily organs. In line with this critique, the political philosopher Claude Lefort has demonstrated that the totalitarian image of society corresponds with an image of a machine. The tendency to re-establish and reassert unified social bodies, however, is not limited to totalitarian forms of organization. As Charlie Chaplin illustrated with his film *Modern Times,* rational bureaucracy with its focus on standardization, regulation and procedures is based on the notion of a perfect, mechanical body. Here the individual is merely a "cog" in the machine, much as Max Weber feared would happen with the rationalization of modern society.

The body of the totalitarian society is a *deformed* body because its head constantly seeks to swallow and absorb its parts.

Without suggesting that the discourse on corporate communication is inherently bureaucratic or has totalitarian implications, we should be open to the possibility that the ambition to restore and maintain an organizational unity and wholeness by aligning and coordinating all organizational messages may, as an unintended consequence, produce a deformed organizational body in which the head is at odds with the rest.

Towards Fluid Bodies?

The dream of bodily coherence defines the corporate communication project. Yet, the ambition of integrating all parts of the organizational body ignores the fact that the "whole" and its components are necessarily interdependent and interrelated. The parts owe their individuality to the whole, which in turn depends on their autonomy to maintain itself as a viable totality. The importance of seeing something in light of its (counter)parts is not new. In 500 BC, the Greek philosopher Heraclitus pointed out that every concept and every "thing" depend on and should be seen in relation to their opposites. Heraclitus pointed out that there is only unity because there are parts: if only unity exists the body will coagulate, and if only fragments exist the body will vanish. Unity and parts are, in other words, each others' logical preconditions: "Things taken together are whole and not whole, something which is being brought together and brought apart, which is in tune and out of tune, out of all things there comes a unity, and out of a unity all things" (cited in Kirk and Raven, 1957: 191).

While the whole is essential for the parts in their pursuit of individuality and innovation, the whole in turn depends on the parts to develop and maintain itself as an endurable entity.

In the last century, literary and rhetorical critic Kenneth Burke (1969) helped us to see the paradox of "sub-stance": in trying to define something's essence, we are inevitably led to consider what "stands" behind it or underneath it, or in a way, "outside" it. Language of course helps to reinforce this tendency and sets up many opposing pairs: that a characteristic like "openness" become clear to us only in relation to its dialectical opposite, "closedness".

On a broader societal level, we see the importance of these insights in comprehending globalization. From the late 1980s until about 2000, there was a strong effort, especially in western corporate and governmental circles, to see the world as moving inevitably toward one system of secular, democratic capitalism. It is now evident that there are many lines of cleavage in the world – in other words, forces of fragmentation. Thus a story, a script of "universality", "totality", of "one body", can be as much self-persuading as it is a fair representation of all the parts of system.

No matter how dedicatedly an organization works on its communications, there will always be fractures: between front stage and backstage, between the values of rank-and-file members and the values professed by the administrative core, between different departments and professions, and between what has previously been said and what one would like to say in the future. It is often in such fractures that development and innovation arise, not to mention profound practical and ethical reflection. Thus, there is a need for corporate communication to appreciate a more fluid corporate body capable of flowing and easily changing shape.

To remain vital corporate bodies, contemporary organizations must appreciate and nurture the fluid interplay between the "whole" and its parts.

Contemporary sociologists have argued that it is a false assumption that different cultures and traditions can co-create unity and consensus in a globalizing world. Instead, sociologist Ulrick Beck (2006) calls for the development of a *cosmopolitanism* that recognizes pluralism and diversity. Beck emphasizes the necessity of inviting plurality and contradictions – even certain types of provincialism and nationalism – and disengaging from an elitist presumption of "one best way" if in fact modern industrialized societies are to achieve their democratic ambitions. Analogous to the call for cosmopolitanism, contemporary organizations need to benefit from poly-phony and multiple voices to maintain an agile body and one which honours its various parts. While we recognize contemporary organizations' powerful desire for certainty, continuity and consistency, we challenge the wisdom and even the expediency of pursuing unity in contemporary communications.

The Artist

Thomas Kiær (born 1954) is a professional artist with a Master of Arts from The Royal Academy of Fine Arts, Copenhagen. Also, he studied at Facultad de Bellas Artes, Universidad Complutense de Madrid. Kjaer has held solo-exhibitions in New York, Stockholm and Copenhagen and has been part of numerous group exhibitions. Recognized by major grants and awards, Thomas's work has been purchased by institutions such as The New Carlsberg Foundation, Sønderjylland's Art Musem, The State Art Foundation, and The Danish Ministry of Foreign Affairs.

The Authors

Lars Thøger Christensen (PhD, Odense University, 1993) is Professor of Communication at the Department of Marketing & Management, The University of Southern Denmark. Also, he is Adjunct Professor at The Copenhagen Business School where he established the CBS Center for Corporate Communications. His research and teaching interests include critical and postmodern approaches to the broad fields of organizational and corporate communications, for example identity, issues management, integration, advertising and transparency. In addition to five books, his research appears in *Organization Studies*, *European Journal of Marketing*, *Consumption, Markets and Culture*, *The New Handbook of Organizational Communication*, *The Handbook of Public Relations*, *Communication Yearbook* and elsewhere.

Mette Morsing (PhD, Copenhagen Business School, 1993) is Professor of Corporate Social Responsibility at the Copenhagen Business School. In addition, she is the founding director of the CBS Center for Corporate Values and Responsibility. Mette's teaching and research interests include communication, organization, identity, learning, ethics, and corporate social responsibility. She has published a number of books, journal articles and book chapters. Mette is also active on a number of boards and committees in Europe on the research and education of corporate social responsibility (CSR), as well as acting as an advisor to the Danish government on CSR.

George Cheney (PhD, Purdue University, 1985) is Professor of Communication at the University of Utah, where he also serves as director of the Barbara and Norman Tanner Human Rights Center together with Peace and Conflict Studies. In addition, he is Adjunct Professor of Management Communication at the University of Waikato, Hamilton, New Zealand. His teaching and research interests include identity and power in the organization, participation and democracy at work, ethics in professional and corporate contexts, the rhetoric of war and peace, and alternative perspectives on globalization and marketization. Alone and with colleagues, he has published six books and over 80 journal articles and book chapters. Recognized for teaching and scholarship, he has lectured, conducted research and consulted in Europe and Latin America.

References

Aaker, D.A. (1996) *Building Strong Brands*. New York: The Free Press.

Aaker, D.A. and Joachimstahler, E. (2000) *Brand Leadership*. New York: Free Press.

Åberg, L.E.G. (1990) 'Theoretical model and praxis of total communications', *International Public Relations Review*, 13(2): 13–16.

Abrahamson, E. (1996) 'Management fashion', *Academy of Management Review*, 21: 254–85.

Achrol, R.S. (1991) 'Evolution of the marketing organization: New forms for turbulent environments', *Journal of Marketing*, 55(4): 77–93.

Achrol, R.S. and Kotler, P. (1999) 'Marketing in the network economy', *Journal of Marketing*, 63(4): 146–63.

Ader, C.R. (1995) 'A longitudinal study of agenda setting for the issue of environmental pollution', *Journalism & Mass Communication Quarterly*, 72: 300–11.

Aguilar, F.J. (1967) *Scanning the Business Environment*. London: Collier-Macmillan.

Albert, S. and Whetten, D.A. (1985) 'Organizational identity', in B.M. Staw and L.L. Cummings (eds), *Research in Organizational Behavior*. Greenwich, CT: JAI Press. pp. 263–95.

Alvesson, M. and Willmott, H. (2002) 'Identity regulation as organizational control: Producing the appropriate individual', *Journal of Management Studies*, 39(5): 619–44.

Andersen, N.A. (2003) 'The Undecidability of Decision', in T. Bakken and T. Hernes (eds), *Autopaetic Organization Theory*, Abstrakt, Liber. Oslo: Copenhagan Business School Press. pp. 235–58.

Andriof, J., Waddock, S., Husted, B. and Rahman, S. (2003) *Unfolding Stakeholder Thinking: Relationships, Communication Reporting and Performance*. Sheffield: Greenleaf Publishing.

Antorini, Y.M. (in progress) 'The AFOL experience. Brand community in a customers value and innovation perspective: An instrumental case study of the Adult Fans of Lego'. PhD thesis, presented at predefence at Copenhagen Business School, 26 June 2006.

Argenti, P.A. (1998) *Corporate Communication*. 2nd edn. Boston, MA: Irwin McGraw-Hill.

Argenti, P.A., Howell, R.A and Beck, K.A (2005) 'The strategic communication imperative', *MIT Sloan Management Review*, Spring: 83–7.

Arnstein, S.R. (1969) 'A ladder of citizen participation', *Journal of the American Planning Association*, 35(4): 216–24.

Ashby, W.R. (1956) 'Self-Regulation and Requisite Variety', in F.E. Emery (ed.), *Systems Thinking*. Volume 1. Harmondsworth: Penguin. pp. 100–20.

Ashby, W.R. (1958) 'Requisite variety and its implications for the control of complex systems', *Cybernetica*, 1(3): 83–99.

Ashforth, B.E. and Gibbs, B.W. (1990) 'The double edge of organizational legitimation', *Organizational Science*, 1(2): 177–94.

Ashforth, B.E. and Mael, F. (1989) 'Social identity theory and the organization', *Academy of Management Review*, 14(1): 20–39.

Backer, L. (2001) 'The mediated transparent society', *Corporate Reputation Review*, 4(3): 235–51.

Bakan, J. (2004) *The Corporation: The Pathological Pursuit of Profit and Power*. London: Constable.

Bakhtin, M.M. (1981) *The Dialogic Imagination: Four Essays*. Edited by Michael Holquist. Austin, TX: University of Texas Press.

Balmer, J.M.T. (1995) 'Corporate branding and connoisseurship', *Journal of General Management,* 21(1): 24–46.

Balmer, J.M.T. (1999) 'Corporate identity', in M. J. Baker (ed.), *The IEBM Encyclopedia of Marketing.* London: International Thomson Business Press. pp. 732–46.

Balmer, J.M.T. and Greyser, S.A. (eds) (2003) *Revealing the Corporation: Perspectives on Identity, Image, Reputation, Corporate Branding, and Corporate-Level Marketing.* London: Routledge.

Barker, J.R. (1993) 'Tightening the iron cage: Concertive control in the self-managing organization', *Administrative Science Quarterly,* 38: 408–37.

Barker, James R. (1999) *The Discipline of Teamwork: Participation and Concertive Control.* Thousand Oaks, CA: SAGE.

Barnard, C.I. (1968) *The Functions of the Executive,* 30th anniversary edition. Cambridge, MA: Harvard University Press.

Barnett, G.A. (1988) 'Communication and organizational culture', in G.M. Goldhaber and G.A. Barnett (eds), *Handbook of Organizational Communication.* Norwood, NJ: Ablex pp. 101–30.

Barrett, R. (1998) *Liberating the Corporate Soul.* Oxford: Butterworth-Heinemann.

Bateson, G. (1972) *Steps to an Ecology of Mind.* New York: Ballentine.

Baudrillard, J. (1983) *In the Shadow of the Silent Majorities.* New York: Semiotext(e).

Baudrillard, J. (1988) *The Ecstasy of Communication.* New York: Semiotext(e).

Baudrillard, J. (1990a) *Seduction.* Trans. Brian Singer. New York: St. Martin's Press.

Baudrillard, J. (1990b) *Fatal Strategies.* New York: Semiotext(e)/Columbia University.

Baudrillard, J. (1994) *Simulacra and Simulation.* Ann Arbour, MI: University of Michigan Press.

Beck, U. (2006) *Cosmopolitan Vision.* London: Polity.

Beder, S. (2005) 'Making energy more'. BP Sustainability Report 2005.

Behr, R.L. and Iyengar, S. (1985) 'Televison news, real-world cues, and changes in the public agenda', *Public Opinion Quarterly,* 49: 38–57.

Belch G.E. and Belch, M.A. (1998) *Introduction to Advertising & Promotion.* 4th edn. Burr Ridge, IL: Irwin McGraw-Hill.

Berg, P.O. (1985) 'Organization change as a symbolic transformation process', in P. Frost et al. (eds), *Organizational Culture.* Beverly Hills, CA: SAGE. pp. 281–99.

Berg, P.O. (1989) 'Postmodern management? From facts to fiction in theory and practice', *Scandinavian Journal of Management,* 5(3): 201–17.

Berg, P.O. and Gagliardi, P. (1985) 'Corporate images: a symbolic perspective of the organization-environment interface'. Paper presented at the SCOS conference on Corporate Images, Antibes, France.

Berg, P.O. and Kreiner, K. (1990) 'Corporate architecture: Turning physical settings into symbolic resources', in P. Gagliardi (ed.), *Symbols and Artifacts: Views of the Corporate Landscape,* Berlin: Walter de Gruyter. pp. 41–67.

Bernstein, D. (1984) *Company Image and Reality: A Critique of Corporate Communications.* Eastbourne: Holt, Rinehart and Winston.

Blackwell, R.D. (1987) 'Integrated marketing communications', in G.L. Frazier and J.N. Sheth (eds), *Contemporary Views on Marketing Practice.* Lexington, MA: Lexington Books. pp. 237–50.

Body Shop (1996) *The Body Shop's Social Statement 1995.* Mission Statement. Littlehampton: The Body Shop.

Boorstin, D. (1964) *The Image: A Guide to Pseudo-events in America*. New York: Random House.

Boyle, M. (2001) 'So where do MBAs want to work?', *Fortune*, 16 April: 408.

'bp: Beyond Petroleum?' (2002) in *Battling Big Business: Countering Greenwash, Infiltration and Other Forms of Corporate Bullying*, E. Lubbers (ed.). London: Green. pp. 26–32.

Brian, H. (2000) 'BP goes green, solar, connected', *Sydney Morning Herald*, 26 July: 25–6.

Broms, H. and Gahmberg, H. (1983) 'Communication to self in organizations and cultures', *Administrative Science Quarterly*, 28: 482–95.

Broom, G.M., Lauzen, M.M. and Tucker, K. (1991) 'Public relations and marketing: Dividing the conceptual domain and operational turf', *Public Relations Review,* 17(3): 219–25.

Brown, M.E. (1969) 'Identification and some conditions of organizational involvement', *Administrative Science Quarterly*, 14(3): 346–55.

Brown, M.H. (1990) 'Defining stories in organizations: Characteristics and functions', *Communication Yearbook,* 13: 162–90.

Brown, S.L. and Eisenhardt, K.M (1998) *Competing on the Edge: Strategy as Structured Chaos*. Boston, MA: Harvard Business School Press.

Brunsson, N. (1985) *The Irrational Organization: Irrationality as a Basis for Organizational Action and Change*. Chichester: Wiley.

Brunsson, N. (2003a) *The Organization of Hypocrisy: Talk, Decisions and Actions in Organizations*. 2nd edn. Copenhagen: Abstrakt, Liber and Copenhagen Business School Press.

Brunsson, N. (2003b) 'Organized hypocrisy', in B. Czarniawska and G. Sevón (eds), *The Northern Lights – Organization Theory in Scandinavia*. Copenhagen: Copenhagen Business School Press. pp. 201–22.

Buhl, C. (1991) 'The consumer's ad: The art of making sense of advertising', in H.H. Larsen, D.G. Mick and C. Alsted (eds), *Marketing and Semiotics: Selected Papers from the Copenhagen Symposium.* København: Handelshøjskolens Forlag. pp. 104–27.

Bullis, C. (1999) 'Organizational values and control', in C. Conrad (ed.), *The Ethical Nexus*. Norwood, NJ: Ablex. pp. 75–102.

Burawoy, M. (1979) *Manufacturing Consent*. Chicago, IL: University of Chicago Press.

Burke, K. (1969/1945) *A Grammar of Motives*. Berkeley, CA: University of California Press.

Burke, K. (1973) 'The rhetorical situation', in L. Thayer (ed.), *Communication: Ethical and Moral Issues*. London: Gordon & Breach. pp. 263–75.

Burke, W.W. (1987) *Organization Development: A Normative View*. Reading, MA: Addison Wesley.

Carroll, A. (1979) 'A three-dimensional conceptual model of corporate social responsibility', *Academy of Management Review*, 497–505.

Cawson, A. (1986) *Corporatism and Political Theory*. Oxford: Blackwell.

Chase, R.B. (1978) 'Where does the customer fit in the service operation?', *Harvard Business Review,* 56: 137–42.

Chase, R.B. and Tansik, D.A. (1983) 'The customer contact model for organization design', *Management Science,* 29(9): 1037–50.

Cheney, G. (1983) 'The rhetoric of identification and the study of organizational communication', *Quarterly Journal of Speech,* 69: 143–58.

Cheney, G. (1992) 'The corporate person (re)presents itself', in E.L. Toth and R.L. Heath (eds), *Rhetorical and Critical Approaches to Public Relations*. Hillsdale, NJ: Erlbaum. pp. 165–83.

Cheney, G. (1998) 'It's the economy, stupid!" A rhetorical communicative perspective an today's market', *Australian Journal of Communication*, special edition: 25–44.

Cheney, G. (1999) *Values at Work: Employee Participation Meets Market Pressure at Mondragón*. Ithaca, NY and London: Cornell University Press.

Cheney, G. (2004) 'Arguing about the "place" of values and ethics in market-oriented discourses', in S. Goldzwig and P. Sullivan (eds), *New Directions in Rhetorical Criticism*. Thousand Oaks, CA: SAGE. pp. 61–88.

Cheney, G. (2005) 'The united consumers of America. Or, is there a citizen in the house?', *The Kingfisher*, Vol. 1. Salt Lake City: College of Humanities, University of Utah.

Cheney, G. and Christensen, L.T. (2001a) 'Organizational identity: linkages between "internal" and "external" organizational communication', in F.M. Jablin and L.L. Putnam (eds), *The New Handbook of Organizational Communication*. Thousands Oaks, CA: SAGE. pp. 231–69.

Cheney, G. and Christensen, L.T. (2001b) 'Public relations as contested terrain. A critical response', in R. Heath and G. Vasquez (eds), *Handbook of Public Relations*. Newbury Park, CA: SAGE. pp. 167–82.

Cheney, G. and Cloud, D.L. (2006) 'Doing democracy, engaging the material: Employee participation and labor activity in an age of market globalization', *Management Communication Quarterly*, 19: 501–40.

Cheney, G., and Ashcraft, K. L. (in progress) 'Considering "the professional" in communication studies: Implications for theory and research beyond the boundaries of organizational communication'. Unpublished paper, University of Utah, Salt Lake City.

Cheney, G. and Vibert, S.L. (1987) 'Corporate discourse: Public relations and issue management', in F.M. Jablin, L.L. Putnam, K.H. Roberts and L.W. Porter (eds), *Handbook of Organizational Communication*. Newbury Park, CA: SAGE. pp. 165–94.

Cheney, G. and Tompkins, P.K. (1987) 'Coming to terms with organizational identification and commitment', *Central States Speech Journal*, 38: 1–15.

Cheney, G., Christensen, L.T., Conrad, C. and Lair, D. (2004) 'Corporate rhetoric as organizational discourse', in D. Grant, C. Hardy, C. Oswick, N. Phillips and L. Putnam (eds), *Handbook of Organizational Discourse*. London: SAGE. pp. 79–103.

Christensen, L.T. (1997) 'Marketing as auto-communication', *Consumption, Markets & Culture*, 1: 197–227.

Christensen, L.T. (2001) 'Intertextuality and self-reference in contemporary advertising', in F. Hansen and L.Y. Hansen (eds), *Advertising Research in the Nordic Countries*. København: Sam funds litteratur pp. 351–6.

Christensen, L.T. (2002) 'Corporate communication: The challenge of transparency', *Corporate Communications: An International Journal*, 7(3): 162–8.

Christensen, L.T. (2004) 'Det forførende medie. Om autokommunikation i markedsføringen', *Mediekultur*, 37: 14–23.

Christensen, L.T. and Askegaard, S. (2001) 'Corporate identity and corporate image revisited. A semiotic perspective', *European Journal of Marketing*, 35(4): 292–315.

Christensen, L.T. and Cheney, G. (2000) 'Self-absorption and self-seduction in the corporate identity game', in M. Schultz, M.J. Hatch and M.H. Larsen (eds), *The Expressive Organization*. Oxford: Oxford University Press. pp. 246–70.

Christensen, L.T. and Cheney, G. (2005) '*The Corporate Anatomy of Integrated Communications: Challenging the "Bodily" Pursuit'*. Paper presented at the Critical Management Studies conference, Cambridge, 4–6 July.

Christensen, L.T. and Morsing, M. (2005) *Bagom Corporate Communication*. København: Samfundslitteratur.

Christensen, L.T., Fuat Firat, A. and Torp, S. (in press) 'The organization of integrated communications: Toward flexible integration', *European Journal of Marketing*, 42.

Cloud, D.L. (2005) 'Fighting words: Labour and the limits of communication at Staley, 1993 to 1996. *Management Communication Quarterly*, 18: 509–42.

Cohen, J.B. and Basu, K. (1987) 'Alternative models of categorization: Toward a contingent processing framework', *Journal of Consumer Research*, 13: 455–72.

Collier, P. and Horowitz, D. (1976) *The Rockefeller*. New York: Holt, Reinhart, and Winston.

Collins, J.C. and Porras, J.I. (2000) *Built to Last: Successful Habits of Visionary Companies*. New York: Horper Collins Publishers.

Connor, S. (2004) *The Book of Skin*. London: Reaktion.

Conant, R.C. and Ashby, W.R. (1970) 'Every good regulator of a system must be a model of that system', *International Journal of System Science*, 1(2): 89–97.

Cooley, C.H. (1983) *Human Nature and the Social Order*. New Brunswick, NJ: Transaction.

Cooper, R. and Burrell, G. (1988) 'Modernism, postmodernism and organizational analysis: An introduction', *Organization Studies*, 9(1): 91–112.

Cooren, F. (1999) *The Organizing Property of Communication*. Amsterdam: John Benjamins.

Cornelissen, J.P. (2001) 'Integrated marketing communications and the language of marketing development', *International Journal of Advertising*, 20(4): 483–98.

Cornelissen, J.P. (2003) 'Change, continuity and progress: The concept of integrated marketing communications and marketing communications practice', *Journal of Strategic Marketing*, 11(4): 217–34.

Cornelissen, J. (2004a) *Corporate Communications: Theory and Practice*. London: SAGE.

Cornelissen, J.P. (2004b) 'What are we playing at? Theatre, organization and the use of metaphor', *Organization Studies*, 25(5): 705–26.

Cornelissen, J.P. and Lock, A.R. (2000) 'Theoretical concept or management fashion: Examining the significance of integrated marketing communications', *Journal of Advertising Research*, 40(5): 7–15.

Cornelissen, J., Christensen, L.T. and Vijn, P. (2006) 'Understanding the development and diffusion of integrated marketing communications (IMC): A metaphorical perspective', *NRG Working Paper Series*, January, No. 06–02.

Coser, L.A. (1977) *Masters of Sociological Thought: Ideas in Historical and Social Context*, 2nd edn. New York: Harcourt Brace Jovanovich. pp. 132–6.

Cova, B. (1996) 'The postmodern explained to managers: Implications for marketing', *Business Horizons*, November–December: 15–23.

Crable, R.E. and Vibbert, S.L. (1983) 'Mobil's epideictic advocacy: "Observations" of Prometheus-bound', *Communication Monographs*, 50: 380–94.

Dachler, H.P. and Wilpert, B. (1979) Conceptual dimensions and boundaries of participation in organizations: A critical evaluation', *Administrative Science Quarterly*, 23: 1–38.

Dahler-Larsen, P. (1997) 'Organizational identity as a "crowded category": A case of multiple and quickly-shifting we-typifications', in S. Sackman (ed.), *Cultural Complexity in Organizations: Inherent Contrasts and Contradictions*. Thousand Oaks, CA: SAGE. pp. 367–90.

Davidson, D.K. (1998) 'Consumers don't really care about brand products' owners', *Marketing News*, 32: 5–6.

Davis, W. (1997) *The Serpent and the Rainbow*. New York: Touchstone.

Deal, T.E. and Kennedy, A.A. (1982) *Corporate Cultures*. Reading, MA: Addison-Wesley.

de Chernatony, L. (1999) 'Brand management through narrowing the gap between brand identity and brand reputation', *Journal of Marketing Management*, 15: 157–79.

de Chernatony, L. (2002) 'Would a brand smell any sweeter by a corporate name?', *Corporate Reputation Review*, 5(2/3): 114–32.

De Pelsmacker, P., Geuens, M. and van den Bergh, J. (2001) *Marketing Communications*. London: Financial Times/Prentice Hall.

Deal, T.E. and Kennedy, A.A (1982) *Corporate Cultures: The Rites and Rituals of Corporate Life*. Reading, MA: Addison-Wesley.

Dearlove, D. (2004) 'Wanted: The next big thing', *The Times* (London), 29 April: 8.

Deephouse, D. (2000) 'Media reputation as a strategic resource: An integration of mass communication and resource-based theories', *Journal of Management*, 26(6): 1091–112.

Deetz, S. (1995) *Transforming Communication, Transforming Business: Building Responsive and Responsible Workplaces*. Cresskill, NJ: Hampton.

Deetz, S. (2006) 'Corporate governance, corporate social responsibility, and communication', in S. May, G. Cheney and J. Roper (eds), *The Debate over Corporate Social Responsibility*. Oxford: Oxford University Press. pp. 267–78.

Dilenschneider, R.L. (2000) *The Corporate Communications Bible: Everything You Need to Know to Become a Public Relations Expert*. Beverly Hills, CA: New Millennium.

Dolphin, R.R. (1999) *The Fundamentals of Corporate Communications*. Oxford: Butterworth Heinemann.

Donnellon, A., Gray, B. and Bougon, M.G. (1986) 'Communication, meaning and organized action', *Administrative Science Quarterly*, 31(1): 43–55.

Douglas, M. (1996) *Natural Symbols: Explorations in Cosmology*. 3rd edn. London: Routledge.

Drobis, D.R. (1997) 'Integrated marketing communications redefined', *Journal of Integrated Communications*, 8: 6–10.

Drucker, P. (1954) *The Practice of Management*. New York: Harper & Row.

Du Gay, P. and Salaman, G. (1992) 'The cult[ure] of the customer', *Journal of Management Studies*, 29(5): 615–33.

Dukerich, J.M. and Carter, S.M. (1998) 'Mismatched image: Organisational responses to conflicts between identity, shared external image, and reputation'. Paper presented at EGOS' 14th Colloquium, Maastricht, 22 June.

Duncan, T. (1993) 'Integrated marketing? It's synergy', *Advertising Age*, 8 March: 22.

Duncan, T. (2005) *Principles of Advertising and IMC*, 2nd edn. Boston, MA: McGraw-Hill.

Duncan, T. and Caywood, C. (1996) 'The concept, process, and evolution of integrated marketing communication', in E. Thorson and J. Moore (eds), *Integrated Communication: Synergy of Persuasive Voices*. Mahwah, NJ: Erlbaum. pp. 13–34.

Duncan, T. and Moriarty, S.E. (1998) 'A communication-based marketing model for managing relationships', *Journal of Marketing*, 62: 1–13.

Dunford, R. and Palmer, I. (1998) 'Discourse, organization and paradox', in D. Grant, T. Keenoy and C. Oswick (eds), *Discourse + Organization*. London: SAGE. pp. 214–21.

Duranti, A. (1986) 'The audience as co-author: An introduction. *Text*, 6: 239–47.

Durkheim, É. (2000/1893) (Reprint 1997) *The Division of Labor in Society*. London: Macmillan.

Dutton, D. (2003) 'Authenticity in art', in J. Levinson (ed.), *The Oxford Handbook of Aesthetics*. New York: Oxford University Press. pp. 258–75.

Dutton, J.E. and Dukerich, J.M. (1991) 'Keeping an eye on the mirror: Image and identity in organizational adaptation', *Academy of Management Journal*, 34: 517–54.

Dutton, J.E., Dukerich, J.M. and Harquail, C.V. (1994) 'Organisational images and member identification', *Administrative Science Quarterly,* 39(2): 239–63.

Eco, U. (1979) *The Role of the Reader: Explorations in the Semiotics of Texts.* Bloomington, IL: Indiana University Press.

Ehnmark, A. (1986) *Magtens hemmeligheder: Et essay om Machiavelli.* København: Samleren.

Eisenberg, E. (1984) 'Ambiguity as strategy in organizational communication', *Communication Monographs,* 51: 227–42.

Eisenberg, E.M. and Witten, M.G. (1987) 'Reconsidering openness in organizational communication', *Academy of Management Review,* 12(3): 418–26.

Elsbach, K.D. and Kramer, R.M. (1996) 'Members' responses to organizational identity threats: encountering and countering the business week rankings', *Administrative Science Quarterly,* 41: 442–76.

Fairhurst, G., Jordan, J.M. and Neuwirth, K. (1997) 'Why are we here? Managing the meaning of the organizational mission statement', *Journal of Applied Communication Research,* 25: 243–63.

Feldman, M.S. and March, J.G. (1981) 'Information in organizations as signal and symbol', *Administrative Science Quarterly,* 26: 171–86.

Ference, T.P. (1970) 'Organizational communications systems and the decision process', *Management Science,* 17: B83–B96.

Firat, A.F. and Christensen, L.T. (2005) 'Marketing communications in a postmodern world', in A.J. Kimmel (ed.), *Marketing Communication: New Approaches, Technologies and Styles.* Oxford: Oxford University Press. pp. 215–35.

Fombrun, C.J. (1996) *Reputation: Realizing Value from the Corporate Image.* Boston, MA: Harvard Business School Press.

Fombrun, C.J. and Rindova, V.P. (2000) 'The road to transparency: Reputation management at Royal Dutch/Shell', in M. Schultz, M.J. Hatch and M.H. Larsen (eds), *The Expressive Organisation: Linking Identity, Reputation and the Corporate Brand.* Oxford: Oxford University Press. pp. 77–98.

Fombrun, C.J. and van Riel, C.B.M (1997) 'The reputational landscape', *Corporate Reputation Review,* 1: 5–13.

Fombrun, C.J. and van Riel C.B.M. (2003) *Fame & Fortune: How Successful Companies Build Winning Reputations.* New York: FT Prentice Hall.

Fombrun, C.J. and van Riel, C.B.M. (2004) *Fame and Fortune: How Successful Companies Build Winning Reputations.* Oxford: Butterworth-Heinemann.

Fornell, C. and Westbrook, R.A. (1984) 'The vicious cycle of consumer complaints', *Journal of Marketing,* 48: 68–78.

Foss, N.J. (2003) 'Selective intervention and internal hybrids: Interpreting and learning from the rise and decline of the spaghetti organization', *Organization Science,* 4(3): 331–49.

Fossgard-Moser, T. (2006) 'Social performance: Key lessons from recent experiences within Shell', in A. Kakabadse and M. Morsing (eds), *Corporate Social Responsibility – Reconciling Managerial Strategies Towards the 21st Century.* London: Palgrave Macmillan. pp. 155–82.

Foucault, M. (1970) *The Order of Things: An Archaeology of the Human Sciences.* New York: Random House.

Foucault, M. (1973) *The Birth of the Clinic: An Archaeology of Medical Perception.* New York: Random House.

Foucault, M. (1977) *Discipline and Punish: The Birth of the Prison.* London: Penguin.

Foucault, M. (1978) *The History of Sexuality: An Introduction. 1.* New York: Random House.

Foucault, M. (1984) *The Foucault Reader*. Edited by P. Rabinow. New York: Pantheon.

Freeman, R.E. (1984) *Strategic Management: A Stakeholder Approach*. Boston, MA: Pitman.

Freeman, R.E. and Daniel, R. Gilbert, Jr (1988) *Corporate Strategy and the Search for Ethics*. Englewood Cliffs, NJ: Prentice Hall.

Freeman, R.E. and Velamuri, R. (2006) 'A new approach to CSR: Company stakeholder responsibility', in A. Kakabadse and M. Morsing (eds), *Corporate Social Responsibility: Reconciling Aspiration with Application*. London: Palgrave Macmillan. pp. 9–23.

French, W.L. and Bell, C.H. (1984) *Organization Development: Behavioural Science Interventions for Organization Improvement*. Englewood Cliffs, NJ: Prentice Hall.

Friedman, M. (1970) 'The social responsibility of business is to increase its profits', *New York Times*, 13 September. Reprinted in H.W. Michael and R.E Frederick (1995) *Business Ethics*. New York: McGraw-Hill.

Friedman, M. (1991) 'Consumer boycotts: A conceptual framework and research agenda', *Journal of Social Issues*, 1: 149–68.

Gallie, D., Felstead, A. and Green, F. (2001) 'Employer policies and organizational commitment in Britain 1992–97', *Journal of Management Studies*, 38(8): 1081–101.

Gardner, B.B. and Levy, S.J. (1955) 'The product and the brand', *Harvard Business Review*, 33(2): 33–9.

Gray, P. du and Salaman, G. (1992) 'The cult(ure) of the customer', *Journal of Management Studies*, 29(5), 615–33.

Gayeski, D.M. and Woodward, B.E. (1996) *Integrated communication: from theory to performance*. Available online at http://www.omnicomassociates.com/omninteg.html

Geertz, C. (1973) *The Interpretation of Cultures*. New York: Basic.

Gelb, B.D. (1995) 'More boycotts ahead? Some implications', *Business Horizons*, 38(2): 70–6.

Gergen, K. (2000) *The Saturated Self: Dilemmas of Identity in Contemporary Life*. New York: Basic.

Giddens, A. (1984) *The Constitution of Society*. Berkeley, CA: University of California Press.

Gilly, M.C. and Wolfinbarger, M. (1998) 'Advertising's internal audience', *Journal of Marketing*, 62: 69–88.

Gioia, D.A., Schultz, M. and Corley, K.G (2000) 'Organizational identity, image and adaptive instability', *Academy of Management Review*, 25(1): 63–81.

Glassman, R.B. (1973) 'Persistence and loose coupling in living systems', *Behavioral Science*, 18: 83–98.

Giroux, H. and Landry, S. (1998) 'Schools of thought in and against total quality management', *Journal of Managerial Issues*, 10(2): 183–203.

Giroux, H. and Taylor, J.R. (2002) 'The justification of knowledge: Tracking the translations of quality', *Management Learning*, 33(4): 497–517.

Goffman, E. (1969) 'The arts of impression management', in M.J. Hatch and M. Schultz (eds), *Organizational Identity: A Reader*. Oxford: Oxford University Press. pp. 35–55.

Goodman, M.B. (1994) *Corporate Communication: Theory and Practice*. Albany, NY: State of New York Press.

Goodman, M.B. (2000) 'Corporate communication: The American picture', *Corporate Communications: An International Journal*, 5(2): 69–74.

Goodpaster, B. and Holloran, T. (2006) 'Exxon Valdez: Corporate recklessness on trial', in K.E. Goodpaster, L. L. Nash and H-C de Bettignies (eds), *Business Ethics: Policies and Persons*. Boston, MA: McGraw-Hill. pp. 396–411.

Gossett (2002) 'Kept an arms length: Questioning the organizational desirability of member identification', *Communication Monographs*, 69: 385–404.

Granovetter, M.S. (1973) 'The strength of weak ties', *American Journal of Sociology,* 81: 1287–303.

Grant, D., Keenoy, T. and Oswick, C. (1998) *Discourse + Organization.* London: SAGE.

Griffin, E.M. (1998) 'The melting pot, vegetable soup, and the martini cocktail: Competing explanations of U.S. cultural pluralism', *The Midwest Quarterly,* 39(2): 133–52.

Gronstedt, A. (1996a) 'Integrated communications in America's leading total quality management corporations', *Public Relations Review,* 22(1): 25–42.

Gronstedt, A. (1996b) 'How agencies can support integrated communications', *Journal of Business Research,* 37: 201–6.

Gronstedt, A. (2000) *The Customer Century: Lessons from World-Class Companies in Integrated Marketing and Communications.* London: Routledge.

Grunig, J.E. (ed.) (1992) *Excellence in Public Relations and Communication Management.* Hillside, NJ: Erlbaum.

Grunig, J.E. and Grunig, L.A. (1991) 'Conceptual differences in public relations and marketing: The case of health-care organizations', *Public Relations Review,* 17(3): 257–78.

Grunig, J.E. and Grunig, L.A. (1998) 'The relationship between public relations and marketing in excellent organizations: Evidence from the IABC Study', *Journal of Marketing Communications,* 4(3): 141–62.

Grunig, J.E. and Hunt, T. (1984) *Managing Public Relations.* Fort Worth, TX: Harcourt Brace Jovanovich.

Gummesson, E. (1999) *Total Relationship Marketing. Rethinking Marketing Management: From 4Ps to 30Rs.* Oxford: Butterworth-Heinemann.

Hale, B. (2000) 'BP goes green, solar, connected'. *Sydney Morning Herald,* 26 July, 25–6.

Hall, R. (1993) 'A framework linking intangible resources and capabilities to sustainable competitive advantage', *Strategic Management Journal,* (14): 607–18.

Hamel, G. and Prahalad, C.K. (1994) *Competing for the Future. Breakthrough Strategies for Seizing Control of Your Industry and Creating the Markets of Tomorrow.* Boston, MA: Harvard Business School Press.

Hammer, M. and Champy, J. (1993) *Reengineering the Corporation.* London: Nicolas Brealey.

Harley, B. and Hardy, C. (2004) 'Firing blanks? An analysis of discursive struggle in HRM', *Journal of Management Studies,* 41(3): 377–400.

Harris, F. and de Chernatony, L. (2001) 'Corporate branding and corporate brand performance', *European Journal of Marketing,* 35(3/4): 441–56.

Harrison, S. (1995) *Public Relations: An Introduction.* London: Routledge.

Harvard Business School (1989) 'Dow Corning Corporation: Business Conduct and Global Values. Case 9-385-018, rev. 2/89', reprinted in K.E. Goodpaster, L.L. Nash and H-C de Bettignies (eds) (2006) *Business Ethics: Policies and Persons.* Boston, MA: McGraw-Hill. pp. 430–47.

Hatch, M.J. and Schultz, M. (2001) 'Are the strategic stars aligned for your corporate brand?', *Harvard Business Review,* 79(2): 3–4, 128–34.

Hazen, M.A. (1993) 'Towards polyphonic organization', *Journal of Organizational Change Management,* 6(5): 15–26.

Heath, R.L. (1980) 'Corporate advocacy: An application of speech communication perspectives and skills – and more', *Communication Education,* 29: 370–7.

Hennessey, D. (1999) 'View from here', *The Ashridge Journal,* July: 23–4.

Hirschhorn, L. and Gilmore, T. (1992) 'The new boundaries of the "boundaryless" company', *Harvard Business Review,* May–June: 104–15.

Ho, N. (2001–02) 'Creating an emotional connection with your employees through marketing communications: A new tool for managing your employees as internal customers', *Journal of Integrated Communications*.http://jimc.medill.northwestern. edu/2001/ho.htm

Hobbes, T. (1988/1651) *The Leviathan*. Buffalo, NY: Prometheus.

Humphreys, M. and Brown, A.D. (2002) 'Narratives of organizational identity and identification: A case study of hegemony and resistance', *Organization Studies*, 23(3): 421–47.

Hutton, J.G. (1996) 'Integrated relationship-marketing communication: A key opportunity of IMC', *Journal of Marketing Communications*, 2: 191–9.

Imberman, W. (1979) 'Strikes cost more than you think', *Harvard Business Review*, 57(3): 133–42.

Ind, N. (1997) *The Corporate Brand*. London: Macmillan.

Ind, N. (1998) 'An integrated approach to corporate branding', *Journal of Brand Management*, 5(5): 323–9.

Ind, N. (2004) *Living the Brand: How to Transform Every Member of Your Organization into a Brand Champion*. London: Kogan Page.

Iser, W. (1974). *The Implied Reader*. Baltimore, MD: Johns Hopkins University Press.

Jackson, J.E. and Schantz, W.T. (1993) 'Crisis management lessons: When push shoved Nike', *Business Horizons*, January–February: 27–35.

Jackson, P. (1987) *Corporate Communication for Managers*. London: Pitman.

Jauss, H.R. (1982) *Toward an Aesthetic of Reception*. Minneapolis, MN: University of Minneapolis Press.

Jordan, J.W. (2003) 'Sabotage or performed compliance: Rhetorics of resistance in temp worker discourse', *Quarterly Journal of Speech*, 89: 19–40.

Kantorowicz, E.H. (1997/1957). *The King's Two Bodies: A study in Mediaeval Political Theology*. Princeton, NJ: Princeton University Press.

Karmark, E. (2005) 'Living the brand', in M. Schultz, Y.M. Antorini and F.F. Csaba (eds), *Towards the Second Wave of Corporate Branding: Purpose/People/Process*. Copenhagen: Copenhagen Business School Press. pp. 103–24.

Kaufman, H. (1960) *The Forest Ranger: A Study in Administrative Behavior*. Baltimore, MD: Johns Hopkins University Press.

Kierkegaard, S. (1997) *The Seducer's Diary*. Princeton, NJ: Princeton University Press.

Kirk, G.S. and Raven, J.E. (1957) 'Heraclitus of Ephesus', *The Pre-Socratic Philosophers*. Cambridge: Cambridge University Press.

Kjærgaard, A. (2004) *Knowledge Management as Internal Corporate Venturing: A Field Study of the Rise and Fall of a Bottom-Up Process*. Department of Informatics, Copenhagen: Copenhagen Business School Press.

Klein, N. (2000a) *No Logo*. London: Flamingo Press.

Klein, N. (2000b) *No Logo: Taking Aim at the Brand Bullies*. London: Penguin.

Knight, G. (2007) 'Activism, risk and communicational politics: Nike and the sweatshop problem', in S. May, G. Cheney and J. Roper (eds), *The Debate over Corporate Social Responsibility*. Oxford: Oxford University Press. pp. 305–20.

Knights, D. and Morgan, G. (1991) 'Corporate strategy, organizations, and subjectivity: A critique', *Organization Studies*, 12(2): 251–73.

Knudsen, H. (2003) Licens til kritik. *Ledersupporten*.

Knudsen, H. (2004) 'Licens til kritik – og Andre Måder at Bruge Værdier på i Organisationer', in D. Pedersen (ed.), *Offentlig ledelse i managementstaten*. København: Samfundslitteratur. pp. 159–75.

Kohli, A.K. and B.J. Jaworksi (1990) 'Market orientation: The construct, research propositions, and managerial implications', *Journal of Marketing,* 54(2): 1–18.

Kotler, P. (1985) Global standardization – courting danger. Panel discussion, 23rd American Marketing Association Conference, Washington, DC.

Krippendorf, K. (1984) 'An epistemological foundation for communication', *Journal of Communication,* 34: 21–36.

Kristian, E. (1998) *Managing the Unmanageable for a Decade.* Copenhagen: Oticon.

Kuhn, M.H. and McPartland, T.S. (1954) 'An empirical investigation of self-attitudes', *American Sociological Review,* 19: 68–76.

Kunda, G. (1992) *Engineering Culture.* Boston, MA: Temple.

Kunde, J. (1997) *Corporate Religion: Vejen til en Stærk Virksomhed.* København: Børsens Forlag.

Kunde, J. (2000). *Corporate Religion: Building a Strong Company through Personality and Corporate Soul.* Tokyo: Financial Times/Prentice Hall.

Lair, D.J., Sullivan, K. and Cheney, G. (2005) 'The rhetoric and ethics of personal branding', *Management Communication Quarterly,* 18: 307–43.

Lakoff, G. (2004) *Don't Think of an Elephant! Know Your Values and Frame the Debate.* White River Junction, VT: Chelsea Green.

Lakoff, G. and Johnson, M. (1989) *Metaphors We Live by.* Chicago, IL: University of Chicago Press.

Laufer, R. and Paradeise, C. (1990) *Marketing Democracy. Public Opinion and Media Formation in Democratic Societies.* New Brunswick, NJ: Transaction.

Lawrence, P.R. and Lorsch, J.W. (1967a) *Organization and Environment: Managing Differentiation and Integration.* Boston, MA: Harvard University.

Lawrence, P.R. and Lorsch, J.W. (1967b) 'Differentiation and integration in complex organizations', *Administrative Science Quarterly,* 12(1): 1–47.

Leitch, S. (1999) 'From logo-centrism to corporate branding? The (r)evolution in organisational identity', *Austrlian Journal of Communication,* 26(3): 1–8.

Levinson, H., Molinari, J. and Spohn, A.G. (1972) *Organizational Diagnosis.* Cambridge, MA: Harvard University Press.

Levitt, T. (1983) 'The globalization of markets', *Harvard Business Review,* 61(3): 92–101.

Lindblom, C.E. (1959) 'The science of "muddling through"', *Public Administration Review,* 19(2): 79–88.

Livesey, S.M. and Graham, J. (2007) 'Greening of corporations? Eco-talk and the emerging social imaginary of sustainable development', in S. May, G. Cheney and J. Roper (eds), *The Debate over Corporate Social Responsibility.* Oxford: Oxford University Press.

Lotman, Y.M. (1977) 'Two models of communication', in D.P. Lucid (ed.), *Soviet Semiotics: An Anthology.* London: Johns Hopkins University Press. pp. 99–101.

Lotman, Y.M. (1990) *Universe of the Mind: A Semiotic Theory of Culture.* London: I.B. Tauris.

Luhmann, N. (1990) *Essays on Self-Reference.* New York.: Colombia University Press.

Luhmann, N. (1995) *Inklusion und Exklusion: Soziologische Aufklärung 6.* Opladen: Westdeutscher Verlag.

Lynn, M.L. (2005) 'Organizational buffering: managing boundaries and cores', *Organization Studies,* 26(1): 37–61.

Lyotard, J.F. (1984) *The Postmodern Condition: A Report on Knowledge.* Minneapolis, MN: University of Minnesota Press.

Machiavelli, N. (1513) *The Prince.*

Manning, P.K. (1986) 'Signwork', *Human Relations,* 39(4): 283–308.

March, J.G. (1988) *Decisions and Organizations.* Oxford: Blackwell.

March, J.G. (1994) *A Primer on Decision Making: How Decisions Happen.* New York: Free.

Marchand, R. (1998) *Creating the Corporate Soul: The Rise of Public Relations and Corporate Imagery in American Big Business.* Berkeley, CA: The University of California Press.

Marsden, C. (2006) 'In defense of corporate responsibility', in A. Kakabadse and, M. Morsing (eds), *Corporate Social Responsibility: Reconciling Aspiration with Application.* London: Palgrave. pp. 31–4.

Martin, J. (1992) *Cultures in Organizations: Three Perspectives.* New York: Oxford University Press.

Martin, J., Feldman, M.S., Hatch, M.J. and Sitkin, S.B. (1983) 'The uniqueness paradox in organizational stories', *Administrative Science Quarterly,* 28: 438–53.

Maturana, H. and Varela, F. (1989) *Autopoiesis and Cognition: The Realization of the Living.* Dordrecht: D. Reidel.

Mayo, E. (1945) *The Social Problems of an Industrial Civilization.* Cambridge, MA: Harvard University Press.

McAlexander, J.H., Schouten, S. and Koenig, H.F. (2002) 'Building brand community', *Journal of Marketing,* 66(1): 38–54.

McCarthy, E.J. (1960) *Basic Marketing: A Managerial Approach.* Homewood, IL: Irwin.

McMillan, G.S. snd Joshi, M.P. (1997) 'Sustainable competitive advantage and firm performance: The role of intangible resources', *Corporate Reputation Review,* 1: 81–5.

McMillan, J.J. (2007) 'Why corporate social responsibility: Why now? How?', in S. May, G. Cheney and J. Roper (eds), *The Debate over Corporate Social Responsibility.* Oxford: Oxford University Press. pp. 15–29.

Mead, G.H. (1934) *Mind, Self and Society.* Chicago, IL: University of Chicago Press.

Meyer, J.W. and Rowan, B. (1977) 'Institutional organizations: Formal structure as myth and ceremony', *American Journal of Sociology,* 83: 340–63.

Miller, A. and Friday, C. (1992) 'Do boycotts work?', *Newsweek,* 120 (1), July: 58–61.

Miller, D.A. and Rose, P.B. (1994) 'Integrated communications: A look at reality instead of theory', *Public Relations Quarterly,* 39(1): 13–16.

Mitchell, A. (1997) *Brand Strategies in the Information Age.* London: Financial Times.

Mitchell, C. (2002) 'Selling the brand inside', *Harvard Business Review,* 80(1): 99–105.

Mongin, O. (1982) 'La democratie a corps perdu', *Esprit,* 2 February: 206–12.

Morgan, A. (1999) *Eating the Big Fish. How Challenger Brands Can Compete Against Brand Leaders.* New York: John Wiley & Sons, Inc.

Morgan, G. (1986) *Images of Organization.* Beverly Hills, CA: SAGE.

Morgan, G. (1993) *Imaginization: The Art of Creative Management.* Newbury Park, CA: SAGE.

Morgan, R.M. and Hunt, S.D. (1994) 'The commitment-trust theory of relationship marketing, *Journal of Marketing,* 58: 20–38.

Morin, E. (1973) *Le Paradigme Perdu: La Nature Humaine.* Paris: Seuil.

Morin, E. (1984) *Sociologie.* Paris: Fayard.

Morin, E. (1986) *La Méthode 3: La Connaissance de la Connaissance. Livre Premier: Antropologie de la Connaisance.* Paris: Seuil.

Morin, E. (1987) *Penser l'Europe.* Paris: Gallimard.

Morin, E. (1992) *Method: Towards a Study of Humankind. Volume 1: The Nature of Nature*. New York: Peter Lang.

Morsing, M. (2005) 'Corporate values – why do companies communicate their identity in stereotype, abstract and banal values?', Paper presented at the European Academy of Management Conference, EURAM, Munich, 6–8 May.

Morsing, M. and Eiberg, K. (1998) *Managing the Unmanageable for a Decade*. Copenhagen: Oticon.

Morsing, M. and Kristensen, J. (2001) 'The question of coherency in corporate branding – over time and across stakeholders', *Journal of Communication Management*, 6(1): 24–40.

Morsing, M. and Oswald, D. (2006) 'Novo Nordisk A/S: Integrating sustainability into business practice', in A. Kakabadse and M. Morsing (eds), *Corporate Social Responsibility – Reconciling Managerial Strategies Towards the 21st Century'*. London: Palgrave Macmillan. pp. 183–216.

Morsing, M. and Schultz, M. (2006) 'Corporate social responsibility communication: stakeholder information, response and involvement strategies', *Business Ethics: a European Review*, 15(4): 323–38.

Motion, J. and Leitch, S. (2002) 'The technologies of corporate identity', *International Studies of Management and Organization*, 32(3): 45–64.

Mulgan, G.J. (1991) *Communication and Control: Networks and the New Economies of Communication*. New York: Guilford.

Muniz, A.M. and O'Guinn, T.C. (2001) 'Brand community', *Journal of Consumer Research*, 27: 412–32.

Narver, J.C. and Slater, S.F. (1990) 'The effect of market orientation on business profitability', *Journal of Marketing*, 54(4): 20–35.

Newsweek (2005) 14 and 17 October.

Niels Åkerstrøm, A. (2003) 'The undecidability of decision', in T. Bakken and T. Hernes (eds), *Autopoietic Organization Theory, Abstakt, Liber*. Oslo: Copenhagen Business School Press. pp. 235–58.

Nike (2004) *Corporate Responsibility Report 2004*, Child Labor, pp. 30–1.

Nisbet, R.A. (1966) *The Sociological Tradition*. London: Heinemann.

Noor-Drugan (2000) 'BP Amoco unveil new global brand to drive growth', BP Press Release, 24 July. *Advertising Age*, 18 September, p. 16. Cited in Beder, S. (2005) 'Making energy more'. *BP Sustainability Report 2005*.

Ogilvy, J. (1990) 'This postmodern business', *Marketing and Research Today*, February: 4–20.

Olins, W. (1989) *Corporate Identity: Making Business Strategy Visible Through Design*. London: Thames and Hudson.

Onkvisit, S. and Shaw, J.J. (1987) 'Standardized international advertising: A review and critical evaluation of the theoretical and empirical evidence', *Columbia Journal of World Business*, 22 (Fall): 43–55.

Orton, J.D. and Weick, K.E. (1990) 'Loosely coupled systems: A reconceptualization', *Academy of Management Review*, 15(2): 203–23.

Parsons, T. (1960) *Structure and Process in Modern Societies*. Glencoe, IL: Free Press.

Pascale, R.T. and Athos, A.G. (1981) *The Art of Japanese Management*. New York: Simon and Schuster.

Peppers, D. and Rogers, M. (1993) *The One to One Future: Building Relationships One Customer at a Time*. New York: Currency Doubleday.

Perniola, M. (1980) *La Societê dei Simulacri*. Bologna: Capelli.

Perrow, C. (1984) *Normal Accidents: Living with High-Risk Technologies*. New York: Basic.

Peters, T.J. (1988) 'Restoring American competitiveness: Looking for new models of organizations', *The Academy of Management EXECUTIVE*, 2(2): 103–9.

Peters, T.J. and Waterman, R.H. (1982) *In Search of Excellence: Lessons from America's Best Run Companies*. New York: Harper & Row.

Pettegrew, L.S. (2000–01) 'If IMC is so good, why isn't it being implemented? Barriers to IMC adoption in corporate America', *Journal of Integrated Communication*, 29(9): 29–37.

Pfeffer, J. (1981) 'Management as symbolic action: The creation and maintenance of organizational paradigms', in L.L. Cummings and B.M. Staw (eds), *Research in Organizational Behavior*. Greenwich, CT: JAI. pp. 1–52.

Pickton, D. and Broderick, A. (2001): *Integrated Marketing Communications*. Marlow: Financial Times/Prentice Hall.

Piercy, N.F. and Cravens, D.W. (1995) 'The network paradigm and the marketing organization: Developing a new management agenda', *European Journal of Marketing*, 29(3): 7–34.

Pine, B.J., Victor, B. and Boyton, A.C. (1993) 'Making mass customization work', *Harvard Business Review*, 71(5): 108–19.

Popper, K.R. (1945) *Open Society and Its Enemies*. Volume 1. London: Routledge.

Porter, M.E. and Kramer, M.R. (2002) 'The competitive advantage of corporate philanthropy', *Harvard Business Review*, 80(12): 56–69.

Potter, J. and Wetherell, M. (1987) *Discourse and Social Psychology*. London: SAGE.

Prensky, D., McCarty, J. and Lucas, J. (1996) 'Integrated marketing communication: An organizational perspective', in E. Thorson and J. Moore (eds), *Integrated Communication: Synergy of Persuasive Voices*. Mahwah, NJ: Erlbaum. pp. 167–83.

PriceWaterhouseCoopers (2005) *Good Practices in Corporate Reporting: Trends*.

Putnam, L.L. and Cheney, G. (1985) 'Organizational communication: Historical development and future directions', in T.W. Benson (ed.), *Speech Communication in the 20th Century*. Carbondale, IL: Southern Illinois University Press. pp. 130–56.

Putnam, L.L., Phillips, N. and Chapman, P. (1996) 'Metaphors of communication and organization', in S.R. Clegg, C. Hardy and W.R. Nord (eds), *Handbook of Organization Studies*. London: SAGE. pp. 375–408.

Quinn, J.B. (1992) *Intelligent Enterprise*. New York: Free.

Rawstorne, P. (1989) 'BP puts on new "public face" to meet the challenges of the 1990s', *The Oil Daily*, 6 February.

Ries, A. and Trout, J. (1986) *Positioning: The Battle for Your Mind*. New York: Warner.

Rindova, V.P. (2000) Panel on Transparency: Condition or Strategy in Reputation Building? Held at the 5th International Conference on Corporate Reputation, Identity & Competitiveness, Paris, 17–19 May, 2001.

Roethlisberger, F.J. and Dickson, W.J. (1947) *Management and the Worker*. Cambridge, MA: Harvard University Press.

Rogers, E.M. and Shoemaker, F.F. (1971) *Communication of Innovations: A Cross Cultural Approach*. 2nd edn. New York: Free.

Roper, J. and Cheney, G. (2003) 'A preliminary analyses of NZ businesses' responses to the Kyoto Protocol'. Paper presented at the annual conference of the European Academy of Business in Society, September, Copenhagen.

Schmidt, J. (2000) *Disciplined Minds: A Critical Look at Salaried Professionals and the Soul-Battering System That Shapes Their Lives*. Lanham, MD: Rowman & Littlefield.

Schneider, K. (1994) 'With 2 Valdez Oil-Spill Trials Down, Big One is Comig Up', *New York Times*, 14 August, Section 1: p. 34.

Scholes, E. and Clutterbuck, D. (1998) 'Communication with stakeholders. An integrated approach', *Long Range Planning,* 31(2): 227–38.

Schön, D. (1983) *The Reflective Practitioner: How Professionals Think In Action.* London: Temple Smith.

Schudson, M. (1993) *Advertising, the Uneasy Persuasion: Its Dubious Impact on American Society.* New York: Basic.

Schultz, D.E. (1993) 'Integration helps you plan communications from outside-in', *Marketing News,* 3(12).

Schultz, D.E. and Kitchen, P.J. (2000) *Communicating Globally: An Integrated Marketing Approach.* London: Macmillan Business.

Schultz, D.E. and Kitchen, P.J. (2004) 'Managing the changes in corporate branding and communication: Closing and re-opening the corporate umbrella', *Corporate Reputation Review,* 6(4): 347–66.

Schultz, D.E. and Schultz, H. (2004) *IMC. The Next Generation: Five Steps for Delivering Value and Measuring Returns Using Marketing Communication.* New York: McGraw-Hill.

Schultz, D.E., Tannebaum, S.I. and Lauterborn, R.F. (1994) *The New Marketing Paradigm: Integrated Marketing Communications.* Chicago, IL: NTC Business Books.

Schultz, M. (2005) 'A cross-disciplinary perspective of corporate branding', in M. Schultz, Y.M. Antorini and F.F. Csaba (eds), *Towards the Second Wave of Corporate Branding: Purpose/People/Process.* Copenhagen: Copenhagen Business School Press. pp. 23–55.

Schultz, M. and de Chernatony, L. (2002) 'Introduction: The challenges of corporate branding', *Corporate Reputation Review,* 5(2/3): 105–12.

Schultz, M. Rubin, J.R. and Hatch, M.J. (N.d.) 'Novo Nordisk: Focusing the corporate brand' University of Virginia Darden School Foundation.

Sellers, C., Goodpaster, K.E. and Bowie, N.E. (1995) reprinted in K.E. Goodpaster, L.L. Nash and H-Cl de Bettignies (eds) (2006), *Business Ethics: Policies and Persons.* Boston, MA: McGraw-Hill. pp. 448–63.

Senge, P. (1990) *The Fifth Discipline: The Art and Practice of the Learning Organisation.* New York: Doubleday.

Sennett, R. (1964) *The Fall of Public Man.* New York: Random House.

Sennett, R. (1996) *Flesh and Stone: The Body and the City in Western Civilization.* New York: Norton.

Sewell, G. (1998) 'The discipline of teams: The control of team-based industrial work through electronic and peer surveillance', *Administrative Science Quarterly,* 43: 397–428.

Shimp, T.A. (2003) *Advertising, Promotion & Supplemental Aspects of Integrated Marketing Communications.* Chicago, IL: NTC Business Books.

Shirley L. (1999) 'From logo-centrism to corporate branding? The (r)evolution in organisational identity', *Australian Journal of Communication,* 26(3): 1–8.

Simon, H.A. (1997) *Administrative Behavior,* 50th Anniversary Edition. New York: Free.

Sirgy, M.J. (1998) *Integrated Marketing Communications: A Systems Approach.* Upper Saddle River, NJ: Prentice Hall.

Skinner, Q. (1981) *Machiavelli.* Oxford: Oxford University Press.

Smith, N.C. (2003) 'Corporate social responsibility: whether or how?', *California Management Review,* 45(4): 52–73.

Smith, P. (1996) 'Benefits and barriers to integrated marketing communications', *Admap*, February: 19–22.

Smith, R.C. and Eisenberg, E. (1987) 'Conflict at Disneyland: A root metaphor analysis', *Communication Monographs*, 54: 367–79.

Smith, V. (1997) 'New forms of work organization', *Annual Review of Sociology*, 23: 315–39.

Smith, V. (2001) *Crossing the Great Divide: Worker Risk and Opportunity in the New Economy.* Ithaca, NY: Cornell University Press.

Sproull, L. and Kiesler, S. (1992) *Connections: New Ways of Working in the Networked Organization.* Cambridge, MA: MIT Press.

Srivastava, R.K., McInish, T.H., Wood, R.A. and Capraro, A.J. (1997) 'The value of corporate reputation: Evidence from the equity markets', *Corporate Reputation Review*, 1: 62–8.

Stohl, C. (1995) *Organizational Communication: Connectedness in Action.* Thousand Oaks, CA: Sage.

Stuart, H. and Kerr, G. (1999) 'Marketing communication and corporate identity: Are they integrated?', *Journal of Marketing Communications*, 5(4): 169–79.

Suchman, M.C. (1995) 'Managing legitimacy: Strategic and institutional approaches', *Academy of Management Review,* 20(3): 571–610.

Swasy, A. (1991) 'P&G to tout name behind the brands', *Wall Street Journal*, 12 December: B1–B3.

Syrett, M. (2004) 'Striking at the Achilles' heel of integrated marketing'. Available online at: http://www.marketingprofs.com/preview.asp?file=/4/syrett2.asp

Taylor, J.R. and van Every, E.J. (2000) *The Emergent Organization: Communication as its Site and Surface.* Mahwah, NJ: Erlbaum.

The Economics (2005) 26 November.

Thompson, J.B. (2005) 'The new visibility', *Theory, Culture & Society,* 22(6): 31–51.

Thompson, J.D. (1967) *Organizations in Action.* New York: McGraw-Hill.

Thompson, M. and Wildavsky, A. (1986) 'A cultural theory of information bias in organizations', *Journal of Management Studies,* 23(3): 273–86.

Thyssen, O. (2003) *Æstetisk Ledelse: Om Organisationer og Brugskunst.* København: Gyldendal.

Tompkins, P.K. and Cheney, G. (1985) 'Communication and unobtrusive control in contemporary organizations', in R.D. McPhee and P.K. Tompkins (eds), *Organizational Communication: Traditional Themes and New Directions.* Thousand Oaks, CA: SAGE. pp. 179–210.

Turner, B.S. (1996) *The Body & Society.* London: SAGE.

Van Houten, B. (2006) Q & A: Barry D. Pressman, *Decisions in Imaging Economics.*

Van Riel, C.B.M (1995) *Principles of Corporate Communication.* London: Prentice Hall.

Van Riel, C.B.M (2000) 'Corporate communication orchestrated by a sustainable corporate story', in M. Schultz, M.J. Hatch and M.H. Larsen (eds), *The Expressive Organization.* Oxford: Oxford University Press. pp. 157–81.

Vardar, N. (1992) *Global Advertising: Rhyme or Reason?* London: Paul Chapman.

Vattimo, G. (1992) *The Transparent Society.* Cambridge: Polity.

Waeraas, A. (2004) 'Den karismatiske offentlige organisasjon. Konstruksjonen av organisasjonslegitimitet ved hjelp av private kommunikatsjonsrådgivere'. Doctoral dissertation, the University of Tromsø.

Walker, R. (2006) 'Faux logo', *The New York Times,* 14 May.

Wall Street Journal (2004) 'Branson's "Rebel" Persona places Halo over U.K. Megacompany'. *The Wall Street Journal,* 15 November.

Walton, S. and Huey, J. (1992) *Sam Walton: Made in America*. New York: Doubleday.

Watson, T.J. (2004) 'HRM and critical social science analysis', *Journal of Management Studies,* 41(3): 447–67.

Wätzold, F. (1996) 'When environmentalists have power: A case study of the Brent Spar', in J.P. Ulhøi and H. Madsen (eds), *Industry and the Environment: Practical Applications of Environmental Management Approaches in Business.* Proceedings of the The 3rd Conference of the Nordic Business Environmental Management Network, The Aarhus School of Business, Aarhus, Denmark, 28–30 March. pp. 327–37.

Weber, M. (1978) *Economy and Society*. Berkeley, CA: University of California Press.

Weick, K.E. (1976) 'Educational organizations as loosely coupled systems', *Administrative Science Quarterly,* 21(1): 1–19.

Weick, K.E. (1979) *The Social Psychology of Organizing*, 2nd edn. Reading, MA: Addison-Wesley.

Weick, K.E. (1987) 'Organizational culture as a source of high reliability', *California Management Review,* 29(2): 112–27.

Weick, K.E. (1995) *Sensemaking in Organizations*. Thousand Oaks: SAGE.

Weick, K.E. and Sutcliffe, K. (2001) *Managing the Unexpected: Assuring High Performance in an Age of Complexity*. San Francisco, CA: Jossey-Bass.

Wightman, B. (1999) 'Integrated communications: organization and education', *Public Relations Quarterly,* 44(2): 18–22.

Wright, E.O. (1989) *The Debate on Classes*. London: Verso.

Yeshin, T. (1998) *Integrated Marketing Communications: The Holistic Approach*. Oxford: Butterworth Heinemann.

Young, E. (1989) 'On the naming of the rose: Multiple meanings as elements of organizational culture', *Organization Studies,* 10(2): 187–206.

Zorn, T., Christensen, L.T and Cheney, G. (1999) *Do We Really Want Constant Change? Beyond the Bottom Line*. San Francisco, CA: Berrett-Koehler.

Zuman, M.L. (1996) 'Editor's Notebook'. *Willamette Week*, 12 June.

Index